MVS—Capacity Planning for a Balanced System

Recent Titles in the IBM McGraw-Hill Series

Open Systems and IBM — Pamela Gray
Integration and Convergence

Risk Management for Software Projects — Alex Down
Michael Coleman
Peter Absolon

The New Organization — Colin Hastings
Growing the Culture of Organizational
Networking

Investing in Information Technology — Geoff Hogbin
Managing the Decision-making Process — David Thomas

Commonsense Computer Security 2nd Edition — Martin Smith
Your Practical Guide to Information Protection

The Advanced Programmer's Guide to AIX 3.x — Phil Colledge

The CICS Programmer's Guide to FEPI — Robert Harris

Business Objects — Oliver Sims
Delivering Cooperative Objects for Client-Server

Reshaping I.T. for Business Flexibility — Mark Behrsin
The I.T. Architecture as a Common Language — Geoff Mason
for Dealing with Change — Trevor Sharpe

Writing OS/2 REXX Programs — Ronny Richardson

Practical Queueing Analysis — Mike Tanner

MVS Capacity Planning for a Balanced System — Brian MacFarlane

Details of these titles in the series are available from:

The Product Manager, Professional Books
McGraw-Hill Book Company Europe
Shoppenhangers Road, Maidenhead, Berkshire, SL6 2QL
Telephone: 0628 23432 Fax: 0628 770224

Brian A Macfarlane

MVS—Capacity Planning for a Balanced System

McGRAW-HILL BOOK COMPANY

London · New York · St Louis · San Francisco · Auckland
Bogotá · Caracas · Lisbon · Madrid · Mexico
Milan · Montreal · New Delhi · Panama · Paris · San Juan
São Paulo · Singapore · Sydney · Tokyo · Toronto

Published by
McGRAW-HILL Book Company Europe
Shoppenhangers Road, Maidenhead, Berkshire SL6 2QL, England
Telephone 01628 23432
Fax 01628 770224

British Library Cataloguing in Publication Data

Macfarlane, Brian A.
  MVS—Capacity Planning for a Balanced
System. - (IBM McGraw-Hill Series)
I. Title II. Series
005.43
ISBN 0-07-709053-5

Library of Congress Cataloging-in-Publication Data

Macfarlane. Brian A.,
    MVS—capacity planning for a balanced system/Brian A.
Macfarlane.
      p. cm.—(IBM McGraw-Hill series)
  Includes index.
  ISBN 0-07-709053-5
    1. Computer capacity—Planning. 2. IBM MVS. I. Title.
II. Series.
QA76.9.C63M33   1994
004.2'52—dc20   94-21735
                                                                                      CIP

Copyright © 1995 McGraw-Hill International (UK) Ltd. All rights reserved. No part of this publication may be reproduced, stored in a retrieval system, or transmitted, in any form or by any means, electronic, mechanical, photocopying, recording, or otherwise, without the prior permission of McGraw-Hill International (UK) Ltd.

1234 CUP 9765

Typeset by Paston Press Ltd, Loddon, Norfolk
and printed and bound in Great Britain at the University Press, Cambridge

Contents

IBM Series Foreword		ix
Preface		xi
Trademarks		xvii
Glossary		xix

1 Justification of central electronic complex analysis — 1
- 1.1 Get it in the budget! — 1
- 1.2 What do you analyse? — 2
- 1.3 Why analyse? — 2
- 1.4 Capacity planning versus the performance study — 3
- 1.5 Performance versus capacity planning roadmap — 3

2 The service unit and the SRM second — 5
- 2.1 Introduction — 5
- 2.2 The relationship between SUs and the SRM second — 5
- 2.3 The relationship between the SRM second, real seconds and the SU — 7
- 2.4 Multi-engined processors — 8

3 External throughput rate, internal throughput rate and CPU service time — 13
- 3.1 Introduction — 13
- 3.2 Useful derivatives — 15
- 3.3 Calculating the external throughput rate — 17
- 3.4 Calculating the internal throughput rate — 18
- 3.5 Is there a relationship between the ETR and the ITR? — 20

4 Internal throughput rate ratio and IBM relative processor power — 23
- 4.1 Introduction — 23
- 4.2 The internal throughput rate ratio — 23
- 4.3 How the LSPR ITRR value is calculated — 24
- 4.4 Calculating your own ITRR value — 25
- 4.5 Relative processor power — 26
- 4.6 Graphic relationship between ETR and ITR using a CICS workload — 28

Contents

5 CPU analysis for capacity planning — 30
- 5.1 Introduction — 30
- 5.2 Recording the resources used by each performance group — 30
- 5.3 The CPU analysis worksheet — 32
- 5.4 The system performance groups — 42
- 5.5 Total URPP for each application PG — 43
- 5.6 Calculating the performance group ETR and ITR — 46

6 CPU analysis for performance — 50
- 6.1 Introduction — 50
- 6.2 The transaction time — 50
- 6.3 Individual capture ratios — 52
- 6.4 What information do we need for a performance study? — 53
- 6.5 How to extract WTST, residency time and transaction time from RMF Monitor I report — 55
- 6.6 The absolute number of SUs absorbed by the transaction — 58
- 6.7 Quick method of finding transaction residency time and WTST — 59
- 6.8 The CPU service time for a transaction — 59
- 6.9 How do we calculate our value of U? — 61
- 6.10 Summary — 74

7 Analysis of the I/O subsystem — 76
- 7.1 Introduction — 76
- 7.2 The balanced system — 76
- 7.3 The anatomy of an I/O — 77
- 7.4 Review of DASD controllers — 82
- 7.5 The I/O rate through the channels — 84
- 7.6 Acceptable utilization, I/O activity rate and response time for a DASD — 90
- 7.7 Breaking down the response time — 91
- 7.8 A few words on device utilization — 96
- 7.9 What is the maximum I/O rate my system will sustain? — 98
- 7.10 Page and swap data sets — 107
- 7.11 The paging rate and the system multi-programming level — 116
- 7.12 Where do the swapped address spaces go? — 116
- 7.13 Primary (PLPA), common and duplex page data sets — 119
- 7.14 Cache candidates—what data sets should you cache? — 120
- 7.15 Data Facility—Systems Managed Storage — 120
- 7.16 ESCON channel support with MVS/ESA version 4.3.0 — 121
- 7.17 RAID devices — 122

8 Storage analysis — 123
- 8.1 Introduction — 123
- 8.2 Managing expanded storage — 125
- 8.3 Managing central storage — 125
- 8.4 Review of the swap process — 125
- 8.5 Swap to expanded storage or auxiliary storage? — 126
- 8.6 Page steals, virtual fetch pages and VIO pages—page-outs — 127
- 8.7 Analysis for storage requirements — 129
- 8.8 How is the storage being used? — 130

	8.9	How do we find out whether we need additional central or expanded storage?	133
	8.10	Page migration and page management	140
	8.11	Storage isolation	144

9 Capacity planning for MVS in LPAR mode — 146
- 9.1 Introduction — 146
- 9.2 RMF Monitor I and LPAR mode — 147
- 9.3 The capture ratio—general point — 147
- 9.4 CPU utilization and LPAR mode — 147
- 9.5 The RMF Monitor I partition data report for LPAR mode — 148
- 9.6 Performance aspects of LPAR — 148
- 9.7 Capacity planning under LPAR — 150
- 9.8 The capture ratio—calculation — 152
- 9.9 Capacity planning for a partition — 154
- 9.10 How efficient is LPAR? — 157

10 Capacity planning for MVS in a VM guest partition — 159
- 10.1 Introduction — 159
- 10.2 VM multiple high-performance guests — 159
- 10.3 Start Interpretive Execution mode — 160
- 10.4 CP mode and involuntary wait time — 161
- 10.5 MVS clocks — 161
- 10.6 The RMF weakness — 162
- 10.7 The capture ratio for an MVS guest under VM — 164
- 10.8 Summary — 165

Appendices

1 Relevant SYS1. PARMLIB members for the system analysed in this book — 166
- A1.1 IEAIPS00 member of SYS1.PARMLIB — 166
- A1.2 IEAICS00 member of SYS1.PARMLIB — 167
- A1.3 IEAOPT00 member of SYS1.PARMLIB — 168
- A1.4 IEASYS00 member of SYS1.PARMLIB — 169
- A1.5 COFVLF00 member of SYS1.PARMLIB — 170
- A1.6 COFDLF00 member of SYS1.PARMLIB — 171
- A1.7 VATLST00 member of SYS1.PARMLIB — 172

2 Formatted worksheet for CPW analysis of RMF I Monitor report — 173

3 IBM internal throughput rates — 175

4 Complete quarter-hour RMF Monitor 1 report for the system analysed in this book — 177

5 The M Value as an alternative to relative processor power — 195
- A5.1 The RIOC versus the I/O per Q — 196

	A5.2 How is the M Value of another processor derived?	196
	A5.3 Summary	197

6 Calculating capture ratios by regression analysis — 198
A6.1 The SAS JOB SUBMITted for execution — 199

7 Recording the number of CICS ended transactions — 201
A7.1 The link between RMF, VTAM and CICS — 201
A7.2 Setting up CICS and RMF to collect CICS transactions — 201
A7.3 What about external networks? — 203
A7.4 CICS/ESA 3.2 and 3.3 — 203

Index — 206

Foreword

The IBM McGraw-Hill Series

IBM UK and McGraw-Hill Europe have worked together to publish this series of books about information technology and its use in business, industry and the public sector.

The series provides an up-to-date and authoritative insight into the wide range of products and services available, and offers strategic business advice. Some of the books have a technical bias, others are written from a broader business perspective. What they have in common is that their authors—some from IBM, some independent consultants—are experts in their field.

Apart from assisting where possible with the accuracy of the writing, IBM UK has not sought to inhibit the editorial freedom of the series, and therefore the views expressed in the books are those of the authors, and not necessarily those of IBM.

Where IBM has lent its expertise is in assisting McGraw-Hill to identify potential titles whose publication would help advance knowledge and increase awareness of computing topics. Hopefully these titles will also serve to widen the debate about the important information technology issues of today and of the future—such as open systems, networking, and the use of technology to give companies a competitive edge in their market.

IBM UK is pleased to be associated with McGraw-Hill in this series.

Sir Anthony Cleaver
Chairman
IBM United Kingdom Limited

Dedicated to IAG

Preface

This book has been written for the systems programmer/analyst and the computer centre manager. It is aimed at the professional computer practitioner and it shows how the information supplied by the technical team, who process the data supplied by the Resource Measurement Facility (RMF) Monitor I report, can be used by the management team to ensure that the optimum system is installed at the least cost to the enterprise.

When computer companies and information systems specialists ask the customer to spend literally millions of pounds, dollars, yen, or whatever, it behoves both the seller and the buyer to ensure that the system being obtained is in fact the 'right' one. *Caveat emptor* still applies, particularly in the IT industry.

The principles incorporated within this book have been applied by the author on many occasions. He was with IBM for 18 years, starting as a systems engineer, and leaving as a large-systems specialist. He had particular responsibility for capacity planning and performance studies of mainframe central electronic complexes (CECs) running under MVS, MVS/XA and MVS/ESA, both native and within logical partitions (LPAR mode) and as VM guest machines.

The author has also written many courses within IBM, to train both its own systems engineers and customers' systems programmers. The courses ranged from one-day introductory seminars, through 'team' development with others, to building ten-day, complex, internal operating system courses. Courses have also been developed in the Middle East, to train both expatriates and Saudi Arabian nationals.

During his latter period within IBM, he was responsible for the mainframe capacity planning curriculum at the IBM Education Centre. A complete inter-linked set of courses was developed in the United Kingdom, the United States of America and many European countries, and combined at the Education Centre to form a capacity planning curriculum.

Who would find this book useful?

Anyone responsible for the *capacity planning* of a mainframe central electronic complex (CEC); anyone responsible for a *performance study* of a mainframe; anyone responsible for the *evaluation* of a processor, in order that the claims of an information system (IS) supplier can be confirmed.

The components to be studied comprise the:

- Processing unit (CPU)
- I/O subsystem
- Processor storage (central and expanded storage)

The people involved with these components will be:

- Systems programmers
- Systems analysts
- Capacity planning and performance specialists
- Application designers
- Database administrators
- Technical managers

Objectives of this book

After reading this book, or using it as a reference work, you will understand the following:

- The necessity and requirement for capacity planning and performance planning
- IBM's principle of the service unit, as an indicator of processor power consumed by an executing task
- IBM's principle of the SRM second, and how the system resources manager (SRM) component of MVS/ESA allocates system resources to executing tasks
- IBM's principle of relative processor power (RPP) to measure processor power
- IBM's principle of external throughput rate (ETR), and why it is essential and at the heart of capacity planning calculations
- IBM's principle of internal throughput rate (ITR), and how it is used to arrive at the CPU service time of any type of transaction
- IBM's principle of internal throughput rate ratio (ITRR), and how it is used to compare the power of two or more processors, not necessarily IBM processors
- The techniques used to measure the use of the processing unit(s), I/O subsystem and both central and expanded storage.
- How to measure for capacity planning or performance purposes an MVS/ESA virtual guest machine running under VM/XA and VM/ESA, or an MVS/ESA system in an MVS/ESA logical partition (LPAR mode).

Pre-requisite knowledge required to get the best use of this book

An understanding of IBM's Resource Measurement Facility (RMF), product number 5685-029. The version used in this book is version 4, release 2, modification level 1 (V4.2.1). This knowledge can be obtained from publications, books and courses. In addition, an understanding of the IBM principle of the service unit (SU) and the system resources manager (SRM) second. Both of these will be reviewed in Chapter 2.

A sound knowledge of the IBM mainframe operating system MVS/ESA, product numbers 5695-047 (MVS/ESA SP JES2 VERSION 4) and 5695-048 (MVS/ESA SP JES3 VERSION 4). The principles incorporated within the SRM second and the SU are embodied in these products. In the last quarter of 1993 the version was version 4, release 3, modification level 0 (4.3.0).

The level of MVS mainly referred to in the book is version 4, release 2, modification level 2 (4.2.2). In capacity planning terms, version 4.3.0 incorporates additional support for ESCON channels and RAID (redundant arrays of independent disks). Chapter 7 briefly covers these features.

Other books by the author will cover the setting up of the SRM parameters in order to achieve the customer's objectives, and how to set up the Resource Measurement Facility (RMF) parameters in order to ensure the correct data is collected for further analysis.

Scope and structure of this book

The content of this book covers the capacity planning and performance studies of MVS systems. MVS in this context includes basic MVS system 370, MVS/XA (MVS Version 2) and MVS/ESA (MVS versions 3 and 4); primarily Version 3 (MVS/ESA) onwards. Generically, all MVS versions are referred to as 'MVS', but where it is necessary to differentiate between them, then this is done in context. The chapters can be read sequentially, randomly, or used as reference.

The hardware referred to is explicitly IBM, but as MVS can run on other manufacturers' processors, then it does not matter if the hardware you have installed is not IBM. The only time this does not apply is in Chapter 9, which deals with MVS in a logical (LPAR mode) partition, defined by IBM's Processor Resource/Systems Manager (PR/SM) feature.

The structure of the book is to define terms in Chapters 1–4, which are intentionally short in order to maintain discrete units for reference purposes. They are light reading for the very experienced practitioner; the real analysis starts at Chapter 5.

Methods

Each chapter stands alone, in that it can be treated as a separate segment. At the same time, if the reader is new to the subject, then it would be beneficial to take the topics in the order they are presented. A grounding in the understanding of some basic capacity planning principles is covered in the earlier chapters, and this is essential knowledge required of a capacity planner, or to make any performance study.

A peak quarter-hour Monitor 1 RMF report is used, and edited pages from the report are included within the relevant chapter where the data is to be extracted. The peak quarter-hour report is the one for the busiest period (usually ranging between 15 minutes and 1 hour). The smaller the peak period, the more accurate will be your data, and hence your calculated information and predictions. It is essential that you always use a peak period report, otherwise you will find that your system will be incapable of supporting your full workload at the busiest time. In addition, a formatted Monitor I CPU analysis worksheet is imbedded at various points throughout the CPU capacity planning analysis chapter (Chapter 5), and is continually updated with the information as we proceed through the topic.

The peak quarter-hour Monitor I RMF report is for a well-tuned system. The rationale of showing the analysis of a 'good' system is to show both how it is done and at the same time what sort of results can be expected from the well-run system. This will allow you to have something to compare against when you carry out your analysis on your own installations. A well-tuned system does not necessarily mean one that comprises the optimum configuration, as you will see as you go through the book.

Storage analysis is covered in the same manner, with an analysis sheet being completed in Chapter 8.

The RMF report

All examples in this book are based upon a peak period Resource Measurement Facility (RMF) Monitor I report (product number 5685-029).

The RMF Monitor I report is installed on a processor of the following configuration:

- IBM ES/9021 Model 340
- MVS/ESA version 4.2.1.
- IBM MVS/DFP version 3.3
- IBM RMF version 4.2.1
- IBM RACF version 1.9
- 128 megabytes of central storage
- 512 megabytes of expanded storage
- 48 channels
- IBM 3880 and IBM 3990 DASD controllers
- 55 IBM DASD comprising 3380-AD4s, AE4s and AJ4s
- 15-minute RMF reporting interval (900 seconds)

- One (1) second RMF cycle time
- RPP of IBM ES/9021 Model 340 taken as 27

Relative processor power

IBM relative processor power (RPP) is used as the basis for power consumed by transactions. All capacity planning calculations will use RPP as the sizing definition of any processor. This will hold true no matter which manufacturer's machine you are considering.

Calculations of RPP per transaction are based upon internal throughput rate (ITR). Comparison of processor power is also based upon ITR allied to the internal throughput rate ratio (ITRR). Capacity planning throughputs for each type of transaction are based upon the external throughput rate (ETR).

Chapter 3 deals with the ITR and ETR, and Chapter 4 with RPP and the ITRR. These topics have been deliberately kept in individual short chapters, in order to allow the book to be used as a reference work, if the need should arise.

Alternative to RPP

In the United States and Canada, an alternative method of comparing processor power is sometimes used, although the RPP method is gaining overall acceptance throughout Europe and the United States. The optional method is based upon the work of one of IBM Canada's performance analysts, Joe Major, and uses what is called the 'M Value' as the basis of comparing processor power. The M Value is not used in this book, but Appendix 5 shows the principle of how it is derived, and how it compares to the corresponding RPP value.

Data collection and setup of the SRM parameters

You will see that there is no chapter on data collection, or on setting up the SRM parameters to achieve your business objectives. This is a conscious decision to not incorporate these topics, as the author feels that they are worthy of an entirely separate book.

Setting up the SRM parameters for MVS/ESA Version 4.2 (and later releases and versions) in order to obtain the optimum distribution of the computer resources, in such a manner that they truly reflect your business requirements, certainly involves less effort than for previous MVS versions and releases. None the less it is still a complex business, which should therefore not be dismissed in one chapter.

Similarly, setting up RMF to ensure that the required data is selected for processing is also a fairly complex business which, to do it full justice, should not be delivered in just one chapter.

These chapters would be very long and out of context with the other chapters in the book. Therefore, an entirely separate book will be developed in due course by the author, which will cover both the setup of the SRM, and RMF.

Acknowledgements

The author would like to thank IBM (UK) Ltd Intellectual Properties for allowing information from IBM documents to be reproduced in this book. He would also like to thank John Larry, a friend and business colleague, for his valuable contribution to Appendix 7, which deals with the thorny point of getting RMF to produce individual CICS transaction counts and times. Finally, he would like to thank a friend, Geoffrey Smith. Geoffrey took the time to review the grammatical/syntactical aspects of the book, a time-consuming and soul-destroying job, for which the author is extremely grateful.

Trademarks

CICS, CICS/ESA, CICS/XA, DFHSM, DLONE, ES/390, ES/3090, ES/9000, ESA/370, ESA/390, GRS, HIPERBATCH, HIPPI, IBM, IMS, JES2, JES3, MVS, MVS/ESA, MVS/SP, MVS/XA, RACF, RMF, S/370, S/390, S/3090, SMF, SMP, SYSPLEX, TCAS, VM, VM/ESA, VM/XA are trademarks of International Business Machines Corporation.

The following are trademarks of features and functions incorporated within IBM products: **DATASPACE, DFSMS, DIV, DLF, ESCON, HIPERSPACE, ISPF, LPAR, PR/SM, SIE, VLF**.

HDS is a trademark of the Hitachi Data Systems Corporation.

MDF is a trademark of the Amdahl Corporation.

Glossary

ACB	access control block
APAR	application for program alteration
ASM	auxiliary storage manager
ASD	address space data
CA	criteria age
CC	clock comparator
CCW	channel command word
CEC	central electronic complex
CICS	Customer Information Control System
CICS/ESA	Customer Information Control System/Enterprise Systems Architecture
CICS/XA	Customer Information Control System/Extended Architecture
CP	control program
CPU	central processing unit
CR	capture ratio
DASD	direct access storage device
DCB	data control block
DFHSM	Data Facility Hierarchical Storage Manager
DFSMS	Data Facility Systems Managed Storage
DIM	data-in-memory
DIV	data-in-virtual
DL1	Data Language 1 (CICS)
DLF	Data Lookaside Facility
DLSE	device level selection extended
EC	engineering change
ES/3090	Enterprise System/3090
ES/390	Enterprise System/390
ESA/370	Enterprise Systems Architecture/370
ESA/390	Enterprise Systems Architecture/390
ESCON	Enterprise Systems Connection
ETR	external throughput rate
FIFO	first in first out
GTF	generalized trace facility
HIPPI	High Performance Parallel Interface
HSA	high storage area
IBM	International Business Machines

IML	initial microcode load
IMS	Information Management System
I/O	input/output
IOS	input/output supervisor
IOSQ	input/output supervisor's queue
ISPF	Integrated Structure Programming Facility
ITR	internal throughput rate
ITRR	internal throughput rate ratio
LCU	logical control unit
LPAR	logical partition
LSPR	large system performance reference
LSR	local shared resource
MA	migration age
MDF	Multiple Domain Facility
MHPG	multiple high-performance guest
MP	multi-processor
MPL	multi-programming level
MVS	Multiple Virtual Storage
MVS/ESA	Multiple Virtual Storage/Enterprise Systems Architecture
MVS/SP	Multiple Virtual Storage/Systems Product
MVS/XA	Multiple Virtual Storage/Extended Architecture
NVS	non-volatile storage
PG	performance group
PLPA	Pageable Link Pack Area
PR/SM	Processor Resource/Systems Manager
PTF	program temporary fix
RACF	Resource Access Control Facility
RAID	redundant array of independent disks
RIOC	relative input/output content
RMF	Resource Measurement Facility
RPP	relative processor power
RPS	rotational position sensing
RSM	real storage manager
RT	response time
SAD	system activity display
SAS	Statistical Analysis System
SCE	system control element
SDC	service definition coefficient
SECP	seldom ending channel program
SI	storage isolation
SIE	Start Interpretive Execution
SIGP	signal processor
SMF	Systems Management Facility
SMP	System Modification Program
SRB	service request block
SRM	systems resources manager
ST	service time
SU	service unit
TAR	transaction absorption rate
TCB	task control block
TIC	transfer-in-channel

TOD	time-of-day (clock)
TS	time in the system (transaction time)
TSO	time share option
TSR	transaction service rate
TTIME	total guest time
TQ	time on the queue
UCB	unit control block
UCW	unit control word
UIC	unreferenced interval count
UMV	utilized M Value
URPP	utilized relative processor power
VF	vector facility
V = F	Virtual = Fixed
VLF	Virtual Lookaside Facility
VM	Virtual Machine
VM/ESA	Virtual Machine/Enterprise Systems Architecture
VM/XA	Virtual Machine/Extended Architecture
V = R	Virtual = Real
VSAM	virtual storage access method
VTIME	virtual guest time
V = V	Virtual = Virtual
WAR	workload activity report
WTST	wait-to-start time

1
Justification of central electronic complex analysis

1.1 Get it in the budget!

One of the most difficult jobs to be undertaken by you—the capacity planning and performance analyst—is to sell your results to senior management in order to obtain the resources that you know are required in the future. To do this, you must ally your technical skills with the ability to present a complex solution in a simplified format; or employ the expertise of someone who is a presenter. The listeners' minds are attuned to a strategical level, and they must fit your plans into an overall company strategical objective. Try to think along the same lines if possible, and try to perceive your presentation from the chairs of the listeners. If possible, discuss your plans with sympathetic board members beforehand, in order to obtain allies.

The important point is to ensure that you get the resource requirements for information processing equipment *into the budget*. If you do not, then no matter how justified you are in your claims at a later date, you will get nothing allocated to your department; other departments will have consumed the year's available pool of money.

You must make a clear distinction between the requirements of the functional line departments, in terms of information they need to achieve their objectives at a *tactical* level, and the *strategical* requirements of the senior managers, who need information to assist them in their decision-making process. By ensuring that you restrict the strategical information to the decision-makers, you will help your case considerably. Strategists do not inspect the carrots, they put into place the environment to grow them at the least cost, and in the optimum manner—do not flood them with unnecessary information. In turn, the senior managers must be educated to be explicit both in their requirements and in stating the timing and form of the information needed.

You have to ensure that there is a defined avenue of authority and responsibility, from the decision-making level through to your IT department. This can sometimes be difficult, but is mainly achieved through having a strong personality as IT manager/director.

Regular, separate meetings should be held at each level of functional management and the IT department, but ensure that they remain within stated time limits, and discuss a prepared agenda. This agenda should be based upon your knowledge of the organization's business objectives, and the requirements of these departments to help achieve these objectives. Get this right and you will avoid later 'alibi' meetings, where you are looking for explanations (excuses?) as to why objectives are not being achieved. In other words, the functional line departments will be working together and with you, to ensure the success of the integrated strategical plan for the company. The IT department is at the centre of this process; ensure that the decision-makers are aware of this.

Make your IT plans clear, simple, systematic, realistic and continuous, and present them in a clear and concise manner to the decision-makers. Concentrate on the key data processing resources required, and do not succumb to the 'nice to have' approach, particularly in stringent financial times.

1.2 What do you analyse?

Any analysis should cover the three fundamental components of a mainframe central electronic complex (CEC)—central processing unit(s) (CPU(s)), I/O subsystem and central/expanded storage—allowing the analyser to establish how well the system is meeting the customer's business objectives, and at the same time, to identify the bottlenecks that are causing holdups. Only when this exercise has been completed can we see what resources (CPU(s), I/O and storage) are required to run the system efficiently, and at the least cost to the customer, i.e. what is the optimum system.

We have all read of, or possibly even know of, the claims made against the consultants and service providers who have been responsible for a computer system that either is not powerful enough to sustain the required number of users simultaneously, or is totally underused, or possibly just will not fit into the available floor space. A lot of money has probably been spent in all these cases to put it right. Correct capacity planning would have avoided these types of situation.

The storage requirement is normally based upon zero paging, which in turn is fundamental to the principle of data-in-memory (DIM). Additional DIM requirements, for example to achieve more Hiperspace use, would be in addition to the zero paging calculation.

1.3 Why analyse?

If we analyse our system properly, we are then in the position to plan for required capacity. Any system (computer or otherwise) is only efficient to the point of the first bottleneck. Our rationale is to identify these bottlenecks and remove them.

Only then can we optimize the information system (IS) CEC, in terms of current and future requirements, in order to achieve the customer's business objectives. The resources we will be optimizing are:

- CPU(s) engine(s)
- I/O subsystem
- Central and expanded storage

Decision-makers do not like surprises. Capacity planning enables us to ensure that surprises are at least kept to a minimum, and hopefully completely avoided. Therefore, capacity planning allows us to:

- Forecast the effect of growth in the current workload on the system.
- Forecast the effect of new applications on the current system.
- Forecast the future system requirements based on known growth rates.
- Define the required system to support merged/combined workloads.
- Arrive at the floor space and power requirements for the total system.

1.4 Capacity planning versus the performance study

Performance studies are essential. They are carried out continuously to ascertain the effectiveness of the system installed as a result of our capacity planning. The performance study enables us to see where the capacity planning was weak. It allows us to monitor the manner in which the system is behaving. Is it doing as we expected? If not, why not? The performance study is usually at a lower level than the capacity plan study. This is necessary, in order to identify where the capacity plan data was insufficient (or inefficient).

1.5 Performance versus capacity planning roadmap

Figure 1.1 is a roadmap showing what *monitoring* is trying to achieve. We monitor a system to ascertain whether the system is meeting its short-term and long-term objectives. The short-term objective is associated with *performance*. Is the system doing as we expect? It is giving the expected response time? Are the batch jobs turning round in the required time? Is there enough power to support the required number of CICS/TSO users during peak periods, and at the same time turn round the required number of batch jobs? Is there a current latent demand which would manifest itself if we added more processor power, which is 'hidden' merely because there is insufficient power to process the queued transactions? If this is so, then by adding another engine for example, we will allow only the queued latent transactions to complete; we will not have added more power to process the transactions that we have in mind perhaps.

Monitoring for performance can be regarded as checking to see if you are meeting your *service-level agreement* (assuming you have one!). This is the agree-

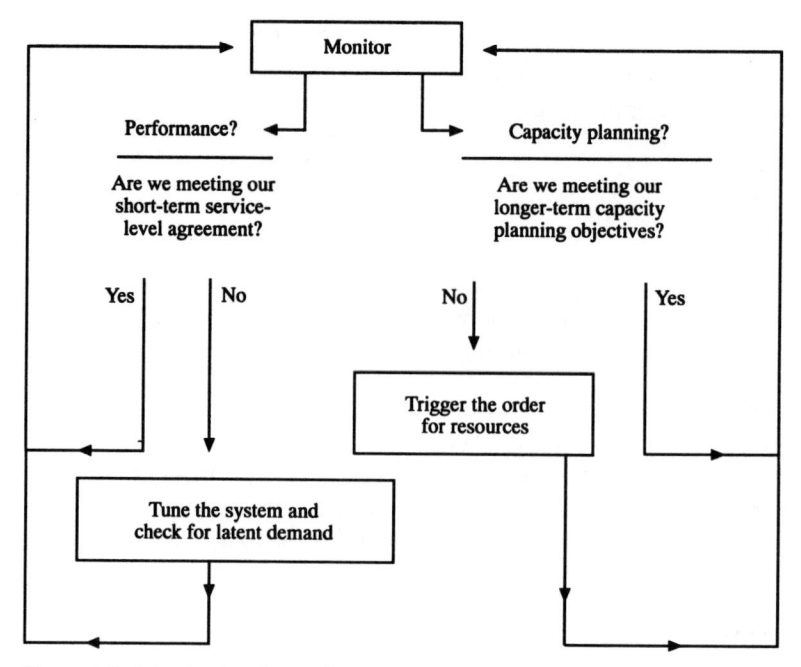

Figure 1.1. Monitoring for performance or capacity planning.

ment that you have with the users of your system to meet the requirements of these users, in order that they can meet their short-term objectives in helping the enterprise. You are all part of the same team. These are short-term objectives which can only be achieved *after* correct capacity planning. In other words, by monitoring for performance, we are checking our earlier capacity planning efforts. Monitoring for capacity planning therefore takes place *first*. We are looking to the *future* with monitoring for capacity planning. Will we be able to handle the extra CICS transactions expected in three months' time? Will we be able to complete the extra batch jobs that will be submitted during prime shift when a new application comes on line?

2
The service unit and the SRM second

2.1 Introduction

This chapter explains the unit of resource absorption, the *service unit* (SU), and the *systems resources manager* (SRM) *second*. It also explains how the number of SUs per SRM second falls as the number of engines rises. In turn, the SRM second has a direct bearing on the overall power of the CEC; the greater the number of SRM seconds per real second, the greater the power of the CEC's engine(s).

The three main hardware resources of the CEC are the CPU(s), the I/O subsystem and storage (both central and expanded). The resources are absorbed by the applications in the form of service units. The rate at which SUs are absorbed varies for each type of resource, and is a function of the weighting associated with the resource (more on this later).

2.2 The relationship between SUs and the SRM second

2.2.1 Service units

The component of the MVS/ESA operating system that measures the amount of resource (CPU, I/O and storage) that a transaction uses, is the *system resources manager* (SRM). The SRM allocates SUs to a transaction based upon the following criteria:

- The amount of processing unit time used while executing
- The amount of central storage used while executing
- The amount of I/O effected by the executing task

The number of SUs per second is the inverse of the the amount of time required to absorb one CPU SU. For example, the IBM ES/9021 Model 340 requires 860.36 microseconds (0.000 860 36 seconds) to absorb one CPU SU. Therefore, the number of SUs per second is:

$$1/0.000\,860\,36 = 1162.39$$

for this particular processor. The value, 1162.39, is referred to as the *CPU factor*, and is a representation of the power of the machine. We will see later how the alliance of the CPU factor and the number of engines (processors) allows us to arrive at relative powers of processors, not just IBM processors, but any manufacturer's machines.

Tables of CPU factors are in the IBM *Initialisation and Tuning Guide* (1993). Manual numbers vary, but the MVS/ESA version 4 manual used during last quarter 1993 was GC28-1634-04, dated March 1993.

2.2.2 Summary of how service units are calculated for a task

The *service definition coefficient* (SDC) is the weight given to each type of SU (CPU, I/O and storage). Its purpose was primarily to allow for the restrictions imposed by a lack of any one type of resource relative to the others. Therefore, the component with the least supply would have the heaviest weighting. With the advent of large amounts of storage and cached I/O, allied to faster and more powerful processors, the requirement to 'play' with this function has diminished.

Calculation of service units is as follows:

$$\text{CPU service units} = \text{CPU time} \times \text{SDC} \times \text{CPU factor} \times \text{No. engines}$$

$$\text{SRB service units} = \text{SRB time} \times \text{SDC} \times \text{CPU factor} \times \text{No. engines}$$

$$\text{I/O service units} = \text{\# EXCPs} \times \text{SDC or I/O connect time} \times \text{SDC}$$

$$\text{MSO service units} = \frac{\text{CS page frames} \times \text{SDC} \times \text{CPU service units}}{50}$$

where MSO main storage occupancy
　　　　CS central storage

2.2.3 The SRM second

As we have seen, the SU is the unit of allocation of a computer's resources. What we have to look at now is how the SRM knows when to invoke its routines that calculate how much resource the executing task is absorbing. This invocation interval differs according to the power of the machine. A faster processor absorbs SUs at a higher rate than a slower one.

Let us consider a base machine, then all other processors can be measured in relative terms against this base machine. In fact, this is what IBM has done; the base machine is a IBM 370/158 Model 3, and it is reckoned to allow a task to absorb 1 CPU SU in 23.81 milliseconds. The inverse of this number is $1/0.02381 = 42$; this is the CPU factor for a 370/158 Model 3. To look at this another way, this is the number of SUs per *real* second that are absorbed by an executing task on a

370/158 Model 3, because there is 1 SRM second per real second on a 370/158 Model 3.

Supposing we now double the power of the processor, maintaining a single CPU (engine). This will mean that the time to absorb a CPU SU is halved to 11.91 milliseconds (0.01191 seconds). The inverse of this is $1/0.01191 = 83.96$ (say 84). Thus the CPU factor for this machine that has doubled in power is 84.

If we now tell the SRM that the time to absorb a CPU SU on this faster processor is 11.91 milliseconds, and in addition, tell the SRM that it must invoke its calculating routines when 42 SUs have been absorbed (the number of SUs that can be absorbed on the base machine, a 370/158 Model 3, in 1 second), then in fact the routines will be invoked every 42×0.01191 seconds $= 0.5$ second. In other words, the routines will be invoked *twice per real second*, as opposed to once per real second on the base machine. The SRM sees the half-second to absorb 42 SUs on the faster machine as the *SRM second*. There will be $2 \times 42 = 84$ SUs per real second on this machine (a CPU factor of 84), and there will be 2 SRM seconds per real second on this faster machine.

Let us take this one stage further. On a machine *four* times as fast as the base machine (still maintaining a single engine), the SRM will invoke its routines *four* times per second. Thus the SRM second will be 0.25 s on this particular machine. It will only take 0.25 s to absorb 42 SUs, and there will be $4 \times 42 = 168$ SUs per real second on this machine; or there will be 4 SRM seconds per real second on this machine.

We now tell the SRM the amount of time to absorb a CPU SU by placing this value into a control block; IRARMCPU in module IEAVNP10. This is done by putting on a program temporary fix (PTF) whenever a machine is upgraded. No change is necessary to the IEAIPSxx, IEAICSxx or IEAOPTxx members of SYS1.PARMLIB. Merely the application of a PTF is required whenever a machine upgrade is installed.

Invocations of the calculating routines are more frequent on the faster processors. In this manner, we have a degree of repeatability, which in turn allows us to manage the computer system, and find out just how much of the processor's resources each type of transaction uses.

The SRM in fact invokes its SU calculating routines every 100 SRM seconds. Therefore, on the base machine this would be every 100 real seconds. On a machine 20 times faster than the base machine, this would be every 5 real seconds.

Tables of service units per real second are in the *Initialisation and Tuning Guide* (1993) already referred to, manual number GC28-1634-04.

2.3 The relationship between the SRM second, real seconds and the SU

Figure 2.1 shows the relationship between the SU real seconds and the SRM second. Maintaining our example of a processor with a single CPU (engine), as the engine speed is doubled, so the time to absorb an SU is halved (in simple terms),

Base processor

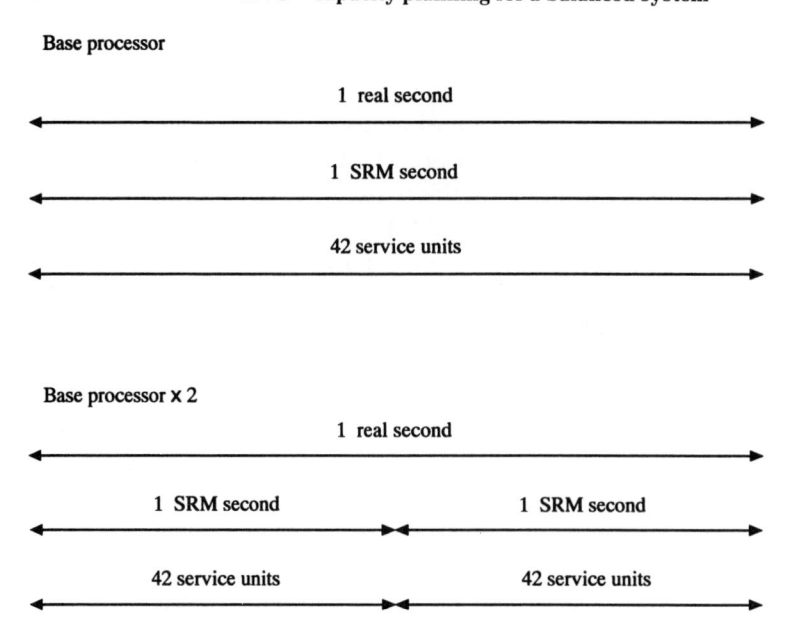

```
|←——————————— 1 real second ———————————→|

|←——————————— 1 SRM second ———————————→|

|←——————————— 42 service units ———————————→|
```

Base processor × 2

```
|←——————————— 1 real second ———————————→|

|←——— 1 SRM second ———→|←——— 1 SRM second ———→|

|←——— 42 service units ——→|←——— 42 service units ——→|
```

Figure 2.1. The relationship between the SRM second, the real second and the service unit.

correspondingly the time associated with an SRM second is halved. As the time to absorb an SU is halved, so the number of SRM seconds per real second doubles. Therefore, there are twice as many invocations of the SRM routines on the faster processor, in order to compensate for the quicker absorption of SUs.

2.4 Multi-engined processors

Finally, we must take into account the number of engines that a processor (CEC) has. If it has two engines, then this means that it can execute two tasks in parallel. Therefore, the number of SUs absorbed per second is in fact doubled, in theory. Because MVS/ESA has to manage these two engines, and ensure that certain parts of its code are not executed on both engines at the same time (that is why we have MVS LOCKS in the code), then in fact the number of SUs per real second falls slightly as the number of engines grows. Therefore, the power of a machine grows as we add engines, but at a diminishing rate as the number of engines increases; this has to be taken into account in arriving at the overall power of the CEC.

So, as the number of engines grows, the power of the processor grows, but the CPU factor per engine falls. The degree to which it falls is a function of the efficiency of the manufacturer's code and architecture. Figure 2.2 indicates how the CPU factor falls as the number of engines increases.

The service unit and the SRM second

Model	No. of engines	CPU factor per engine
IBM ES/9021 Model 520	1	2324.76
IBM ES/9021 Model 640	2	2208.52
IBM ES/9021 Model 740	3	2138.78
IBM ES/9021 Model 820	4	2045.79
IBM ES/9021 Model 860	5	1976.04
IBM ES/9021 Model 900	6	1883.05

Figure 2.2. Showing how the CPU factor falls as engines are added.

2.4.1 By how much does efficiency fall as engines are added?

Taking the single engine machine as the 'base', we can calculate the diminishing power from each engine, as more engines are added:

From 1 to 2 engines $2208.52/2324.76 = 0.95$ (95%)

From 1 to 3 engines $2138.78/2324.76 = 0.92$ (92%)

From 1 to 4 engines $2045.79/2324.76 = 0.88$ (88%)

From 1 to 5 engines $1976.04/2324.76 = 0.85$ (85%)

From 1 to 6 engines $1883.05/2324.76 = 0.81$ (81%)

Therefore, for example, we can see that the output from each engine in a four-way processor (IBM ES/9021 Model 820) is 88% of a single engine machine. The value of 0.88 (88%) is referred to as the *multi-processor ratio* (MP ratio). We can check this by the following calculations:

$4 \times 2324.76 \times 0.88 = 8183$ (4 × single engine CPU factor × MP ratio)

or:

$4 \times 2045.79 = 8183$ (4 × reduced CPU factor per engine)

8183 (which is close enough for our purposes) represents the number of SUs per real second that are available for absorption on an IBM ES/9021 Model 820, *across all four engines*. The CPU factor per engine is 2045.79. Recalling that the SRM second incorporates 42 SUs, then if we divide 2045.79 by 42, we arrive at the number of SRM seconds per engine for this particular processor:

$2045.79/42 = 48.7$ SRM seconds per engine

As this is a four-way processor, then:

$4 \times 48.7 = 194.8$ (say 195) SRM seconds for the entire processor

Does this number 195 look familiar? Perhaps not, but if you look up the claimed *relative processor power* (RPP) value of the IBM ES/9021 Model 820, you will see it is the same as the number of SRM seconds available. In fact, the RPP figure for the IBM ES/9021 Model 820 is given as 195, but RPP values of this magnitude are rounded to the nearest integer as you will see later in Chapter 4. Therefore, our calculated value of 195 SRM seconds begins to look acceptable as a measure of processor power, which is normally measured in RPP units.

So, RPP values are in fact the number of SRM seconds per real second per processor, taking into account the number of engines and the reduction factor (MP ratio) associated with the additional engines. Now that you know just what the SRM second is, you know now how to ascertain the processor power of any machine, and see if it really matches the claims of the manufacturer. The whole basis of power measurement is the time to absorb one SU; the value in the IRARMCPU control block. IBM and its mainframe competitors are honourable companies, which would not place a value in this control block which was incorrect (although mistakes can be made—IBM's five-engine processor values always seemed a bit out).

Figure 2.3 indicates the relationship between the number of engines and the CPU factor for a transaction absorbing 42 SUs. Figure 2.4 indicates the relationship between the number of engines and the SRM second for a transaction absorbing 42 SUs.

Processor type	Number of engines	CPU factor (SU per real second per engine)	Millisecs per SU	Total SUs per transaction	Millisecs per transaction
	A	B	$C = (1/B) \times 1000$	D	$E = C \times D$
		CPU FACTOR			
370/158-3	1	42.0	23.8	42	1000
3090/120J	1	477.28	2.095	42	88
3090/180J 9021/340	1	1162.38	0.860	42	36.12
3090/200J 9021/500	2	1104.26	0.906	42	38.05
3090/300J 9021/580	3	1069.39	0.935	42	39.27
3090/400J 9021/620	4	1022.89	0.978	42	41.08
3090/500J	5	988.02	1.012	42	42.50
3090/600J 9021/720	6	941.53	1.062	42	44.60
9021/820	4	2045.79[1]	0.489	42	20.54
9021/860	5	1976.04[1]	0.506	42	21.25
9021/900	6	1883.05[1]	0.531	42	22.30

Note:
1 Extracted from Fig. 2.2.

Figure 2.3. Relationship between number of engines and CPU factor.

Processor type	Nominal SRM seconds per real second per engine	Multi-processor ratio	Effective SRM seconds per real second per engine	Effective SRM seconds per processor (RPP value)	Milliseconds per SRM second
	F	G = B/1162.38	H = F × G	J = A × H	K = 1000/H
370/158-3	1	1	1	1	1000
3090/120J	11.36	1	11.36	11.36	88
3090/180J 9021/340	27.67	1	27.67	27.67	36.14
3090/200J 9021/500	27.67	0.95	26.29	52.58	38.04
3090/300J 9021/580	27.67	0.92	25.46	76.38	39.28
3090/400J 9021/620	27.67	0.88	24.35	97.40	41.07
3090/500J	27.67	0.85	23.52	117.60	42.52
3090/600J 9021/720	27.67	0.81	22.41	134.46	44.62
9021/820	55.20[1]	0.88[2]	48.58	194.32	20.58
9021/860	55.20[1]	0.85[2]	46.92	234.60	21.31
9021/900	55.20[1]	0.81[2]	44.71	268.26	22.37

Notes:
1 1.995 × 27.67.
2 The last three values in column B in Fig. 2.3 divided by 2324.76 (from the SUs per real second column for the IBM ES/9021 Model 520).

Figure 2.4. Relationship between number of engines and the SRM second.

As the transaction absorbs 42 SUs, and there 42 SUs in an SRM second, then column E in Fig. 2.3 (milliseconds per transaction) will be the same as column K in Fig. 2.4 (milliseconds per SRM second). In fact, there are differences due to rounding, but as you can see, they are very small.

2.4.2 Execution time per SU

In Fig. 2.5 the execution times for a service unit on the IBM ES/9021 520-based processors are approximately 1.995 times the IBM 9021 Model 340-based machines, which in turn are the same as the IBM 3090 Model 180J-based machines. The increase of 1.995 (i.e. the execution time per service unit is almost halved) is based upon internal throughput rate (ITR) improvements on the IBM 9021 processors, with MVS/ESA SP 3.1.3 installed.

Figure 2.6 shows how the factor of 1.995 was derived for the increase in power from the IBM 9021 340-based processors, to the IBM 9021 520 based (Summit) processors. The information in the table is based upon IBM announcement material in September 1991. Note that the 'power increase' of 1.995 referred to in

Processor model	Execution time per SU	SUs per real second	No. of engines	Total SUs	Calculated power
		A	B	C = A × B	C/42
9021-520	0.000430[1]	2324.76	1	2324.76	55
9021-640	0.000453[1]	2208.52	2	4417.04	105
9021-740	0.000468[1]	2138.78	3	6416.34	153
9021-820	0.000489[1]	2045.79	4	8183.16	195
9021-860	0.000506[1]	1976.04	5	9880.20	235
9021-900	0.000531[1]	1883.05	6	11 298.30	269
9021-340	0.000860	1162.38	1	1162.38	27
9021-500	0.000906	1104.26	2	2208.52	52
9021-580	0.000935	1069.39	3	3208.17	76
9021-620	0.000978	1022.89	4	4091.56	97
9021-720	0.001062	941.53	6	5649.18	134
3090-180 J	0.000860	1162.38	1	1162.38	27
3090-200 J	0.000906	1104.26	2	2208.52	52
3090-300 J	0.000935	1069.39	3	3208.17	76
3090-400 J	0.000978	1022.89	4	4091.56	97
3090-500 J	0.001049	988.02	5	4940.10	117
3090-600 J	0.001062	941.53	6	5649.18	134
3090-200 S	0.001033	997.50	2	1995.00	47
3090-300 S	0.001035	966.00	3	2898.00	69
3090-400 S	0.001082	924.00	4	3696.00	88
3090-500 S	0.001120	892.50	5	4462.50	106
3090-600 S	0.001176	850.50	6	5103.00	121

Note:
1 Estimates based on announcement material issued by IBM in September 1991.

Figure 2.5. Calculated processor power from the SRM constant.

Upgrade	CB84	CIC3	DB2	IMS	TSO	Total	Average
340 to 520	2.08	2.04	1.95	1.93	2.00	10.00	2.00
500 to 640	2.06	2.03	1.90	1.93	1.93	9.85	1.97
580 to 740	2.04	2.00	1.87	1.94	1.91	9.76	1.95
620 to 820	2.08	2.09	2.01	2.00	1.98	10.16	2.03
500J to 860	2.07	2.05	1.98	2.02	1.97	10.09	2.02
720 to 900	2.06	2.00	1.98	2.01	1.97	10.02	2.00
					Overall average		1.995

Figure 2.6. Power increase for the '520' based (Summit) processors.

Fig. 2.6 is based upon IBM's internal throughput rate ratio (ITRR). This will be covered in Chapter 4, but suffice to say for the moment, that it is a proven and accepted means of comparing the power of processors, derived from the rate at which known types of transactions (e.g. CICS, TSO or batch) are executed on the processors being compared.

3
External throughput rate, internal throughput rate and CPU service time

3.1 Introduction

This chapter describes the *external throughput rate* (ETR), the *internal throughput rate* (ITR), the relationship between them, and how they are used in mainframe capacity planning and performance studies. The *internal throughput rate ratio* (ITRR) and how it is used to ascertain the relative powers of any manufacturer's mainframe computers are also explained.

Before we start, it would be advisable to ensure a reasonable understanding of basic queuing theory. This will not be an in-depth study of this topic, as there are many textbooks that cover it in great detail. It is essential, however, to have an understanding of how some of our more fundamental formulae are derived and used in capacity planning and performance studies.

3.1.1 A single server system

A post office counter with only one person attending to the public who require service is a good example of a single server system. Figure 3.1 is a diagrammatic representation of a single server system.

The queue →	The servee	The server
(Many)	(One)	(One)

←──────────── The system ────────────→

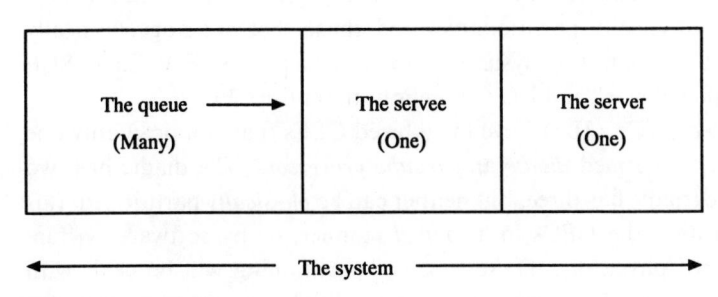

Figure 3.1. A single server system.

Another example of a single server system is a uni-processor, which has only one engine to process the transactions arriving at the CEC.

3.1.2 Defining the terms

- *Central electronic complex (CEC)* The entire computer processor system.
- *The system* The entire structure set up to serve potential clients. It includes the queue of waiters, who are waiting to be served. Once clients join a queue they are 'in the system'. A computer CEC, made up of the CPU, the I/O subsystem and its associated storage, is a good example of a system. Transactions arriving at the processor complex, like customers in a post office system, will probably have to wait to be served by the CPU, i.e. they will be queued.
- *The queue* The transactions (or customers) waiting to be served. The queue can be processed first in first out (FIFO) as for a post office, but is usually a little more sophisticated in a computer system. Different transactions are usually ranked according to their type. For example, a CICS teleprocessing transaction normally ranks higher than a batch transaction, and so even if the batch transaction 'arrives' first, it may have to wait until a later arriving CICS transaction has been processed.
- *The servee* In a uni-processor system, as with a single serving counter in the post office, there can only be one transaction (customer) being served at any one time. In a multi-engined system, or a post office with more than one serving counter, a number of transactions (customers) can be served in parallel. The transaction being processed, or the customer being served, is known as the servee. There can be more than one transaction being served in a multi-engined system, each transaction being processed by a different engine at the same time.
- *The server* In a post office, the server is serving a customer (or customers). In a computer processor, the server will be the central processing unit (CPU). Multi-engined processors will have more than one CPU (engine), each engine working in parallel with the others.
- *Multi-engined processors* This term was used in the earlier discussion, but it should be explained. The definition of a multi-engined processor can include CECs that are physically partitionable, and those that are not. Physically dividable CECs contain *two* system control elements (SCEs). Each SCE controls the traffic of work and I/O throughout the entire CEC.
- *Non-partitionable CECs* IBM have introduced CECs that comprise only one SCE, and these are termed *diadic* and *triadic processors*. The diadic has two engines, and the triadic has three, but neither can be *physically* partitioned. It is possible to partition the CECs in a *logical* manner, or by software (virtual machine), but not physically. These types of partitioning will be dealt with in Chapters 9 and 10. The diadic and triadic CECs are *not* '*n*-way' multi-

processors—that term is restricted to defining physically partitionable machines (see next item—they are multi-engined processors though).
- *Partitionable CECs* Partitionable CECs comprise those that can be divided along power boundaries into two physically separate CECs. Each half can run a different operating system, and has its own set of channels/DASD and storage, and is entirely standalone. For example, the IBM ES/9021 Model 620 is a four-way multi-processor that can be partitioned into two diadics; it is *not* a quadratic machine. The IBM ES/9021 Model 720 is a six-way multi-processor that can be partitioned into two triadics; it is *NOT* a sexadic! Perhaps there is a more fundamental reason why IBM prefers to call it a six-way multi-processor!

3.2 Useful derivatives

In order to arrive at information such as the amount of time that a transaction has either to wait to be processed, or to wait for I/O, we need to understand some basic queuing theory; nothing elaborate, but none the less essential to our ability to analyse properly. This is particularly true of performance studies, which will be enlarged upon in Chapter 6 along with capacity planning analysis.

A single server system is made up of one server, a servee (the person being currently served), and a queue of potential servees (waiters). There is a time associated with each of these components, which can be calculated. What we need to know is the following information in order to calculate these times:

- The *arrival rate* of potential servees (transactions)
- The *service rate* of the server (engine)

3.2.1 The utilization of the system for single or multi-server systems

The *utilization* (U) of the total system is the ratio of the rate of arrival to the rate of service. This is also a representation of how busy the system is. It is, in effect, the probability that the system is busy when a new transaction enters the system. As the number of servers (engines) increases, then the service rate will also increase, thereby reducing the utilization.

The utilization formula is:

$$\text{Utilization (U)} = \frac{\text{Arrival rate}}{\text{Service rate}}$$

3.2.2 The service time for single or multi-server systems

As the reciprocal of the service rate is the service time (ST), then utilization can also be defined as the arrival rate multiplied by the service time. The service time will *not* vary as the number of servers vary.

An alternative formula for system utilization is therefore:

Utilization (U) = Arrival rate × Service time (ST)

3.2.3 The time on the queue for a single server system

The time on the queue (TQ) is calculated by service time × average number on queue, where the average number on the queue is represented by the ratio of the probability that the system is busy, to the probability that it is *not* busy; that is, the ratio of the utilization of the system, to one minus the utilization:

Average number on the queue = $U/(1 - U)$

The formula for time on the queue for a single server (engine) system is as follows:

$$TQ = ST \times \frac{U}{1 - U}$$

As the number of servers (engines) increases, then the formula for time on the queue will change. In Chapter 6 we will go into this in more detail, when we derive the time that a transaction has to wait for a CPU (engine).

3.2.4 The time in the system for a single server system

The time in the system (TS) is the time on the queue (TQ) plus the time taken to be served (ST):

$$TS = TQ + ST$$

The time in the system can be represented in another way for a single server system—the time required to be served multiplied by the average number in the system. The average number in the system is made up of the servee (the *only* one in a single server system) plus the average number on the queue. Therefore, the following holds true in a single server system:

TS = ST × Average number in the system

where average number in the system is 1 + average number on the queue. Therefore:

Average number in the system = $1 + (U/(1 - U))$

but:

$1 + (U/(1 - U)) = 1/(1 - U)$

Thus the formula for time in the system (TS) is:

$$TS = ST \times \frac{1}{1 - U}$$

Note: 'time in the system' (TS) is analogous to 'transaction time'.

We will now look at how these principles work within the CEC. The arrival rate and service rate of transactions have their own terminology in capacity planning and performance studies, but they are still based upon the fundamental ideas just described.

3.3 Calculating the external throughput rate

The external throughput rate (ETR) is the rate at which the total CEC system, which is made up of the processing unit(s), the storage (central and expanded) and the I/O subsystem, can process a transaction of a particular type. Examples of a transaction can be a batch job, a TSO interaction with a local or remote user, or a CICS interaction with a local or remote user. Each type of transaction will have its own ETR, depending upon the degree of use of system components and amount of I/O required to effect the transaction, and the current load of various types of other transactions currently being executed on the system. As you can see, the ETR will not be constant, but, as you will see later, is very much a function of how busy the system is, and it *changes at a constant rate*, for practical purposes.

The ETR measures the rate at which the total configuration (CPU, storage and I/O subsystem), can process transactions. There is a different ETR for each type of transaction, and it is very useful for capacity planning purposes as we will see, because it reflects the reality of your total configuration's throughput, not any theoretical limit that may be quoted.

The ETR of any transaction is a function of:

- The operating system
- The current PTF level
- The current I/O configuration
- The current architecture of the system
- The amount of both central and expanded storage currently installed
- The current workload of all types on the system
- The current engineering change (EC) level on the system

Recall that any system is only as efficient as its first bottleneck. Therefore, in a computer system, all components other than the CPU will act as a limiting factor on the efficiency of the processor (because the CPU is the fastest component). The ETR reflects the limiting effect of all the other components, and thus shows you the real throughput of transactions in your system. It shows the 'warts and all' effect for each different type of transaction. For example, if your paging level is high, indicating a shortage of central storage, then this will affect your ETR; it will fall.

Accepting also that the units that make up the CEC work together to form a system in the real sense, then we can see that, in effect, the ETR for any transaction is in fact the rate of arrival of the transactions at the fastest component, the processing unit (CPU). Therefore, the CPU is the server in our computer system, and in a multi-engined system, we thus have multi-servers.

We know that the ETR varies according to the load on the system, but *providing all other variables remain constant*, we will see that the ETR varies at a constant rate for practical purposes; and remember, capacity planning is about practicality. Indeed IBM has plotted figures (more on this later) which show this information, known as the *large system performance reference (LSPR)*.

If the ETR changes at a constant rate, then we can use this information to arrive at the amount of processor power used per transaction (of each type). This information (again for practical purposes) is a constant, therefore it can be used for capacity planning purposes.

We calculate the ETR from the following formula:

$$\text{ETR} = \frac{\text{Number of completed transactions}}{\text{Elapsed interval time (seconds)}}$$

3.4 Calculating the internal throughput rate

The calculated internal throughput rate (ITR) is not the same as the IBM LSPR ITR. This is because the LSPR ITR is based upon a 'standard' workload, whereas the calculated ITR is based upon the actual workload on the customer's installation. Therefore, the calculated ITR is the more accurate, and reflects the real workload of the customer. The LSPR ITR has its uses, which we will see later.

If you recall that the ETR was the rate of arrival of the transactions at the fastest component making up the computer system (the processing unit), then the ITR is the *rate of service* of the processing unit itself. There is an ITR for each type of transaction, as there is for the ETR. Thus, we can see that the computer system is a 'system' in the true sense; it has a rate of arrival (ETR) of transactions, allied to the service rate (ITR) of those transactions once they are in the system. We can use this understanding to our advantage.

The ITR measures the speed of the processing unit(s). Therefore, once a transaction is dispatched on an engine, it is running at its maximum speed. It is unfettered by any other component, therefore it reflects the speed in a totally unconstrained environment, within which the theoretical maximum transaction rate for this type of transaction may be achieved. The ITR is showing the service rate of the system for this type of transaction. Once the transaction requests an I/O, then it will give up this privileged position, and revert to being held up while the I/O is processed; a slower process than executing on a CPU. It is back in ETR country.

Thus the ITR is a measurement of the processing unit(s) only, not of the entire system as the ETR is. The speed and power of the processing unit, or the engine, for a uni-processor, reflects the service rate of the processor—the ITR. There is a different ITR for each type of transaction, as for the ETR.

The ITR for any transaction is almost a constant, whereas the ETR is not a constant (but it does change at a constant rate). The ITR usually falls slightly as the processor gets busier with transactions (of any type, including transactions of the type currently being measured). The increase in the rate of CICS transactions has a different effect on the ITR—it *rises* slightly! This apparent paradox is because CICS transactions are usually the quickest in the processor, and the code is optimized for many concurrent transactions. This optimization is sometimes referred to as *multi-threading*.

The ITR is calculated as follows:

$$\text{ITR} = \frac{\text{Number of completed transactions}}{\text{Total number of CPU seconds}}$$

As the ITR measures the service rate of the engine in a uni-processor, then this is in fact an upper bound towards which the ETR tends, but never reaches, as the processor rises towards 100 per cent utilization. In mathematical terms this is referred to as an asymptote. That is, the ETR is asymptotic to the ITR; it tends toward the ITR but will never attain the same value.

3.4.1 Using the ITR to calculate the CPU service time

Recall that the reciprocal of the service rate is the service time. Therefore, as the ITR is the service rate, then $1/\text{ITR}$ = the service time. Multiplying $1/\text{ITR}$ by 1000 will give the service time in milliseconds. The following gives CPU service time in milliseconds for a uni-processor:

$$\text{CPU service time (ST) (in milliseconds)} = \frac{1000}{\text{ITR}}$$

3.4.2 How ITR is affected by multi-engined processors

As we add engines, so the ITR will increase by an amount which is a function of the type of transaction, allied to the already existing number of engines. This is because each engine will execute a transaction in parallel with the other engines. The ETR will be about the same, and will still change at about the same rate, as any increase in the ITR would be compensated by a corresponding reduction in the CPU busy percentage (ETR = ITR × CPU busy %). This change in the ITR has to be taken into account, as it has an impact on our formula for milliseconds of CPU time per transaction. Recall that the formula for a single server is:

$$\text{CPU service time (ST) (in milliseconds)} = \frac{1000}{\text{ITR}}$$

As the number of engines has no effect on the individual service time for a transaction on any of the engines, we must remove the effect on the ITR of the additional engines. This is done simply by multiplying the CPU service time by the number of engines. The following modified formula gives the CPU service time on a multi-processor:

$$\text{CPU service time (ST) (in milliseconds)} = \frac{1000 \times \text{No. of engines}}{\text{ITR}}$$

3.5 Is there a relationship between the ETR and the ITR?

There is a relationship between the ETR and ITR which we can make good use of. Let us look at the formula for the calculated ETR:

$$\text{ETR} = \frac{\text{Number of completed transactions}}{\text{Elapsed seconds in the interval}}$$

and the formula for the calculated ITR:

$$\text{ITR} = \frac{\text{Number of completed transactions}}{\text{Total number of CPU seconds}}$$

The 'number of completed transactions' is common to both formulae, therefore:

$$\text{ETR} \times \text{Elapsed seconds in the interval} = \text{Number of completed transactions}$$

and

$$\text{ITR} \times \text{Total number of CPU seconds} = \text{Number of completed transactions}$$

Therefore:

$$\text{ETR} \times \text{Elapsed seconds in interval} = \text{ITR} \times \text{Total number of CPU seconds}$$

Therefore:

$$\frac{\text{ETR}}{\text{ITR}} = \frac{\text{Total number of CPU seconds}}{\text{Elapsed seconds in the interval}}$$

and as

$$\frac{\text{Total number of CPU seconds}}{\text{Elapsed seconds in the interval}} = \text{CPU per cent busy}$$

then

$$\frac{\text{ETR}}{\text{ITR}} = \text{CPU per cent busy}$$

Therefore:

$$\text{ETR} = \text{ITR} \times \text{CPU per cent busy}$$

and

$$\text{ITR} = \text{ETR}/\text{CPU per cent busy}$$

3.5.1 Calculating the ITR, ETR and CPU service time

Remember, we are calculating the CPU service time, which is part of the overall transaction time that is spent on the CPU. Therefore, the service time is a component part of the transaction time.

Using the information in the case study RMF Monitor I report, which we will go into in more detail later, let us suppose the following data was extracted in response to a request for information:

> TSO production performance group 42
> Number of completed transactions (all periods) = 3268
> CPU seconds calculated = 103.1 seconds (expanded later)
> Total elapsed time = 900 seconds

The following information can be derived from this extracted data:

$$ITR = \frac{\text{Number of completed transactions}}{\text{Total number of CPU seconds}}$$

$$= \frac{3268}{103.1} = 31.7 \text{ transactions per second}$$

and:

$$ETR = \frac{\text{Number of completed transactions}}{\text{Elapsed time in the interval}}$$

$$= \frac{3268}{900} = 3.63 \text{ transactions per second}$$

and:

$$ST = \frac{1000 \times \text{Number of engines}}{ITR}$$

$$= \frac{1000 \times 1}{31.7} = 31.5 \text{ milliseconds}$$

3.5.2 How do we use the calculated ETR and ITR?

As we have seen, the calculated ITR can be used to find the CPU milliseconds per transaction. This is essential information when we are analysing for performance as opposed to capacity planning, as will be seen later. A transaction has many components all taking a certain amount of time, which make up the total time for the transaction. For example, queuing for the processor along with other transactions of equal and higher priority (specified in the installation performance specification—IEAIPSxx), waiting for I/O to complete, and waiting to be swapped in (for a TSO transaction possibly).

The ETR is very useful for capacity planning studies. For example, supposing the following question were asked of you (as you are the capacity planning expert!): 'What is going to be the additional load on my processor, if I add another 100 production TSO users during the peak period of the day?'

MVS—capacity planning for a balanced system

To start answering this question you would need the following data extracted from a peak period RMF Monitor I report:

The total RPP output of the processor	An IBM 9021/340 of 27 RPP
The number of production TSO users	65
Current number of (peak) transactions	3268 per 15 minute interval
Utilized RPP (URPP) of the PG	3.527 RPP (covered later)

From this data we can now derive the following information:

$$\text{ETR} = \frac{3268}{900} = 3.63 \text{ transactions per second}$$

$$\text{RPP/transaction} = \frac{\text{Utilized RPP for PG}}{\text{ETR}}$$

$$= \frac{3.527}{3.63} = 0.97 \text{ URPP per transaction}$$

$$\text{Transactions per user (average)} = \frac{\text{Ended transactions}}{\text{No. of users}} = \frac{3268}{65} = 50$$

Expected no. of transactions over period $= 100 \times 50 = 5000$

$$\text{No. of transactions per second increase} = \frac{5000}{900} = 5.6$$

Additional load on processor $=$ URPP/transaction $\times$ transaction/second
$$= 0.97 \times 5.6 = 5.44 \text{ RPP}$$

or more simply:

$$(100/65) \times 3.527 = 5.43 \text{ RPP}$$

(very close to our value already calculated by the longer method).

4
Internal throughput rate ratio and IBM relative processor power

4.1 Introduction

Now that we have covered the ITR, we can look at the internal throughput rate ratio (ITRR), which is used to compare the power of CECs' engines. You will see that the ITRR is an established method of comparing any manufacturer's processor's power against any other processor's power, not necessarily from the same supplier.

You will also see that the ITRR is a volatile value, and so the introduction of the relative processing power (RPP) unit is really quite necessary for capacity planning and performance studies. The establishment of the RPP as the measure of processor power, and of comparing powers, allows us to bring a degree of stability to the capacity planning and performance study process.

4.2 The internal throughput rate ratio

Recall that the ITR is a measure of the rate at which the engine (processing unit) can service the type of transaction in question (i.e. there is an ITR for TSO transactions, one for CICS transactions, one for batch transactions, one for vector processor transactions, and yet another for a scientific number-crunching type of transaction). If we calculate the ITR for a particular type of transaction, on a particular processor, and then put the same type of transaction onto a processor of twice the engine speed, we would expect (in simple terms) a doubling of the service rate, i.e. a doubling of the ITR. In fact the laws of diminishing returns will have an impact on the ITR as we already know.

We can use this philosophy to compare processor powers (speeds), by taking the ratio of one ITR to another. Thus we will have an *internal throughput rate ratio* (ITRR). This is what IBM does to generate LSPR tables, which are normally internal use only documentation, but can be seen on request by the customer. An example of the type of information obtained from IBM ITR tables, that can be used for calculating ITRRs, can be found in Appendix 3.

4.3 How the LSPR ITRR value is calculated

For any ITR table of the type in Appendix 3 to be of use, there must be a base machine against which all other machines can be related. In fact, the original base machine that IBM used for all measurements, but which it does not make too public, is the IBM 370/158 Model 3. Subsequent updates still use this machine as the base, although periodic calibrations tend to obscure this. The IBM 370/158 Model 3 is the machine against which *all* other IBM mainframe machines are measured, including the ES/9021/9121/9221 series.

The rationale has already been explained, whereby the ratio of the ITR of each type of workload, on each machine being measured, represents the relative power of the two machines. To be of more practical use, IBM has loaded a 'representative' machine with four types of workload: 25 per cent batch, 25 per cent CICS, 25 per cent IMS, and 25 per cent TSO, and has taken the four ITRs of each type of workload on one machine, and compared them to the same four ITRs on another machine. As you now know, the relationship between each of the two ITRs is referred to as the internal throughput rate ratio. The average of the aggregated ITRRs is then used as the measure of the difference in processing power between the machines.

IBM has not used a 100 per cent fully loaded machine, but has taken the 70 per cent workload, made up of 25 per cent of each of the four types of work (batch, CICS, IMS, TSO—about 17.5% per cent of each). It used to take the 50 per cent and the 90 per cent workload as well, but because of the principle of practicality, and acceptance that the ITR is constant for practical purposes, it now takes only the 70 per cent workload figure for its LSPR data.

For example, if one were upgrading from an IBM ES/9021/340 (RPP 27), to an IBM ES/9021/580 (RPP 75), then the relative power of the IBM ES/9021/580 to the IBM ES/9021/340 would be the aggregate of the four ITRRs. Figure 4.1 shows how IBM arrives at the aggregate ITRR for the IBM LSPR.

	Batch ITR	CICS ITR	IMS ITR	TSO ITR
IBM 9021/340	0.430	84.90	53.30	19.94
IBM 9021/580	1.231	239.63	141.47	54.36
Individual ITRR calculation	$\frac{1.231}{0.430}$	$\frac{239.63}{84.90}$	$\frac{141.47}{53.30}$	$\frac{54.36}{19.94}$
Individual ITRR	2.86	2.82	2.65	2.73
0.25 × ITRR	0.715	0.705	0.663	0.683
Aggregate ITRR of the four quarter ITRRs = 2.766				

Figure 4.1. Calculating the aggregated ITRR.

Thus, the IBM ES/9021/580 is 2.766 times more powerful than the IBM ES/9021/340. This can be seen from the *relative processor powers* (RPPs) of the two machines:

$$2.766 \times 27 = 74.68$$

which is very close to 75, the stated RPP of the more powerful machine.

4.4 Calculating your own ITRR value

Now that we see how IBM calculates the ITRR values for its LSPR tables, we can take this a step further. It is very unlikely that your own system has a workload that is made of 25 per cent CICS, 25 per cent TSO, 25 per cent IMS and 25 per cent batch, therefore the LSPR data will always be an approximation of your own system. It would be better surely, if we could be more exact. Well, we can.

Let us take the same example, an IBM ES/9021 Model 340 system that is in reality 90 per cent loaded, and moreover, that the breakdown of the load is 10 per cent TSO, 60 per cent CICS and 20 per cent batch. What will be the effect on the ITRR now? Remember that our LSPR ITRR is 2.766. Figure 4.2 shows the calculations on our differently loaded system. The LSPR ITRRs will be weighted by the real amount of each type of transaction on our system, not the fictitious one of 25 per cent.

So, whereas the LSPR ITRR gives us a reasonably accurate figure, certainly useful for a first-cut exercise, the calculated ITRR, based upon our real workload, shows a different figure. The LSPR figure tells us that if we migrate our workload from the IBM ES/9021 Model 340 to the IBM ES/9021 Model 580, we will use $1/2.766 = 0.3615$ (36.15 per cent) of the new processor's capacity of CPU(s).

Our calculated figure tells us that, in reality, we will use $1/2.82 = 0.3546$ (35.46 per cent) of the new processor's capacity of CPU(s). The difference is only 0.69 per cent, apparently not much, until you think that this possibly represents a large

$\leftarrow \frac{1}{2.766} - \frac{1}{2.82}$

	(20% load) Batch ITR	(60% load) CICS ITR	(0% load) IMS ITR	(10% load) TSO ITR
IBM 9021/340	0.430	84.90	53.30	19.94
IBM 9021/580	1.231	239.63	141.47	54.36
Individual ITRR calculation	$\frac{1.231}{0.430}$	$\frac{239.63}{84.90}$	$\frac{141.47}{53.30}$	$\frac{54.36}{19.94}$
Individual ITRR	2.86	2.82	2.65	2.73
% of the load of 90%	(0.2/0.9) × 100 = 0.222	(0.6/0.9) × 100 = 0.67	(0.0/0.9) × 100 = 0.0	(0.1/0.9) × 100 = 0.11
Calculated ITRR	0.22 × 2.86 = 0.64	0.67 × 2.82 = 1.88	0.0 × 2.65 = 0	0.11 × 2.73 = 0.30
Aggregate ITRR of the four quarter ITRRs = 2.82				

Figure 4.2. Calculating the true weighted aggregated ITRR.

sum of money: 0.69 per cent of 1 000 000 = 6900. Be this pounds sterling, dollars or yen, this is not an unusual number to be playing with when we talk about upgrades for modern mainframe processors.

So the result of our exercise is to realize that we are getting more from our upgrade than we at first thought. Ally this to the compounding effect over time, and the delay in spending expensive money (inflation) today, and we have a worthwhile exercise. When the results (not the figures themselves!) are presented to the budget committee, your expertise and professionalism will help your case, as well as show that you care about the company's finances. Do not forget to make the points mentioned above in your presentation.

This would be a particularly useful exercise for overnight batch-only loads. In fact, the overnight load would be only 34.97 per cent for 100 per cent batch runs; this represents a difference of 1.18 per cent of the processor; 1.18 per cent of 1 000 000 = 18 000. Consider this when you are thinking of upgrading, and it becomes another very useful exercise. Again, if there are differing types of workload at different times of the day, do not forget to include this information in your presentation.

4.5 Relative processor power

The aggregated ITRRs are very useful, and should always be used by the IBM field marketing staff, unless you specifically ask for the relative processor power (RPP) figure for a particular processor. Ensure that you ask for the most representative figure—the ITRR.

The RPP value is in fact a 'frozen' ITRR. The ITRR is constantly changing, for example, if a new release of the MVS/ESA operating system is announced, then this will change the ITR for each machine, and hence change any ITRR calculated using that ITR. Other events which will affect the ITRR are:

- A program temporary fix (PTF)
- An application for program alteration (APAR)
- A hardware modification, e.g. microcode installation
- An engineering change (EC)

As can be seen, the ITRR is very volatile and it is constantly changing. IBM decided that to be of practical use, the ITRR had to be frozen, at least for a period of time, and so the RPP unit was introduced.

4.5.1 Setting the RPP value

The current setting of the RPP values at the time of writing is based on the latest calibration, which used the IBM 3090 'S' series. This in effect freezes the ITRRs. The calibrated machine to be used as the base may change, but the principle will not. The aggregated ITRRs of the 3090 'S' machines against the base machine

(IBM 370/158 Model 3) were established, and these were taken as the RPP for that machine against the base machine. For example, the IBM 3090/180S had an ITRR of 24.5 against the IBM 370/158 Model 3, that is, it is reckoned to be 24.5 times more powerful than the IBM 370/158 Model 3. This was taken as the RPP for the IBM 3090/180S. The IBM 3090/180J machine has an ITRR of 27.08, but for practical purposes, this value is frozen at 27 until a revision of the ITRRs is undertaken.

In this manner, IBM has established what is a useful and practical measure of processor powers. Periodically the RPPs will be modified by another recalibration, but in the mean time, there is a practical basis for comparing processor powers, which will not change overnight as ITRRs are apt to do. Therefore, by comparing the two RPPs instead of the aggregated ITRRs of a pair of machines, we can establish the relative power of the two machines.

The RPPs are rounded to the nearest 0.1 if less than 10, 0.2 if between 10 and 20, 0.5 if between 20 and 50, and the nearest 1.0 if greater than 50.

The definitive document on IBM RPPs is *IBM RPPs—Relative Processor Powers*. This is an IBM internal use only document, but may be shown to customers at the representative's discretion if you, the customer, ask to see it.

4.5.2 So which one should you use? RPP or ITRR?

You should always use the ITRR if possible, as this is always the latest value. In addition, you should always weight the ITRRs according to the relative workloads that are actually on your own machine. RPPs will always vary slightly from the latest ITRR, but are of practical use if you are asked for a quick decision.

Let us take an example of using RPP, LSPR ITRR and weighted ITRR. Each of these in sequence is more accurate. The example we will use is an IBM 3090/180E running 60 per cent CICS, 20 per cent TSO and 10 per cent batch. Thus we have a 90 per cent loaded IBM 3090/180E. We are looking to upgrade to a second user IBM 3090/200J. What is the relative difference in processing power, and hence the load on the 200J when we migrate the workload?

RPP versus LSPR ITRR versus weighted ITRR

- Using RPP ratio

    RPP of IBM 3090/180E = 19.4
    RPP of IBM 3090/200J = 52.0
    RPP ratio = 52/19.4 = 2.68

- Using the latest LSPR ITRR

    Aggregated ITRR of IBM 3090/180E = 18.89
    Aggregated ITRR of IBM 3039/200J = 51.82
    25 per cent aggregated ITRR of IBM 3090/200J = 51.82/18.89 = 2.74

	CICS (60%)	TSO (20%)	Batch (10%)
180E ITR	56.21	14.29	0.327
200J ITR	165.36	38.41	0.839
ITRR	2.94	2.69	2.57
Load on processor	0.67	0.22	0.11 ← $\Sigma = 1.00$
Weighted ITRR	1.97	0.59	0.28
Aggregated ITRR = 2.84			

Figure 4.3. Example of calculating the weighted ITRR.

- *Using the weighted ITRR*
  See Fig. 4.3.

  Summary

- Using the RPP values, the 200J is 2.68 times more powerful than the 180E.
- Using the latest LSPR ITRRs this rises to 2.74.
- Using the calculated weighted ITRR this rises again to 2.84.

The range (2.84–2.68) will make a difference to how much more powerful the 200J is than the 180E. Taking the RPP of the 180E as 19.4, the following differences will apply:

- Using RPP   2.68 × 19.4 = 51.99
- Using LSPR ITRR   2.74 × 19.4 = 53.16
- Using weighted ITRR   2.84 × 19.4 = 55.10

The range in RPP is 55.10–51.99 = 3.11, very expensive RPP. This represents almost 6 per cent of the accepted RPP of an IBM 3090 Model 200J (52 RPP); 6 per cent of 1 000 000 = 60 000 (dollars, pounds, etc.). So, by taking the trouble to calculate a weighted ITRR, we have in fact shown that we are getting more for our money than we originally thought. This can be a telling point in a constrained budget situation, and can make the difference on the timing of the upgrade.

4.6 Graphic relationship between ETR and ITR using a CICS workload

The relationship is shown in Fig. 4.4. Note that:

1 The average ITR lies between 218 and 226. As IBM now uses only the 70 per cent utilization for its LSPR data, then the 70 per cent value of the ITR can be taken as the average for this workload; this is 223. By taking only the 70 per cent value, IBM implies acceptance of the practicality of the average ITR being used for capacity planning purposes, although it will never expressly say so.

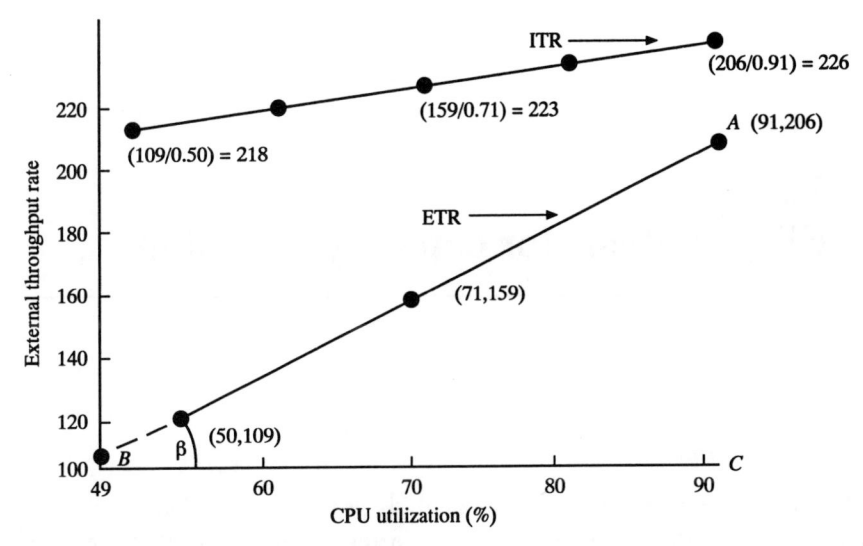

Figure 4.4. The relationship between ETR and ITR. (*Source*: IBM document ZZ05-0450 'MVS ITRs'.)

2   We can see that the CPU utilization to ETR representation is a straight line for practical purposes (a first degree curve for the purists). This means that any change in the ETR brought about by a change in the CPU utilization percentage, is at a constant rate. This rate is indicated by tan β (AC/BC). As the ITR is obtained by dividing the ETR (which is rising as the CPU gets busier), by the CPU utilization percentage (which is also rising as the CPU gets busier!), then this means that the ITR is, for practical purposes, a constant.

5
CPU analysis for capacity planning

5.1 Introduction

We will now start our capacity planning analysis proper. This chapter will cover the analysis of the CPU power, and how it is currently being used. By the end of this chapter, you will know just what power is being consumed by the various types of transactions entering the system. You will also know how to apply this information to 'what if' questions, in order to arrive at a forecast of power requirements for any future work that may be coming on the system, and therefore allow you to state when an upgrade may be necessary in good time. In other words, you will be able to avoid unpleasant surprises in terms of processor power. You will be able to get it into the budget for the following year, as a true capacity planning professional should.

5.2 Recording the resources used by each performance group

The *workload activity report* (WAR) of the RMF Monitor I report records the amount of each type of resource used by each performance group (PG). The recovery is in the form of SUs, and the resources used are the CPU(s), use of the I/O subsystem, and use of central and expanded storage.

We can then transfer the SUs used by each PG into CPU seconds, and then into a percentage of the CPU, and finally into relative processor power used by each PG. We can then derive the utilized RPP (URPP) used by each transaction in the PG. This is necessary if we are evaluating the increased use of power because we are thinking of adding more users of a particular type.

In theory, if we take all the SUs recorded by the RMF Monitor I report in the WAR, and transfer them to CPU seconds, then this should equal the number of seconds that the CPU was busy, i.e. the percentage of time the CPU was busy during the interval, multiplied by the interval duration. In fact, this is not the case, because RMF will not record all the SUs used.

SUs used by MVS/ESA on behalf of all the users in the system are not recovered. For example, some of the I/O supervisor's code is not recorded. In addition, different types of users have varying use of system resources. TSO users, for example, are subject to SWAP/IN SWAP/OUT cycles which batch jobs do not (should not) suffer at anything like the same rate, and which CICS transactions do not (must not) have to tolerate at all. Therefore, a TSO user usually has fewer SUs recovered than (say) a CICS transaction; TSO users are said to have a lower *capture ratio*.

Recalling that practicality must be our guiding principle, we will calculate an *average capture ratio* recovery for *all* types of applications. It is not necessary to find the amount of resource captured for each type of transaction, unless we are involved in a performance study (more on this in Chapter 6) whereby we are comparing the same workload on (say) an IBM ES/9021 Model 340 and an IBM ES/9021 Model 860.

The purists will say that a capture ratio must be calculated for each application currently running on the system. If you wish to be absolutely accurate, then this is indeed the case, and you will have to carry out multiple regression analysis to find them (see Appendix 6 for an example of calculating capture ratios by this method). On the other hand, if you recall that our calculations are a means to an end, not an end in itself, and if you wish to be accurate within acceptable bounds, which will give you satisfactory figures upon which to base your financial case, then in most cases the average capture ratio will suffice. Practicality is our watchword, so we will use the average capture ratio (CR). The multiple regression method has also been used on testbed occasions and, in every case, it has been found to be unjustified in terms of both the amount of time, and the differences in the final outcome.

5.2.1 The average capture ratio

Take the total time *recovered* in the RMF Monitor I workload activity report (WAR) in seconds, referred to as the *captured time*, and divide it by the number of CPU seconds, which is derived from the product of the CPU busy percentage, and the interval length in seconds. This product is referred to as the *CPU busy seconds*. The resulting quotient is the average capture ratio. Figure 5.1 illustrates the captured seconds and the CPU busy seconds.

The derived average capture ratio can now be used to account for the 'uncaptured' time in the application PGs, and to apportion it across these PGs. The apportionment is carried out on a pro rata basis, based on the amount of RPP used by the PG relative to other PGs. Some people use a different means of spreading the uncaptured time across the application PGs, based upon the number of I/O service units used by each PG relative to the other PGs. There is no hard and fast rule on this, as both methods work out at about the same spread. In this manner, each PG bears its share of the uncaptured component, weighted by the amount of resource actually used by the PG.

32 MVS—capacity planning for a balanced system

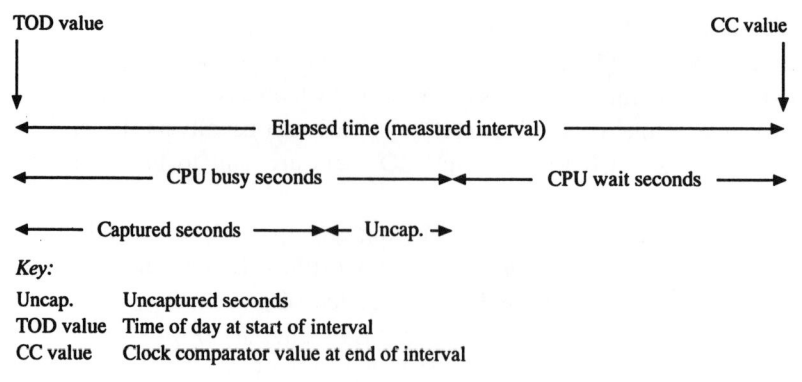

```
TOD value                                                    CC value
  │                                                             │
  ▼                                                             ▼
  ◄─────────────── Elapsed time (measured interval) ──────────►
     ◄──────────── CPU busy seconds ──────────►◄─ CPU wait seconds ─►
     ◄──── Captured seconds ────►◄─ Uncap. ─►
```

Key:
Uncap.   Uncaptured seconds
TOD value Time of day at start of interval
CC value   Clock comparator value at end of interval

Figure 5.1. Captured seconds, CPU busy seconds and elapsed seconds.

Hence the average capture ratio is:

$$\text{Average capture ratio} = \frac{\text{Captured seconds}}{\text{CPU busy seconds}}$$

5.3 The CPU analysis worksheet

Figure 5.2 is a formatted worksheet, which will be used to accumulate the information we are going to extract from the RMF Monitor I report. Notice that the date, time, system id, cycle time, number of samples, processor type, interval duration, the CPU busy percentage, MVS/ESA version and RMF version have already been filled in. This information is obtained from the the top of the CPU activity report (Fig. 5.3), which shows the relevant information highlighted. In addition, the processor power has been entered, 27 RPP, the power of the IBM ES/9021 Model 340.

5.3.1 *Calculating the total CPU busy seconds*

Among the data extracted from the RMF Monitor I CPU activity report (Fig. 5.3) and placed on the worksheet were:

- The CPU busy percentage—89.19
- The interval in seconds—900 (15 minutes)

Now we can calculate the *total* CPU busy seconds as follows:

$$\text{CPU busy seconds} = \text{Busy time percentage} \times \text{Interval in seconds}$$
$$= 0.8919 \times 900$$
$$= 802.7 \text{ seconds (say) 803 seconds}$$

RMF MONITOR I REPORT—ANALYSIS WORKSHEET

DATE 28/06/93 PROC'R ES9021-340			TIME 09.00 DUR'N 900 secs	SYSID CPU %	MAC1 89.19	CYCLE 1 second PROC'R RPP 27			SAMPLES 900 URPP		TOTAL CPU SECS	AVE. CAPTURE RATIO MVS VER. 4.2.0 RMF VER. 4.2.1			
APPL. PERF. GROUP	CPU SECS	PG %	PG URPP	←——— SYSTEM PGs ———→					TOTAL PG URPP	TOTAL CPU %		No. TRANS	No. USERS	ETR	ITR
TOTAL URPP ——→															

Figure 5.2. CPU analysis worksheet.

CPU ACTIVITY

OS/VS2 SP4.2.0	SYSTEM ID MAC1 RPT VERSION 4.2.1	DATE 28/06/93 TIME 09.00.00	INTERVAL 15.00.000 CYCLE 1.000 SECOND

CPU MODEL 9021 VERSION 49 ←——— The Version Code for the IBM ES/9021 Model 340

CPU NUMBER	VF ONLINE	VF AFFINITY PERCENTAGE	BUSY TIME PERCENTAGE	WAIT TIME PERCENTAGE	CPU SERIAL NUMBER	% I/O TOTAL INTERRUPT RATE	% I/O INTERRUPT HANDLED VIA TP
1	—	****	89.19	10.80	******	744.9	3.39
TOTAL/AVERAGE		****	89.19	10.80		744.9	3.39

SYSTEM ADDRESS SPACE ANALYSIS

Samples = 900

	NUMBER OF ASIDS						DISTRIBUTION OF QUEUE LENGTHS (%)							
TYPE	MIN	MAX	AVE	0	1	2	3	4	5	6	7–8	9–10	11–12	13–14	14+
READY	0	34	9.0	11.2	6.2	6.3	4.7	5.5	4.5	5.0	8.7	9.8	8.0	6.4	23.1
IN				0	1–2	3–4	5–6	7–8	9–10	11–15	16–20	21–25	26–30	31–35	35+
OUT	34	69	48.9	0.0	0.0	0.0	0.0	0.0	0.0	0.0	0.0	0.0	0.0	0.0	99.8
READY OUT	0	17	4.1	17.8	25.6	19.7	11.8	10.0	6.3	8.0	0.4	0.0	0.0	0.0	0.0
WAIT LOGICAL OUT RDY	149	195	175.1	0.0	0.0	0.0	0.0	0.0	0.0	0.0	0.0	0.0	0.0	0.0	100.0
LOGICAL OUT WAIT	0	7	0.3	79.6	17.8	2.4	0.0	0.0	0.0	0.0	0.0	0.0	0.0	0.0	0.0
BATCH	35	79	56.5	0.0	0.0	0.0	0.0	0.0	0.0	0.0	0.0	0.0	0.0	0.0	99.9
STC	14	20	19.8	0.0	0.0	0.0	0.0	0.0	0.0	0.0	99.9	0.0	0.0	0.0	0.0
TSO	21	27	21.3	0.0	0.0	0.0	0.0	0.0	0.0	0.0	0.0	99.9	0.0	0.0	0.0
ASCH	240	249	243.9	0.0	0.0	0.0	0.0	0.0	0.0	0.0	0.0	0.0	0.0	0.0	100.0
	0	0	0.0	100.0	0.0	0.0	0.0	0.0	0.0	0.0	0.0	0.0	0.0	0.0	0.0

Figure 5.3. RMF Monitor I CPU report.

5.3.2 Calculating the average capture ratio

In order to calculate the average capture ratio, we need to extract some data from the RMF Monitor I WAR summary, which is shown in Fig. 5.4. Again, the data has been highlighted.

The data required to calculate the captured seconds:

$$\text{Captured seconds} = \frac{\text{Total (SRB + CPU) SUs for } all \text{ PGs}}{\text{SDC (for CPU and SRB)} \times \text{SU/second} \times \text{No. of engines}}$$

where:

SDC   Service definition coefficient for CPU and SRB (should be equal)
SU/second   Service units per second per engine for that processor
No. of engines   Number of engines in a multi-engine processor

Here is the data extracted from the WAR summary:

Total CPU service units = 6 638 865
Total SRB service units = 600 186
SDC for CPU and SRB = 10
SUs per second per engine = 1162.3 (IBM ES/9000 Model 340)
Number of engines = 1 (IBM ES/9000 Model 340)

Therefore

$$\text{Captured seconds} = \frac{6\ 638\ 865 + 600\ 186}{10 \times 1162.3 \times 1}$$

$$= \frac{7\ 239\ 051}{11\ 623}$$

$$= 622.8 \text{ seconds}$$

(say) 623 seconds

and thus:

$$\text{Average capture ratio} \approx \frac{\text{Captured seconds}}{\text{CPU busy seconds}}$$

$$= \frac{623}{803}$$

$$= 0.776$$

5.3.3 Applying the average capture ratio

Now that we have calculated the average capture ratio (CR), we can apply it to each of the PGs. Therefore, using the TSO production PG 42 as the example, we

WORKLOAD ACTIVITY

MVS/ESA
SP4.2.0

SYSTEM ID MAC1
RPT VERSION 4.2.1

DATE 28/06/93
TIME 09.00.000

INTERVAL 15.00.000
IPS = IEAIPS00

OPT = IEAOPT00
ICS = IEAICS00

SYSTEM SUMMARY

SERVICE DEFINITION COEFFICIENTS
IOC = 5.0   CPU = 10.0   SRB = 10.0   SU/SEC = 1162.3   MSO = 0.1000

PGN	PGP	DMN	TIME SLICE GROUP	INTERVAL SERVICE		AVERAGE AVE TRX TCB + SRB	ABSORPTION SERV RATE SECONDS, %	PAGE-IN RATES	RATES	STORAGE		TRANSACTIONS		AVE TRANS TIME, STD DEVIATION HHH.MMM.SSS.TTT	
ALL	ALL	ALL	ALL	IOC	2 760 090	ABSRPTN	247	SINGLE	0.05	AVERAGE	982.41	AVE	50.59	TRX	000.00.01.688
				CPU	6 638 865	TRX SERV	226	BLOCK	0.04			MPL	46.20	SD	000.00.12.340
				MSO	305 398	TCB	571.1	HSP	0.00	TOTAL	45 396	ENDED	15 815		
				SRB	600 186	SRB	51.6	HSP MISS	0.00	CENTRAL	13 844	END/SEC	17.57	QUE	000.21.16.965
				TOT	10 304 539	TCB + SRB %	69.1	EXP SNGL	14.78	EXPAND	31 552	#SWAPS	16 288		
				PER SEC	11 449			EXP BLK	0.38					TOT	000.21.18.654

Figure 5.4. RMF Monitor I Workload Activity report—system summary.

CPU analysis for capacity planning

will calculate the CPU seconds used by this PG, incorporating the average capture ratio. The following data is obtained from the RMF Monitor I WAR for PG 42 (Fig. 5.5) from the 0042 ALL ALL ALL block and from the top of the report. The data is highlighted.

Calculating the CPU seconds for PG 42

$$= \frac{\text{Total (SRB + CPU) SUs for the PG}}{\text{SDC (CPU and SRB)} \times \text{SU/second} \times \text{No. of engines} \times \text{CR}}$$

$$= \frac{888\,462 + 41\,968}{10 \times 1162.3 \times 1 \times 0.776}$$

$$= \frac{930\,430}{9019.4}$$

$$= 103.1 \text{ seconds}$$

Calculating the percentage of processor time used by PG 42

$$\% \text{ CPU used by PG 42} = \frac{\text{CPU seconds}}{\text{Interval time in seconds}} \times 100$$

$$= \frac{103.1}{900.0} \times 100 = 11.5$$

Calculating the URPP of PG 42

URPP of PG 42 = CPU utilization of PG × RPP of the processor

$$= 0.115 \times 27 = 3.1 \text{ URPP}$$

We can now place our derived CPU seconds (incorporating the CR), the CPU percentage and the URPP for PG 42, on the worksheet on Fig. 5.6.

An easier way to find CPU seconds and URPP per PG

Now that you know *how* the CPU seconds are arrived at from the CPU and SRB service units, i.e. you know the theory, we can now look at an improvement in the RMF Monitor I report, which was added with RMF 4.2.1. If you look at the WAR in Fig. 5.5, the 'ALL ALL ALL' totals PG 42, you will see that there are some rows entitled ABSRPTN (absorption), TRX SERV, TCB, SRB and TCB + SRB%. The values associated with PG 42 ALL ALL ALL are:

```
ABSRPTN    = 755
TRX SERV   = 731
TCB        = 76.4
SRB        = 3.6
TCB+SRB%   = 8.9
```

WORKLOAD ACTIVITY

```
MVS/ESA                  SYSTEM ID MAC1              DATE 28/06/93         INTERVAL 15.00.000
SP4.2.0                  RPT VERSION 4.2.1           TIME 09.00.000        IPS = IEAIPS00

  OPT = IEAOPT00         REPORT BY PERFORMANCE GROUP      SERVICE DEFINITION COEFFICIENTS    SU/SEC = 1162.3
  ICS = IEAICS00                PERIOD                    IOC = 5.0   CPU = 5.0   SRB = 10.0  MSO = 0.1000
```

			TIME SLICE			AVERAGE AVE TRX	ABSORPTION SERV RATE	PAGE-IN					TRANSACTIONS			AVE TRANS TIME, STD DEVIATION	
PGN	PGP	DMN	GROUP	INTERVAL SERVICE		TCB + SRB	SECONDS, %	RATES	RATES		STORAGE					HHH.MM.SS.TTT	
				SUBSYS = TSO TRXCLASS =			ACCTINFO = NO										
				USERID = TRXNAME =													
0042	1	031	**	IOC =	58 875	ABSRPTN	1059	SINGLE	0.74		AVERAGE	470.88	AVE	0.39	TRX	000.00.00.049	
				CPU =	276 936	TRX SERV	1024	BLOCK	0.77				MPL	0.38	SD	000.00.00.225	
				MSO =	12 696	TCB	23.8	HSP	0.00		TOTAL	180.69	ENDED	2564			
				SRB =	17 391	SRB	1.4	HSP MISS	0.00		CENTRAL	91.06	END/SEC	2.84	QUE	000.00.00.000	
				TOT =	365 898	TCB + SRB%	2.8	EXP SNGL	304.67		EXPAND	89.63	#SWAPS	2554			
				PER SEC =	406			EXP BLK	0.00						TOT	000.00.00.049	
0042	2	032	**	IOC =	134 290	ABSRPTN	724	SINGLE	0.20		AVERAGE	479.25	AVE	0.91	TRX	000.00.01.217	
				CPU =	407 099	TRX SERV	699	BLOCK	0.11				MPL	0.88	SD	000.00.01.087	
				MSO =	21 769	TCB	35.0	HSP	0.00		TOTAL	424.72	ENDED	573			
				SRB =	14 934	SRB	1.2	HSP MISS	0.00		CENTRAL	252.38	END/SEC	0.63	QUE	001.15.14.522	
				TOT =	578 092	TCB + SRB%	4.0	EXP SNGL	19.33		EXPAND	172.34	#SWAPS	609			
				PER SEC =	642			EXP BLK	0.01						TOT	001.15.15.739	
0042	3	033	**	IOC =	96 205	ABSRPTN	605	SINGLE	0.01		AVERAGE	513.31	AVE	0.60	TRX	000.00.06.913	
				CPU =	204 427	TRX SERV	589	BLOCK	0.00				MPL	0.59	SD	000.00.05.150	
				MSO =	12 502	TCB	17.5	HSP	0.00		TOTAL	304.19	ENDED	131			
				SRB =	9643	SRB	0.8	HSP MISS	0.00		CENTRAL	198.22	END/SEC	0.14	QUE	000.00.00.000	
				TOT =	322 777	TCB + SRB%	2.0	EXP SNGL	6.24		EXPAND	105.97	#SWAPS	137			
				PER SEC =	358			EXP BLK	0.00						TOT	000.00.06.913	
0042	ALL	ALL	ALL	IOC =	289 370	**ABSRPTN**	**755**	SINGLE	0.25		AVERAGE	488.36	AVE	1.92	TRX	000.00.00.529	
				CPU =	**888 462**	**TRX SERV**	**731**	BLOCK	0.21				MPL	1.86	SD	000.00.01.789	
				MSO =	46 967	**TCB**	**76.4**	HSP	0.00		TOTAL	909.61	ENDED	3268			
				SRB =	**41 968**	**SRB**	**3.6**	HSP MISS	0.00		CENTRAL	541.66	END/SEC	3.63	QUE	000.13.11.560	
				TOT =	1 266 767	**TCB + SRB%**	**8.9**	EXP SNGL	73.95		EXPAND	367.95	#SWAPS	3300			
				PER SEC =	1407			EXP BLK	0.00						TOT	000.13.12.090	

Figure 5.5. The WAR for performance group 42.

RMF MONITOR I REPORT—ANALYSIS WORKSHEET

DATE 28/06/93		TIME 09.00		SYSID CPU %	MAC1 89.19	CYCLE 1 second PROC'R RPP		SAMPLES 900 URPP		AVE. CAPTURE RATIO 0.776 MVS VER. 4.2.0 RMF VER. 4.2.1			
PROC'R ES/9021-340		DUR'N 900 secs					27						
APPL. PERF. GROUP	CPU SECS	PG %	PG URPP	←——SYSTEM PGs——→				TOTAL PG URPP	TOTAL CPU %	TOTAL CPU SECS	No. TRANS	No. USERS	ETR	ITR
42	103.1	11.5	3.1											
TOTAL URPP ——→														

Figure 5.6. CPU analysis worksheet, partially completed.

The ABSRPTN and TRX SERV will be explained later. TCB is the number of CPU task (TCB) seconds used by this PG, and SRB is the number of CPU SRB seconds used by the PG. If you add them together, you will arrive at 80 seconds. If you now divide 80 by the average capture ratio (0.776), you will arrive at 103.1 seconds. This is the same as our calculated value, arrived at by transferring the CPU and SRB service units into CPU seconds.

The TCB + SRB% element is the amount of CPU time used by this PG (42), as a percentage of the measured interval. You can calculate this yourself, by adding the TCB and SRB values (76.4 and 3.6) to give a total of 80 seconds, dividing by 900 (the measured interval), and then multiplying by 100 to arrive at the percentage value:

$$((76.4 + 3.6)/900) \times 100 = 8.9\%$$

This value of 8.9% does *not* include the capture ratio weighting, therefore if you divide 8.9% (0.089) by 0.776 (the average capture ratio), we arrive at 11.5%—our calculated value of CPU per cent used by PG 42. If you now multiply this known (and average capture ratio weighted) CPU percentage by the accepted RPP of the processor (in our case 27), you will arrive at the URPP for the performance group:

$$0.115 \times 27 = 3.1 \text{ URPP for PG 42}$$

So you can see that, in future, all you need to do is pick up the TCB and SRB seconds from the TCB and SRB fields in the RMF Monitor I WAR, and divide the total of these two by your calculated average capture ratio to give the CPU seconds for that PG. You can then pick up the CPU % from the TCB+SRB% field, again divide it by your calculated average capture ratio, and you have the capture ratio weighted CPU percentage for that PG. Finally, by multiplying the RPP of the machine by the weighted CPU percentage you will have the URPP for the PG.

You now quickly and easily have the necessary information to calculate the ITR for the PG, by dividing average capture ratio weighted CPU seconds for the PG into the number of completed transactions. This value is also picked up from the WAR shown in Fig. 5.5. See the field ENDED which has a value of 3268 in it. Remember though, this ITR does not include all the CPU seconds for PG 42; we have to add the system component yet to give a truer picture.

$$\text{ITR for PG 42} = 3268/103.1 = 31.7 \text{ transactions per second}$$

Therefore, we can now place the TCB and SRB seconds, and the CPU percentage (inflated by the average capture ratio), for all the other application PGs onto the worksheet. These are the PGs 1, 2, 11, 111 and 999.

Finally, we can add the URPP for each PG, by multiplying the percentage of CPU used by each PG (weighted by the average capture ratio) by the RPP of the processor (27). Figure 5.7 shows the completed details of these application PGs. It

RMF MONITOR I REPORT—ANALYSIS WORKSHEET

DATE 28/06/93 PROC'R ES/9021-340				TIME 09.00 DUR'N 900 secs	SYSID CPU %	MAC1 89.19	CYCLE 1 second PROC'R RPP 27				SAMPLES 900 URPP		AVE. CAPTURE RATIO 0.776 MVS VER. 4.2.0 RMF VER. 4.2.1			
APPL. PERF. GROUP	CPU SECS	PG %	PG URPP		←——— SYSTEM PGs ———→					TOTAL PG URPP	TOTAL CPU %	TOTAL CPU SECS	No. TRANS	No. USERS	ETR	ITR
1	127.2	14.8	3.8													
2	335.4	37.3	10.1													
11	132.3	14.7	4.0													
42	103.1	11.5	3.1													
111	0.3	0.03	0.01													
999	7.9	8.8	0.2													
TOTAL URPP ———→			21.21													

Figure 5.7. CPU analysis worksheet, partially completed.

is all much simpler than it used to be, but as not all products give you this information, you should still know how it is arrived at.

Recording the number of CICS transactions

If you need to know how to set up RMF, VTAM and CICS, in order to collect the number of CICS ended transactions, see Appendix 7.

5.4 The system performance groups

We have arrived at the amount of CPU time used by each application PG, but we have not finished yet. The system PGs have to be apportioned across the application PGs. When we have done this, we will have accounted for all the CPU seconds used (and of course, all the URPP).

The PGs that report on the resources used by the system components should be spread across the application performance groups. The normal way of doing this is to charge each application PG with a share represented by the amount of URPP of the PG relative to the other PGs being measured. Again, the number of I/O SUs per PG relative to other PGs can be used instead if you wish.

Not all system PGs will be spread across all application groups. For example, VTAM is used mainly by the transaction processing applications such as IMS, CICS and TSO. It is not used by the batch performance groups, therefore the batch PG is not charged with any of the VTAM overhead.

The system PGs, like the application PGs, are specified in the IEAICSxx member of SYS1.PARMLIB (in our case 'xx' = '00' to give us IEAICS00). The associated values to achieve the requirements of the installation are stated in the IEAIPSxx (again, 'xx' = '00' in our case) member of SYS1.PARMLIB. Both of these parameter lists are in Appendix 1.

The URPP of each of the system PGs is calculated in exactly the same manner as for an application PG. The RMF Monitor I workload activity reports (WARs) showing the system PGs are in Appendix 4. Again, with RMF 4.2.1, it is possible to pick the amount of TCB and SRB seconds directly from the RMF Monitor I report. These can then be turned into a percentage of the processor and URPP of each PG as described earlier.

5.4.1 *Example of apportioning a system PG*

From the IEAICS00 member, see Appendix 1, the following system PGs are used:

- PG 0 for the master scheduler (this is defaulted)
- PG 100 as the default PG for all started tasks
- PG 101 for the catalog

- PG 102 for LLA
- PG 103 for VLF
- PG 104 for VTAM
- PG 105 for JES2
- PG 106 for RMF
- PG 107 for MOUNT

Some of the system PGs do not have any resource use recorded against them (101, 103 and 107). We will take system PG 100 (the default system PG) and apportion it over the application PGs, on a pro rata basis, according to the amount of URPP used by each application PG relative to each of the other application PGs.

Figure 5.8 shows the WAR of the system performance group 100. From this we can pick out the number of TCB and SRB seconds from the RMF Monitor I WAR associated with PG 100, and modify the total by the average capture ratio:

13.1 TCB seconds and 3.6 SRB seconds = 16.7 CPU seconds
16.7/0.776 (the capture ratio) = 21.52 seconds
21.52/900 (the interval duration) × 100 = 0.024 (2.4%); or
0.018/0.766 = 0.024 (rounding makes for small differences)
0.024 × 27 (the processor RPP) = 0.648 (say) 0.65 URPP

The total URPP for the application PGs is 21.21 URPP (see Fig. 5.7). So now we can apportion 0.65 URPP for system PG 100 across the application PGs:

- Share for appl. PG 1 = (3.8/21.21) × 0.65 = 0.12 URPP
- Share for appl. PG 2 = (10.1/21.21) × 0.65 = 0.31 URPP
- Share for appl. PG 11 = (4.0/21.21) × 0.65 = 0.12 URPP
- Share for appl. PG 42 = (3.1/21.21) × 0.65 = 0.10 URPP
- Appl. PGs 111 and 999 have such a small share they can be ignored.

These values are placed on the worksheet shown in Fig. 5.9. All system PGs have been treated in a similar manner, and their respective values also placed onto the worksheet. You may notice that the VTAM PG (104) has not been allocated to the batch PGs (1 and 11).

The calculation for VTAM apportioning is:

- For PG 2:

    $(10.1/(10.1 + 3.1)) \times 0.08 = 0.06$ URPP

- For PG 42:

    $(3.1/(10.1 + 3.1)) \times 0.08 = 0.02$ URPP

5.5 Total URPP for each application PG

Now that we have allocated the system PGs across the application PGs, we have to total the URPP for each PG, turn it into CPU percentage used per application

```
                                          WORKLOAD ACTIVITY

MVS/ESA                    SYSTEM ID MAC1                    DATE 28/06/93                              INTERVAL 15.00.000
SP4.2.0                    RPT VERSION 4.2.1                 TIME 09.00.000
                                                                                                        IPS = IEAIPS00
  OPT = IEAOPT00           REPORT BY PERFORMANCE GROUP              SERVICE DEFINITION COEFFICIENTS     SU/SEC = 1162.3
  ICS = IEAICS00                   PERIOD                            IOC = 5.0   CPU = 10.0  SRB = 10.0 MSO = 0.1000

           TIME                      AVERAGE   ABSORPTION
           SLICE                     AVE TRX   SERV RATE   PAGE-IN
PGN  PGP   GROUP  DMN  INTERVAL SERVICE  TCB+SRB  SECONDS, %  RATES   RATES             STORAGE                 TRANSACTIONS

SUBSYS = STC              TRXCLASS =
USERID =                  TRXNAME =

0100  1    100    **   IOC =     22426   ABSRPTN     24     SINGLE    0.00   AVERAGE      3011.2   AVE MPL     10.13  TRX     000.03.55.622
                       CPU =    152676   TRX SERV    24     BLOCK     0.00                         ENDED       10.13  SD      000.00.00.000
                       MSO =      4709   TCB         13.1   HSP       0.00   TOTAL       30 526    END/SEC     1
                       SRB =     42501   SRB          3.6   HSP MISS  0.00   CENTRAL      4733.6   #SWAPS      0.00   QUE     547.50.56.559
                       TOT =    222312   TCB+SRB%     1.8   EXP SNGL  0.12   EXPAND      25 793                0
                       PER SEC =   247                      EXP BLK   0.00                                            TOT     547.54.52.181
```

Figure 5.8. WAR for system performance group 100.

RMF MONITOR I REPORT—ANALYSIS WORKSHEET

DATE 28/06/93 PROC'R ES/9021-340				TIME 09.00 DUR'N 900 secs	SYSID CPU %	MAC1 89.19			CYCLE 1 second PROC'R RPP 27			SAMPLES 900 URPP		AVE. CAPTURE RATIO 0.776 MVS VER. 4.2.0 RMF VER. 4.2.1			
APPL. PERF. GROUP	CPU SECS	PG %	PG URPP			—SYSTEM PGs—					TOTAL PG URPP	TOTAL CPU %	TOTAL CPU SECS	No. TRANS	No. USERS	ETR	ITR
				0	100	102	104	105	106								
1	127.2	14.1	3.8	0.28	0.12	0.002	0.00	0.086	0.013	4.30							
2	335.4	37.3	10.1	0.75	0.31	0.005	0.06	0.230	0.033	11.49							
11	132.3	14.7	4.0	0.30	0.12	0.002	0.00	0.092	0.013	4.53							
42	103.1	11.5	3.1	0.23	0.10	0.001	0.02	0.072	0.011	3.53							
111	0.3	0.03	0.01	0.01	0.00	0.00	0.00	0.00	0.00	0.02							
999	7.9	8.8	0.2	0.01	0.00	0.00	0.00	0.00	0.00	0.21							
TOTAL URPP →	21.21			1.58	0.65	0.01	0.08	0.48	0.07	24.08							

Figure 5.9. CPU analysis worksheet, partially completed.

PG, and finally calculate the CPU seconds used by each application PG. The way in which we do this is the reverse of the process used to generate the three columns on the worksheet shown in Fig. 5.9: CPU SECS, PG % and PG URPP. Recall that we calculated the PG % by dividing the PG CPU SECS by the interval duration, in our case 900 seconds, and multiplying by 100. Secondly, we multiplied the PG % by the RPP of the processor, in our case 27, to give URPP of the application PG. Therefore, if we take the TOTAL URPP of the application PG, and now divide by the processor RPP (27), then multiply by 100, we arrive at the CPU percentage of the application PG. Finally, if we then multiply the CPU percentage by the interval duration (900 seconds), we arrive at the TOTAL CPU SECONDS for the performance group.

5.6 Calculating the performance group ETR and ITR

Once we have the TOTAL CPU seconds, we can then ally this to the number of transactions, which we can pick out from the RMF Monitor I WAR, and we can then calculate the ETR and ITR. Once we have the ETR and ITR, we are well on the way to answering our 'what if' capacity planning questions.

First, let us find the total CPU seconds for each application PG. For example, the total CPU seconds for application PG 1:

$$\text{Total URPP} = 3.8 + 0.28 + 0.12 + 0.002 + 0.086 + 0.013 = 4.3 \text{ URPP}$$

$$\text{Total CPU percentage} = (4.30/27) \times 100 = 15.93\%$$

$$\text{Total CPU seconds} = 0.1593 \times 900 = 143.4 \text{ seconds}$$

Now let us calculate the ITR for application PG 1. The formula for the ITR is as follows:

$$\text{ITR} = \frac{\text{Number of completed transactions}}{\text{Total CPU seconds used}}$$

Thus:

$$\text{ITR} = \frac{214}{143.4} = 1.49 \text{ transactions per second}$$

From where did we get the value of 214 completed transactions? Look at the RMF Monitor I WAR for application PG 1 in Fig. 5.10. You will see a field in the 0001 ALL ALL ALL section, on the right-hand side, called ENDED. This is the number of completed transactions in the interval for all performance group periods—in our case, 214. Looking above this field, you will see the respective values for each of the performance group periods: 202 for PG period 1, and 12 for PG period 2, making a total of 214.

To remind ourselves, the formula for the ETR is as follows:

$$\text{ETR} = \frac{\text{Number of completed transactions}}{\text{Total elapsed seconds in interval}}$$

WORKLOAD ACTIVITY

```
MVS/ESA                    SYSTEM ID MAC1                          DATE 28/06/93                              INTERVAL 15.00.000
SP4.2.0                    RPT VERSION 4.2.1                       TIME 09.00.000                             IPS = IEAIPS00

    OPT = IEAOPT00         REPORT BY PERFORMANCE GROUP             SERVICE DEFINITION COEFFICIENTS            SU/SEC = 1162.3
    ICS = IEAICS00                 PERIOD                          IOC = 5.0    CPU = 10.0    SRB = 10.0      MSO = 0.1000
```

PGN	PGP	DMN	TIME SLICE GROUP	INTERVAL SERVICE	AVERAGE AVE TRX TCB + SRB	ABSORPTION SERV RATE SECONDS, %	PAGE-IN RATES	RATES	STORAGE		TRANSACTIONS		AVE TRANS TIME, STD DEVIATION HHH.MM.SS.TTT	
SUBSYS = JES2			TRXCLASS =		ACCTINFO = NO									
USERID =			TRXNAME =											
0001	1	001	**	IOC = 602955	ABSRPTN 216		SINGLE	0.00	AVERAGE	224.42	AVE	9.58	TRX	000.00.35.345
				CPU = 795915	TRX SERV 172		BLOCK	0.00			MPL	8.63	SD	000.00.51.890
				MSO = 31690	TCB 68.4		HSP	0.00	TOTAL	1713.5	ENDED	202		
				SRB = 56777	SRB 4.8		HSP MISS	0.00	CENTRAL	1277.4	END/SEC	0.22	QUE	003.40.53.885
				TOT = 1487337	TCB + SRB% 8.1		EXP SNGL	1.05	EXPAND	436.09	#SWAPS	169		
				PER SEC = 1652			EXP BLK	0.51					TOT	003.41.29.230
0001	2	002	**	IOC = 262405	ABSRPTN 148		SINGLE	0.00	AVERAGE	440.75	AVE	4.75	TRX	000.04.26.383
				CPU = 275065	TRX SERV 132		BLOCK	0.00			MPL	4.21	SD	000.02.38.300
				MSO = 7792	TCB 23.6		HSP	0.00	TOTAL	1859.8	ENDED	12		
				SRB = 20364	SRB 1.7		HSP MISS	0.00	CENTRAL	495.88	END/SEC	0.01	QUE	038.53.38.679
				TOT = 565626	TCB + SRB% 2.8		EXP SNGL	0.49	EXPAND	1363.9	#SWAPS	36		
				PER SEC = 628			EXP BLK	0.27					TOT	038.58.05.062
0001	ALL	ALL	ALL	IOC = 865360	ABSRPTN 192		SINGLE	0.00	AVERAGE	301.42	AVE	14.33	TRX	000.00.48.300
				CPU = 1070980	TRX SERV 159		BLOCK	0.00			MPL	11.85	SD	000.01.21.700
				MSO = 39482	TCB 92.1		HSP	0.00	TOTAL	3573.3	**ENDED**	**214**		
				SRB = 77141	SRB 6.6		HSP MISS	0.00	CENTRAL	1773.3	END/SEC	0.23	QUE	005.39.22.191
				TOT = 2052963	TCB + SRB% 10.9		EXP SNGL	0.85	EXPAND	1800.0	#SWAPS	205		
				PER SEC = 2281			EXP BLK	0.42					TOT	005.40.10.492

Figure 5.10. WAR for performance group 1.

Thus, the ETR for application PG 1 is:

$$\text{ETR} = \frac{214}{900} = 0.238 \text{ transactions per second}$$

This can be checked by multiplying the ITR (1.49) by the CPU per cent (15.93% or 0.1593) to give:

$$1.49 \times 0.1593 = 0.2374 \text{ (close enough)}$$

Remember, rounding will give us slightly different answers, depending upon which method we use. Practicality is our credo, and so being correct to two decimal places is perfectly acceptable for capacity planning purposes, even though we have gone to three!

5.6.1 What can we do with the calculated ETR and ITR?

Now that we have calculated the ETR and ITR for our own system, we can really get to grips with our capacity planning and performance studies. For example, with the calculated ETR for each type of transaction, we can answer our 'What if' questions, such as: 'What is the effect of adding another 50 TSO users during peak period in PG 42?' (2.72 RPP—see if you get the same answer.) Or 'What will be the effect on the system if the number of (say) TSO (PG 42) transactions increases by 30%?' (An extra 3.93 URPP from 13.09 × 0.3.) We can see what the effect *really* is on our system.

With the ITR, we can calculate the effect of transferring our workload from the current system to another processor, by deriving the ITRR. With our calculated ITRs for each type of transaction, we can also make an accurate prediction of the percentage of the new processor that will be used for each of these types of transaction. We can ensure that we help the enterprise by optimizing both the necessary degree of accuracy and the amount of time used in systems analysis. It also means we can compare our findings to those of the seller.

A very important point regarding the ITR is that you can accurately calculate the CPU milliseconds per transaction for any and all types of transactions within your system. For a performance study, this would be absolutely essential, and this will be dealt with in Chapter 6.

The LSPR data from IBM will be useful to start with, and will also be useful to compare with your own figures. If your figures are wildly different from the LSPR figures, then there may be an area of research, both for you and for IBM.

Figure 5.11 shows the completed CPU formatted worksheet. The ETRs and ITRs have been added to give a complete picture. Notice also, that the total URPP at the bottom of the worksheet is the same as the processor RPP × CPU busy percentage (27 × 0.8919 = 24.08 URPP). The same figure is arrived at from two directions.

RMF MONITOR I REPORT—ANALYSIS WORKSHEET

DATE 28/06/93 PROC'R ES/9021-340			TIME 09.00 DUR'N 900 secs		SYSID CPU %	MAC1 89.19			CYCLE 1 second PROC'R RPP 27			SAMPLES 900 URPP 24.08			AVE. CAPTURE RATIO 0.776 MVS VER. 4.2.0 RMF VER. 4.2.1			
APPL. PERF. GROUP	CPU SECS	PG %	PG URPP	0	100	102	— SYSTEM PGs — 104	105	106	TOTAL PG URPP	TOTAL CPU %	TOTAL CPU SECS	No. TRANS	No. USERS	ETR	ITR
1	127.2	14.1	3.8	0.28	0.12	0.002	–	0.086	0.013	4.30	15.93	143.4	214		0.238	1.49
2	335.4	37.3	10.1	0.75	0.31	0.005	0.06	0.230	0.033	11.49	42.55	382.9	11814		13.13	30.85
11	132.3	14.7	4.0	0.30	0.12	0.002	–	0.092	0.013	4.53	16.77	150.9	130		0.144	0.86
42	103.1	11.5	3.1	0.23	0.10	0.001	0.02	0.072	0.011	3.53	13.09	117.8	3268		3.63	27.74
111	0.3	0.03	0.01	0.01	–	–	–	–	–	0.02	0.07	0.65	9		0.01	13.85
999	7.9	8.8	0.2	0.01	–	–	–	–	–	0.21	0.79	7.15	388		0.431	54.27
TOTAL URPP →	21.21			1.58	0.65	0.01	0.08	0.48	0.07	24.08	89.2	802.8				

Figure 5.11. CPU analysis worksheet, completed.

6
CPU analysis for performance

6.1 Introduction

This chapter deals with more detail than Chapter 5. If you have a service-level agreement, then it is sometimes necessary to derive such information as: the number of SUs absorbed within a performance group period, in order to find out if the agreed percentage of transactions complete within the specified period; or the delay between the time a transaction becomes 'ready' and the time it is dispatched on an engine—this would be required to see if the multi-programming levels (MPL) for domains are correct; or again, the amount of I/O wait time (and the number of I/Os) incorporated within a transaction, in order to check for excessive I/O times. All of this information is required to monitor for performance.

6.2 The transaction time

We will take as our example period 3 of performance group 42. The WAR for PG 42 is shown in Fig. 6.1, and you will see that the *overall* transaction service time (in the 0042 ALL ALL ALL block, TRX field) is 0.529 seconds—looks good, yes? What about the individual period transaction service times? For the three periods they are respectively 0.049 seconds (excellent), 1.217 seconds (good) and 6.913 seconds (ouch!). Quite a drop after period 2. In fact, in relative terms the transaction time has increased by over five times after period 2 (6.913/1.217).

Remember, the transactions in period 2 *HAVE ALREADY BEEN THROUGH PERIOD 1*, therefore they have already accumulated 49 milliseconds of transaction time before they get to period 2. Period 2's time includes the 49 milliseconds of period 1's time in the 1.217 seconds. Similarly, period 3's time includes the 49 milliseconds from period 1 and the 1.217 seconds from period 2. Therefore 5.647 seconds (6.913 − (0.049 + 1.217)) are actually used in period 3 by the 131 transactions that drop through periods 1 and 2 into period 3.

These figures are averages, and the standard deviation shown in Fig. 6.1 shows the 'spread' of the data around these averages. The standard deviation assumes a

WORKLOAD ACTIVITY

```
MVS/ESA                SYSTEM ID MAC1              DATE 28/06/93         INTERVAL 15.00.000
SP4.2.0                RPT VERSION 4.2.1           TIME 09.00.000        IPS = IEAIPS00

           OPT = IEAPT00      REPORT BY PERFORMANCE GROUP     SERVICE DEFINITION COEFFICIENTS   SU/SEC = 1162.3
           ICS = IEAICS00              PERIOD                 IOC = 5.0    CPU = 10.0           MSO = 0.1000
                                                              SRB = 10.0
```

PGN	PGP	DMN	TIME SLICE GROUP	INTERVAL SERVICE	AVERAGE AVE TRX TCB + SRB	ABSORPTION SERV RATE SECONDS, %	PAGE-IN RATES	RATES	STORAGE		TRANSACTIONS		AVE TRANS TIME, STD DEVIATION HHH.MM.SS.TTT	
			SUBSYS = TSO		TRXCLASS =	ACCTINFO = NO								
			USERID =		TRXNAME =									
0042	1	031	**	IOC = 58 875	ABSRPTN	1059	SINGLE	0.74	AVERAGE	470.88	AVE	0.39		
				CPU = 276 936	TRX SERV	1024	BLOCK	0.77			MPL	0.38	TRX	000.00.00.049
				MSO = 12 696	TCB	23.8	HSP	0.00	TOTAL	180.69	**ENDED**	**2564**	SD	000.00.00.225
				SRB = 17 391	SRB	1.4	HSP MISS	0.00	CENTRAL	91.06	END/SEC	2.84		
				TOT = 365 898	TCB + SRB%	2.8	EXP SNGL	304.67	EXPAND	89.63	#SWAPS	2554	QUE	000.00.00.000
				PER SEC = 406			EXP BLK	0.00						
0042	2	032	**	IOC = 134 290	ABSRPTN	724	SINGLE	0.20	AVERAGE	479.25	AVE	0.91	TOT	000.00.00.049
				CPU = 407 099	TRX SERV	699	BLOCK	0.11			MPL	0.88	**TRX**	**000.00.01.217**
				MSO = 21 769	TCB	35.0	HSP	0.00	TOTAL	424.72	ENDED	573	SD	000.00.01.087
				SRB = 14 934	SRB	1.2	HSP MISS	0.00	CENTRAL	252.38	END/SEC	0.63		
				TOT = 578 092	TCB + SRB%	4.0	EXP SNGL	19.33	EXPAND	172.34	#SWAPS	609	QUE	001.15.14.522
				PER SEC = 642			EXP BLK	0.01						
0042	3	033	**	IOC = 96 205	ABSRPTN	605	SINGLE	0.01	AVERAGE	513.31	AVE	0.60	TOT	001.15.15.739
				CPU = 204 427	**TRX SERV**	**589**	BLOCK	0.00			MPL	0.59	**TRX**	**000.00.06.913**
				MSO = 12 502	**TCB**	**17.5**	HSP	0.00	TOTAL	304.19	ENDED	131	SD	000.00.05.150
				SRB = 9643	**SRB**	**0.8**	HSP MISS	0.00	CENTRAL	198.22	**END/SEC**	**0.14**		
				TOT = 322 777	**TCB + SRB%**	**2.0**	EXP SNGL	6.24	EXPAND	105.97	**#SWAPS**	**137**	QUE	000.00.00.000
				PER SEC = 358			EXP BLK	0.00						
0042	ALL	ALL	ALL	IOC = 289 370	ABSRPTN	755	SINGLE	0.25	AVERAGE	488.36	AVE	1.92	TOT	000.00.06.913
				CPU = 888 462	TRX SERV	731	BLOCK	0.21			MPL	1.86	TRX	000.00.00.529
				MSO = 46 967	TCB	76.4	HSP	0.00	TOTAL	909.61	ENDED	3268	**SD**	**000.00.01.789**
				SRB = 41 968	SRB	3.6	HSP MISS	0.00	CENTRAL	541.66	END/SEC	3.63		
				TOT = 1 266 767	TCB + SRB%	8.9	EXP SNGL	73.95	EXPAND	367.95	#SWAPS	3300	QUE	000.13.11.560
				PER SEC = 1407			EXP BLK	0.00						

Figure 6.1. Workload Activity report for PG 42.

normal distribution, and is indicated in the field highlighted SD; the value is 1.789 seconds. In fact though, the distribution is quite skewed, ranging between 0 and 5.896 seconds ($0.529 \pm (3 \times 1.789)$ taking six standard deviations to cover the complete distribution). Breaking down period 3 of PG 42 will show us where the pain is in the third period, if any.

One of the first things we may have to arrive at, is an individual capture ratio for TSO, as well as the average capture ratio that we have used for capacity planning purposes so far. As you will see, it is usually only because a TSO capture ratio is so volatile, that it makes such an exercise possibly necessary.

6.3 Individual capture ratios

Recall that in Chapter 5 we considered the average capture ratio. For capacity planning analyses this was sufficient for our purposes. For a performance study, where we are comparing the speed of transactions, or the power required for a transaction between different types of processor, an average capture ratio may not suffice.

We can make some assumptions regarding IMS, CICS and batch transactions, or we can calculate the individual capture ratios by multiple regression analysis (see Appendix 6 for an example of using this method), although the comments on this in the previous chapter should be borne in mind. Practicality should be foremost in our minds, and so in most performance studies we accept that TSO is the most volatile type of transaction, and so that is the one for which we possibly should force out a capture ratio. The other type of transactions (IMS, CICS and batch) have capture ratios that alter little for any type of processor, and so we can accept standard values.

Normally, we take the IMS and CICS capture ratios as 97 per cent, and the batch capture ratio as 95 per cent. Continual studies have shown that these values are consistent over many different types of environment, and so we will use them too. As an exercise, you may wish to see if your installation capture ratios are close to these values.

6.3.1 Calculating the TSO capture ratio

Let us assume that:

X	Total CPU recovered seconds (CPU busy × interval time) from RMF
TSOsecs	TSO recovered seconds from RMF Monitor I report
IMSsecs	IMS recovered seconds from RMF Monitor I report
Batch	Total batch recovered seconds from RMF Monitor I report
System	Total system and STC recovered seconds from RMF Monitor I report
AveCR	Average capture ratio (calculated)
TSOcaprat	TSO capture ratio (to be calculated)

The total recovered seconds (X) can be calculated from:

$$X = \frac{\text{TSOsecs}}{\text{TSOcaprat}} + \frac{\text{IMSsecs}}{0.97} + \frac{\text{Batch}}{0.95} + \frac{\text{System}}{\text{AveCR}}$$

So the following formula can be used to calculate the TSO capture ratio:

$$\text{TSOcaprat} = \frac{\text{TSOsecs}}{X - ((\text{IMSsecs}/0.97) + (\text{Batch}/0.95) + (\text{System}/\text{AveCR}))}$$

For our system (TSO, batch and system seconds; no IMS):

$$\text{TSOcaprat} = \frac{346.40}{802.71 - ((201.6/0.95) + (74.89/0.776))}$$

$$= 0.70 \text{ (This is a normal value.)}$$

The TSO, batch and system recovered seconds can be picked up from the WAR fields TCB and SRB. Sum these two fields from the relevant section of the WAR, and plug the values into the above formula. Remember, the above may be necessary only if we are measuring for a *performance* study. If we are measuring for a *capacity planning* study then an average capture ratio will usually suffice. If you are fairly new to capacity planning, then try both methods to begin with (if you have the time!). You will soon see which one suits your requirements best.

6.4 What information do we need for a performance study?

- Wait-to-start time (WTST) made up of:
  —Swap-in-wait time
  —Swap-in time
- CPU queue time
- CPU execution time
- I/O waiting time
- Possibly the percentage of transactions completing within period 1 of a PG 42.

The last item above may be required to find out if you are meeting a service-level agreement value, which states for example, that 90 per cent of all production TSO transactions will complete in period 1 (which will have the highest level of service). If 90 per cent of your production TSO transactions are *not* completing within period 1, then perhaps the value associated with the DURATION parameter is too low, or the lower bound of the MPL parameter associated with the domain is too low. All of the above can be calculated from data in the RMF Monitor I report. The above list does not represent all the possible components of a transaction's service time, but it does cover the major ones which will account for virtually all the service time. What is left can be labelled 'other', and will be both small in value and low in meaning.

6.4.1 A terminal transaction's component parts

In order to understand the relationship between the list of a terminal transaction's component parts, see Fig. 6.2. This shows the breakdown of a transaction, and the relationship between the components. It also defines the terms that will be used throughout this chapter.

As you can see, the transaction time is made up of all the individual tranches of time. The major breakdown is between the WTST (wait-to-start time) and the residency time. The wait-to-start time is made up of two parts; the swap-in-delay time and the swap-in time. The swap-in time is the amount of time required actually to 'swap' the address space into central storage from expanded or auxiliary storage (DASD), *or* swap a logically swapped user, and put the control blocks associated with the address space onto the relevant queues (e.g. the ASCB onto the 'ready' queue). The swap-in-delay time is the amount of time the address space has to wait, from the moment it becomes 'ready' until the swap-in process starts. Therefore, for a logically swapped TSO user, the swap-in-delay time could be the same as for a physically swapped TSO user, but the swap-in time will be much less, as there is no real I/O to perform. Residency time is the time that the transaction is actually *absorbing* SUs after swap-in is complete. It includes the time that the transaction is waiting for an engine (CPU).

The total WTST time is a good indicator of a possible too low value of multi-programming level (MPL) for a domain. If the WTST is greater than 10 per cent (a good starting point) of the total transaction time, and yet expanded storage is installed, then this would almost certainly be the problem. Look for a high value of 'exchange on recommendation value swaps' and high 'out & ready' queue value too. These are respectively on the paging activity report and the CPU activity report.

The queue time for the CPU is the time that the transaction has to wait for a CPU, commencing from the time that it is ready to be dispatched. This time is a function of the dispatching priority for the transaction, allied to the number of other transactions of equal to or greater than dispatching priority already in the dispatcher's queue for the CPU(s).

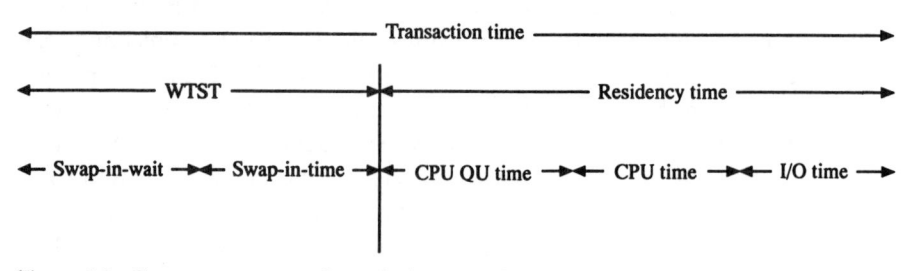

Figure 6.2. Component parts of a typical transaction.

CPU analysis for performance

CPU time is the amount of time the task is dispatched on a CPU (engine); the time which is derived from the ITR. Remember, the CPU time is a *subset* of the residency time, which in turn is a subset of the total transaction time.

I/O time is the amount of time the transaction was waiting for I/Os to complete. There could be more than one I/O, and there could also be more than one *type* of I/O, for example, real I/O to a DASD, DASD controller cached I/O, hiperspace I/O, virtual fetch I/O. All of these have varying times associated with them.

Figure 6.2 does not show a teleprocessing line, it accounts for only a locally attached terminal transaction. A quick rule of thumb for the allowance of a teleprocessing line is that a full screen of 1920 characters takes about 2 seconds to fill the monitor screen. This is based upon a 9600 bits per second (bps) line, with an associated modem of the same baud rate, translating analogue/digital–digital/analogue, and transferring characters at about 1000 characters per second (every 10 bits being taken as a character and its associated parity flags).

6.5 How to extract WTST, residency time and transaction time from RMF Monitor I report

A number of terms have now been introduced, some of which may be new, and so let us first assure ourselves that we understand the relationship between them. Figure 6.3 shows some basic trigonometric ratios which can be used to

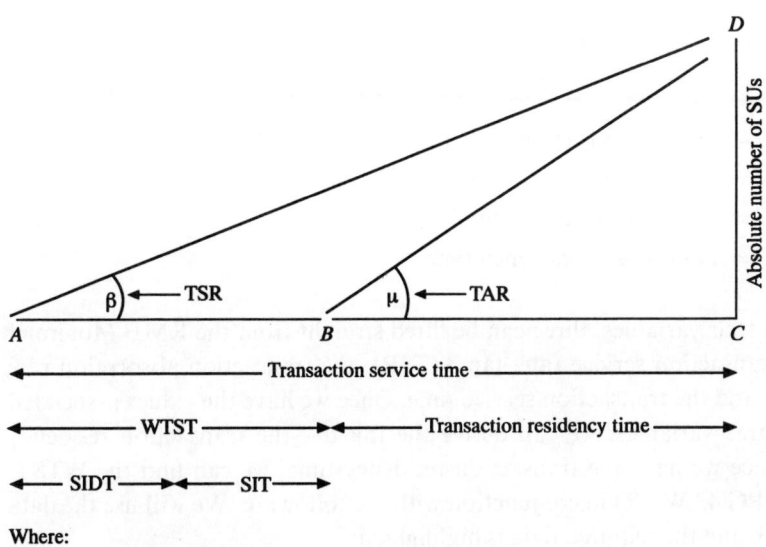

Where:
  SIDT Swap-in-delay time
  SIT   Swap-in time
  TSR   Transaction service rate
  TAR   Transaction absorption rate

Figure 6.3. The transaction service rate and the transaction absorption rate.

indicate how the RMF Monitor I report data all hinges together. For example, tan β (DC/AC) represents the *transaction service rate* (TSR); the rate at which SUs are absorbed throughout the *transaction service time*. Tan μ (DC/BC) represents the *transaction absorption rate* (TAR); the rate at which SUs are absorbed throughout the *transaction residence time*. As the total number of absolute SUs will be the same in both equations, it follows that the TAR will be higher than the TSR; the steeper line indicates the higher absorption rate.

The TSR is the time associated with the transaction *including* the WTST, and the TAR is the time associated with the transaction only while it is *resident*, i.e. *after* swap-in has completed. The only time that we can extract from the RMF Monitor I report is the transaction service time; the transaction residency time and the WTST have to be calculated. We will see how this is done. In fact, we will also show how the actual number of SUs absorbed by the task can calculated as well (DC in Fig. 6.3).

6.5.1 Calculating the residency time and WTST for period 3 PG 42

From Fig. 6.3, we can see the following relationships:

$$\tan \beta = DC/AC \quad \text{therefore } DC = \tan \beta \times AC$$
$$\tan \mu = DC/BC \quad \text{therefore } DC = \tan \mu \times BC$$

As

$$DC = \tan \beta \times AC \quad \text{and} \quad DC = \tan \mu \times BC$$

then:

$$\tan \beta \times AC = \tan \mu \times BC$$

where:

$$\tan \beta = \text{Transaction service rate (TSR)}$$
$$\tan \mu = \text{Transaction absorption rate (TAR)}$$
$$AC = \text{Transaction service time}$$
$$BC = \text{Transaction residency time}$$

Of the above four variables, three can be lifted straight from the RMF Monitor I report: the transaction service rate, tan β (TSR); the transaction absorption rate tan μ (TAR); and the transaction service time. Once we have the values associated with these three variables, we can derive the fourth—the transaction residency time—and once we have the transaction residency time, we can find the WTST. See Fig. 6.1 (PG 42 WAR) in conjunction with the following. We will use the data from period 3, and the required data is highlighted:

- The transaction service rate, tan β (TSR) is taken from the TRX SERV field; the value is 589.
- The transaction absorption rate, tan μ (TAR), is taken from the ABSRPTN field; the value is 605.

CPU analysis for performance

- The transaction service time is taken from the TRX field on the right-hand side of the report. This field has the format 000.00.00.000, representing hours, minutes, seconds and thousandths of a second. The value associated with this field is 000.00.06.913 seconds.

Therefore, according to the relationships we have established, the following is true:

$$\tan \beta \text{ (TSR)} \times \text{Transaction service time}$$
$$= \tan \mu \text{ (TAR)} \times \text{Transaction residency time}$$

Therefore:

$$\text{Transaction residency time} = \frac{\tan \beta \text{ (TSR)} \times \text{Transaction service time}}{\tan \mu \text{ (TAR)}}$$

$$= \frac{589 \times 6.913}{605} = 6.73 \text{ seconds}$$

As:

$$\text{WTST} = \text{Transaction service time} - \text{Transaction residency time}$$
$$= 6.913 - 6.73 = 0.183 \text{ (183 milliseconds)}$$

Is this swap-in delay or swap-in time? Well, if we look at the swap placement activity report (see Fig. 7.11), we will see that there were only three *real* swaps to auxiliary storage. Therefore, it is reasonable to assume that the transactions were at worst expanded storage swaps, a subset of processor storage swaps, and this is acceptable. So, this is probably swap-in delay, and we would therefore look at the domain MPLs.

Also, when we look at the WTST time relative to the total third period transaction service time (0.183 relative to 6.913), we can see that it represents a fairly small proportion of this time (only 2.6 per cent in fact). We would start to examine WTSTˆ only if it represents more than 10 per cent of the transaction service time. Remember, practicality is our guideline, and so using a 10 per cent rule of thumb is a good start and avoids unnecessary calculations which will not give us any additional information.

The swap placement activity report will be dealt with in greater detail in Chapter 7, the I/O subsystem chapter. As well as being incorporated within Chapter 7, it is also on Fig. A4.5(c), Appendix 4, and the value we are looking at is the third figure from the bottom of the column headed AUX STOR TOTAL. This field indicates the total number of *real* swaps to auxiliary storage (page data sets).

6.6 The absolute number of SUs absorbed by the transaction

If we look at Fig. 6.3 the perpendicular DC represents the absolute number of SUs absorbed during the life of the transaction. This is useful for first-cut derivations of values to be associated with the DUR parameter for a domain in the IEAIPSxx parameter member of SYS1.PARMLIB. In fact, if you wish to be reasonably scientific in arriving at the DUR value, then it is essential that you calculate DC. How do we do it?

Well, remember that:

$$\tan \beta \times AC = \tan \mu \times BC$$

and that both sides of the above equation equal DC, then taking the left-hand side:

$$\tan \beta \times AC = DC$$
$$= 589 \times 6.913 = 4072 \text{ SUs (rounded)}$$

Taking the right-hand side:

$$\tan \mu \times BC = DC$$
$$= 605 \times 6.73 = 4072 \text{ SUs (rounded)}$$

This value of 4072 SUs represents the number absorbed throughout the life of the average transaction in period 3. The same exercise can be done for all periods to ensure that the correct value is related to the DUR parameters for each period of the domain. This would be an essential exercise if you had a service-level agreement that stated that a particular percentage of TSO transactions should finish in period 1. This will be necessary only for TSO transactions, as CICS transactions should have only one period anyway.

For example, using Fig. 6.1 we can see that the percentage of TSO transactions completing in periods 1 and 2 is 96 per cent ((2564 + 573)/3268). This looks fine, and providing this is what your service-level agreement specifies, then it is not necessary to change the DUR values.

6.6.1 What about the number of swaps per transaction?

The number of swaps per transaction for TSO should ideally be 1. This would be particularly true for period 1 transactions. As long as this value in close to 1 then we know that our MPL values for the domain are OK. How do we check it? Look at the #SWAPS field on the WAR report for period 3 of PG 42 in Fig. 6.1. You will see a value of 137. Compare this to the number of ended transactions in the period (131). This means that we were almost at our ideal $137/131 = 1.046$ swaps per transaction; not bad at all.

CPU analysis for performance

6.7 Quick method of finding transaction residency time and WTST

Finally, there is a quick way of arriving at the transaction residency time and hence the WTST. Perhaps you will have noticed that if the TAR (tan μ) and TSR (tan β) are equal, then there is no WTST, i.e. the transaction is resident in storage, possibly not even logically swapped. This is possible if transactions are frequent, and the related IEAOPTxx parameters allow this on a lightly loaded system. It follows that the ratio of the TSR (tan β) and TAR (tan μ) has a direct bearing on the WTST value and the transaction residency time. The nearer this is to 1, the smaller will be the WTST, and the closer the transaction residency time will be to the transaction service time. In our case:

$$TSR/TAR = \tan\beta / \tan\mu$$

In the case of period 3 of PG 42 this is:

$$589/605 = 0.974$$

Multiply the transaction service time (the TRX value from the RMF Monitor I report) by this ratio, and you have the transaction residency time. Again, in our case this is:

$$0.974 \times 6.913 = 6.73 \text{ seconds}$$

the same value as we calculated by the longer method.

Now that we have arrived at the WTST and the total transaction residency time, and have made a provisional attempt to explain the WTST, we will start to break down the residency time into its component parts, beginning with the CPU service time for a transaction.

6.8 The CPU service time for a transaction

Now we will take another component of the the transaction residency time—the CPU service time. This is the time during which the transaction is actually dispatched on an engine. Recall that the ITR is the rate at which the transactions of a particular type can be executed on a processor engine, and that the CPU service time can be derived from the ITR. (See Chapter 3 for a revision if necessary.) The CPU service time is calculated as follows:

$$\text{Transaction CPU service time in milliseconds} = \frac{1000 \times \text{No. of engines}}{\text{ITR}}$$

So, what is the ITR in the case of period 3 of PG 42? If you look at the WAR for PG 42 in Fig. 6.1 you will be able to pick up the necessary data to calculate the ITR for period 3 PG 42. The TCB and SRB fields contain 17.5 and 0.8 respectively. The total of these two fields is 18.3 seconds. If we divide this sum by the average capture ratio (0.776), we will arrive at the average capture ratio weighted seconds for period 3 PG 42. We can then pick up the value in the ENDED field for the number of completed transactions, to calculate the ITR.

CPU seconds = 18.3/0.776 = 23.58 seconds

ITR = 131/23.58 = 5.56 transactions per second

CPU MS per transaction = $(1000 \times 1)/5.56$

= 179.86 milliseconds (say 180 ms)

6.8.1 CPU queue time

Chapter 3 introduced the idea of a single server system, and we derived a formula to give the total time on the queue (TQ). Recall that the formula for a single server system was shown by:

TQ = Service time × Average number on the queue

where average number on the queue for a single server is $U/(1 - U)$ where U is the utilization of the system given by the ratio of the arrival rate to the service rate, *or* ETR to ITR. Therefore:

TQ = Service time × $(U/(1 - U))$

6.8.2 CPU queue time for multi-engined processors

Before we go any further, we have to understand how a change in the number of servers (engines in our case) makes a difference to the average number on the queue, and hence to the time on the queue. If the time on the queue is reduced, then intuitively we can accept that the total time in the system will also be reduced. We will not be going through the mathematics of queuing theory here, as there are plenty of better sources of references from which to obtain this information. What we will do, though, is to borrow from Mr Erlang's tables, one of which is in Fig. 6.4. Erlang's tables show how the average number on the queue reduces as the number of servers increases, for any given value of utilization (U).

Just to introduce the way the number on the queue formula changes, let us look at the change when going from one to two servers (and that is as far as we will go!). The formula for the average number on the queue for one server is $(U/(1 - U))$, and it will become $(U^2/(1 - U^2))$. So for example, if the utilization is 0.3 seconds, and the service time is 0.5 seconds, the time on the queue for a single server is:

TQ = $0.5 \times (0.3/(1 - 0.3)) = 0.214$ seconds

For two servers this time reduces to:

TQ = $0.5 \times (0.3^2/(1 - 0.3^2)) = 0.049$ seconds

U	N							
	1	2	3	4	5	6	7	8
0.05	0.053	0.003	0.000	0.000	0.000	0.000	0.000	0.000
0.10	0.111	0.010	0.001	0.000	0.000	0.000	0.000	0.000
0.15	0.176	0.023	0.004	0.001	0.000	0.000	0.000	0.000
0.20	0.250	0.042	0.010	0.003	0.001	0.000	0.000	0.000
0.25	0.333	0.067	0.020	0.007	0.003	0.001	0.000	0.000
0.30	0.429	0.099	0.033	0.013	0.006	0.003	0.001	0.001
0.35	0.538	0.140	0.053	0.023	0.011	0.006	0.003	0.002
0.40	0.667	0.190	0.078	0.038	0.020	0.011	0.006	0.004
0.45	0.818	0.254	0.113	0.058	0.033	0.020	0.012	0.008
0.50	1.000	0.333	0.158	0.087	0.052	0.033	0.022	0.015
0.55	1.222	0.434	0.217	0.126	0.079	0.053	0.037	0.026
0.60	1.500	0.563	0.296	0.179	0.118	0.082	0.059	0.044
0.65	1.857	0.732	0.401	0.253	0.173	0.124	0.093	0.071
0.70	2.333	0.961	0.547	0.357	0.252	0.187	0.143	0.113
0.75	3.000	1.286	0.757	0.509	0.369	0.281	0.221	0.178
0.80	4.000	1.778	1.079	0.746	0.554	0.431	0.347	0.286
0.85	5.667	2.604	1.623	1.149	0.873	0.693	0.569	0.477
0.90	9.000	4.263	2.724	1.969	1.525	1.234	1.029	0.877
0.95	19.000	9.256	6.047	4.457	3.511	2.885	2.441	2.110

Figure 6.4. Erlang's table for average queue length with multiple servers.

The time on the queue has dropped by more than a factor of four; quite a difference, hence quite a difference to the total time in the system—the total transaction time.

Erlang's table to show average number on a queue for multi-engined processors (N) and different utilizations (U) is shown in Fig. 6.4. This table is based upon the $M(1)/M(2)/N$ values, where:

> $M(1)$ is the arrival rate of transactions (ETR)
> $M(2)$ is the service rate of transactions (ITR)
> N is the number of servers (engines)

The left-hand column shows the utilization (U), and the top row shows the number of servers (N) ranging from 1 to 8 (you never know how many engines tomorrow's mainframe processors will have). The body of the table shows the average number on the queue. For example, if U is 0.45 and there are two servers, the average number on the queue is 0.254.

6.9   How do we calculate our value of U?

Well, we have our CPU service time, and all we need now is our value for U (utilization). This is the tricky bit.

Let us do a short review of what we found out in Chapter 3. We know that the utilization for any system is given by the ratio of the arrival rate to the service rate; this will give the probability that the system is busy (single server). We also know that the arrival rate for a mainframe computer is given by the ETR for each type of transaction, and that the service rate for a mainframe computer system is given by the ITR for each type of transaction. So far so good. Further, we know that the utilization is the ratio of the ETR to the ITR, and that we can calculate the ETR, ITR and hence the utilization of the processor, for each type of transaction in the system, i.e. for each PG period.

But what we are looking for now, is an *overall* value for the utilization that represents how busy the system is for a particular type of transaction. The case that we are currently pursuing is for period 3 in TSO PG 42. Therefore, we want the utilization of the system *from period 3 of PG 42's perception*.

When a transaction arrives at the processor, it is queued with other transactions of the same and different types to wait for the use of an engine; the only engine in the case of a uni-processor. What dictates the position on the queue for the engine? It is nothing else but the *dispatching priority*. Therefore, if we aggregate all the ETR/ITR ratios (system utilizations) for all PGs and PG periods of *equal to or greater than* dispatching priority than for period 3 of PG 42, then we will arrive at an overall utilization of the system from the perception of period 3 of PG42. We must include all PGs of equal dispatching priority, as well as the PGs of greater dispatching priority, because the transactions of the same dispatching priority will be competing against each other, on a FIFO basis.

So, we need first of all to find all other PGs and periods, including system PGs, that have a dispatching priority equal to or greater than period 3 of PG 42. This data is obtained from the IEAIPS00 member of SYS1.PARMLIB in Fig. 6.5. We can then pick up the TCB+SRB% field value of these periods and PGs. This data, when it has been divided by the capture ratio, will give us the CPU busy percentage; or utilization (U) of the PG or period. Once we have the individual utilization of the periods and PGs, we can sum them to arrive at the utilization of the processor from the perception of period 3 of PG 42.

We can then arrive at the CPU queue time, by entering Erlang's table for the required number of servers (in our case 1), and the utilization that we have calculated. We will find that the nearest 0.05 boundary is the best we can do in Erlang's table. But again, as always, our credo is practicality, and experience has shown that the 0.05 boundaries are sufficient for our purposes. All we do if we show all the possible 0.01 boundaries is to be about a third decimal place more accurate, and so it is not necessary. That is the theory—let's do it.

6.9.1 *Calculating the CPU queue time for period 3 of PG 42*

Period 3 of PG 42 has a dispatching priority of M7, therefore we are looking for dispatching priorities equal to or greater than this value. Figure 6.6 shows the CPU utilization for all PGs of dispatching priority equal to or greater than period 3 of PG 42. The utilizations have been divided by the capture ratio, 0.776. The aggregated total is the utilization of the system from period 3 of PG 42's view.

CPU analysis for performance

```
COL     ----+----1----+----2----+----3----+----5----+----6----+----7----+----8
 2      /*                IEAIPS00 FOR THE MAC1 SYSTEM              */ 00010001
 2      /*                                                          */ 00020001
 1      CPU=10.0,IOC=5.0,MSO=0.1,SRB=10   /* MSO REDUCED            */ 00030001
 1      APGRNG=(0,15)                     /* ALL APGs INCLUDED      */ 00040001
 1      PVLDP=F7                          /* PRIV. USER DISP PRTY.  */ 00050001
 1      IOQ=PRTY                          /* I/O QUEUED BY DISP PTY */ 00060001
 2      /*                                                          */ 00070001
 2      /*                                                          */ 00080001
 1      DMN=1,DSRV=(0,2800)        /* TEST BATCH FIRST PERIOD       */ 00090001
 1      DMN=2,DSRV=(0,1600)        /* TEST BATCH SECOND PERIOD      */ 00100001
 2      /*                                                          */ 00110001
 1      DMN=11,DSRV=(1150,2200),   /* PROD BATCH FIRST PERIOD       */ 00120001
 8           ESCRTABX=4                                              */ 00130001
 1      DMN=12,DSRV=(400,800),     /* PROD BATCH SECOND PERIOD      */ 00140001
 8           ESCRTABX=4                                              */ 00150001
 2      /*                                                          */ 00160001
 1      DMN=21,ASRV=(460,600)      /* DEV TSO SHORT                 */ 00170001
 1      DMN=22,ASRV=(460,600)      /* DEV TSO MEDIUM                */ 00180001
 1      DMN=23,ASRV=(375,500)      /* DEV TSO LONG                  */ 00190001
 2      /*                                                          */ 00200001
 1      DMN=31,ASRV=(700,1000),    /* PROD TSO SHORT                */ 00210001
 8           ESCRTABX=3                                              */ 00220001
 1      DMN=32,ASRV=(675,900),     /* PROD TSO MEDIUM               */ 00230001
 8           ESCRTABX=3                                              */ 00240001
 1      DMN=33,ASRV=(675,900),     /* PROD TSO LONG                 */ 00250001
 8           ESCRTABX=3                                              */ 00260001
 2      /*                                                          */ 00270001
 1      DMN=80,ASRV=(460,2000),    /* HOT BATCH                     */ 00280001
 1      DMN=99,CNSTR=(0,0)         /* DELAY DOMAIN                  */ 00290001
 1      DMN=100,CNSTR=(0,30)       /* SYSTEM ADDRESS SPACES         */ 00300001
 1      DMN=128,CNSTR=(5,15),      /* SYSPROGS DOMAIN               */ 00310001
 8           ASRV=(4000,4000)     /*                                */ 00320001
 2      /*                                                          */ 00330001
 2      /*                                                          */ 00340001
 1      PGN=1,(DMN=1,DP=M3,DUR=30K)         /* PERIOD 1 TEST BATCH  */ 00350001
 7            (DMN=2,DP=M2)                 /* PERIOD 2 TEST BATCH  */ 00360001
 1      PGN=11,(DMN=11,DP=M6,DUR=30K)       /* PERIOD 1 PROD BATCH  */ 00370001
 8             (DMN=12,DP=M5)               /* PERIOD 2 PROD BATCH  */ 00380001
 1      PGN=2,(DMN=21,DP=F43,DUR=200)       /* DEV TSO SHORT        */ 00390001
 7            (DMN=22,DP=F42,DUR=1800)      /* DEV TSO MEDIUM       */ 00400001
 7            (DMN=23,DP=M4)                /* DEV TSO LONG         */ 00410001
 1      PGN=42,(DMN=31,DP=F73,DUR=200)      /* PROD TSO SHORT       */ 00420001
 8             (DMN=32,DP=F72,DUR=850)      /* PROD TSO MEDIUM      */ 00430001
 8             **(DMN=33,DP=M7,PWSS=(500,*))) /* PROD TSO LONG**    */ 00440001
 1      PGN=3, (DMN=80,DP=F30)              /* HOT BATCH            */ 00450001
 1      PGN=13,(DMN=1,DP=M0)                /* LOW PRTY BATCH       */ 00460001
 1      PGN=99,(DMN=99,DP=M1)               /* DELAY JOBS           */ 00470001
 1      PGN=100,(DMN=100,DP=M8)             /* STARTED TASKS        */ 00480001
 1      PGN=101,(DMN=100,DP=M8)             /* CATALOG              */ 00490001
 1      PGN=102,(DMN=100,DP=M8)             /* LLA                  */ 00500001
 1      PGN=103,(DMN=100,DP=M8)             /* VLF                  */ 00510001
 1      PGN=104,(DMN=100,DP=M8)             /* VTAM                 */ 00520001
 1      PGN=105,(DMN=100,DP=M8)             /* JES2                 */ 00530001
 1      PGN=106,(DMN=100,DP=M8)             /* RMF                  */ 00540001
 1      PGN=107,(DMN=100,DP=M8)             /* MOUNT                */ 00550001
 1      PGN=999,(DMN=128,DP=F9)             /* HIGH PRIORITY WORK   */ 00560001
```

Figure 6.5. The IEAIPS00 member of SYS1.PARMLIB used with this system.

Where a performance group has no utilization, or no ended transactions, then it has been omitted.

If we enter Erlang's table in Fig. 6.4 at the 0.20 utilization, which is as near as we can get to our calculated value of U, and pick out the element corresponding to

Performance group/period no.	DP	Utilization % (U)
0 (master)	FF	5.80
100	M8	2.32
104	M8	0.26
105	M8	1.68
106	M8	0.26
42 period 1	F73	3.61
42 period 2	F72	5.15
999	F9	0.77
Total utilization (U)		19.85

Figure 6.6. Calculating the CPU utilization for period 3 of PG 42.

server 1, we see the value 0.25. This represents the average number on the queue, as far as period 3 of PG 42 is concerned.

We are looking for the average time on the queue (TQ), which is represented by:

$$TQ = \text{CPU service time} \times \text{Average number on the queue}$$

We have a CPU service time of 0.180 from Sec. 6.8, therefore TQ is:

$$TQ = 0.180 \times 0.25 = 0.045 \text{ (45 milliseconds)}$$

6.9.2 The story so far

Let us update Fig. 6.2 and fill in the times that we have calculated so far. This will allow us to take a checkpoint on the information for period 3 of PG 42. Figure 6.7 shows the values we have calculated so far.

6.9.3 Summary of transaction residency time breakdown

So we have 45 milliseconds CPU queue time; is this good? Well, on a system that is close to 90 per cent loaded this is indeed quite good, but not less than we could reasonably expect. Only the two initial periods of PG 42 and the system PGs were of

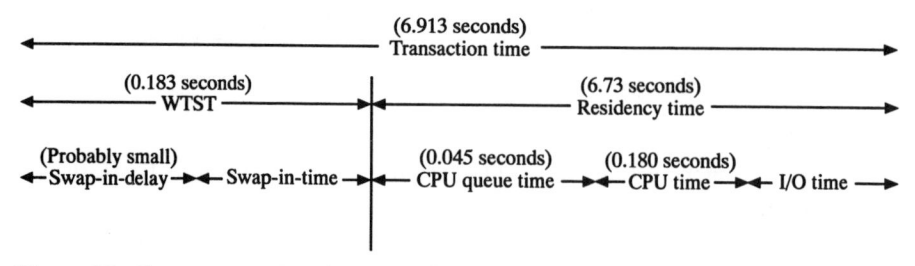

```
                          (6.913 seconds)
                          Transaction time

         (0.183 seconds)                    (6.73 seconds)
              WTST                          Residency time

(Probably small)                 (0.045 seconds)    (0.180 seconds)
← Swap-in-delay →← Swap-in-time →← CPU queue time →← CPU time →← I/O time →
```

Figure 6.7. Component parts of a transaction—with values.

CPU analysis for performance

higher dispatching priority, therefore we could expect this, particularly as the system PGs have little activity.

Regarding the CPU service time of 180 milliseconds, this merely emphasizes that the sudden increase in transaction time is not the result of the type of manipulation of the application data, but is more likely to be because of I/O, but we will confirm this.

The WTST of 183 milliseconds, is primarily made up of swap-in delay not swap-in time.

The total amount of residency time accounted for so far is the sum of the CPU queue time and the CPU time; $0.045 + 0.180 = 0.225$ seconds. This leaves $6.730 - 0.225 =$ (say 6.5) seconds to be accounted for yet. Disregarding 'other' factors within residency time, we can accept that I/O time explains this amount. The question is though, how many I/Os does this represent? If it takes 6.5 seconds for only one I/O per transaction; well, this would need investigating. Our next step therefore is to see how many I/Os are accounted for by this value of 6.5 seconds. In other words, what is the average number of I/Os per transaction?

6.9.4 Calculating the average I/O rate per transaction for period 3 of PG 42

So what do we need to know in order to arrive at the average I/O rate for period 3 of PG 42? In the order they are listed we need to extract the following data:

- The paging and swapping I/O rate; this has to be deducted from 'normal' I/O
- The share of the total I/O rate that 'belongs' to period 3 of PG 42
- The ETR of period 3 PG 42 in order to find the I/Os per transaction
- The average response time (RT) per I/O for period 3 of PG 42
- We should also compare the RT per I/O against the system average I/O RT

Calculating the page and swap I/O rate

We should always subtract the page and swap I/O from application I/O, before we manipulate any application data. The rationale for doing this is that the application should not suffer the page and swap I/O in any calculations based upon I/O rate, because it is no fault of the application that it has to be subjected to paging and swapping; it is the system that does this, in order to optimize the use of resources and achieve the customer's business objectives. Therefore, our first task is to arrive at the page and swap I/O rate for the system. To do this we need the page/swap data set activity report. This report shows all the activity of each of the page and swap data sets. We will pick out other information as we need it, but for now we require the total number of I/Os to and from each of the data sets.

Figure 6.8 shows the page/swap data set activity report. We shall extract some data from it to arrive at the page/swap I/O rate for the system. The total number

PAGE/SWAP DATA SET ACTIVITY

MVS/ESA SP/4.2.0			SYSTEM ID MAC1 RPT VERSION 4.2.1						DATE 28/06/93 TIME 09.00.00				INTERVAL 15.00.00 CYCLE 1 SECOND

NUMBER OF SAMPLES = 900

PAGE DATA SET USAGE

PAGE SPACE TYPE	VOLUME SERIAL	DEV NUM	DEVICE TYPE	SLOTS ALLOC	SLOTS USED MIN	MAX	AVE	BAD SLOTS	% IN USE	PAGE TRANS TIME	NUMBER IO REQ	PAGES XFER'D	V I O	DATA SET NAME
PLPA	MVSCAT	C15	3380E	3000	2986	2986	2986	0	0.06	0.018	38	28		PAGE.VMVSCAT.PLPA
COMMON	MVSCAT	C15	3380E	1950	520	525	521	0	0.06	0.062	8	8		PAGE.VMVSCAT.COMMON
LOCAL	MVS576	576	3380J	60000	5998	6985	6333	0	1.50	0.010	525	1402	Y	PAGE.VMVS576.LOCAL
LOCAL	AKESM1	C12	3380E	42000	6723	7747	7097	0	0.83	0.005	515	1417	Y	PAGE.VAKESM1.LOCAL
LOCAL	ESCCAT	C17	3380E	32100	6827	7899	7276	0	2.06	0.011	596	1678	Y	PAGE.VESCCAT.LOCAL
LOCAL	MVS577	577	3380J	16050	5469	6060	5693	0	1.33	0.011	687	1064	Y	PAGE.VMVS577.LOCAL
LOCAL	CB84LB	567	3380J	60000	6189	7138	6568	0	1.83	0.012	518	1362	Y	PAGE.VCB84LB.LOCAL
LOCAL	CICIPO	C11	3380E	60000	6460	7476	6876	0	1.89	0.011	850	1528	Y	PAGE.VCICIPO.LOCAL

TOTAL PAGE & SWAP I/Os = 3737

Figure 6.8. Page/Swap Data Set Activity report.

of page/swap I/Os (which has been edited onto the report and highlighted) will be divided by the elapsed measured interval time—in our case, 900 seconds. The resulting figure is the page/swap I/O rate for the system. This value will be subtracted from the total system I/O rate to find the total application I/O rate.

Page/swap I/O rate = 3737/900 = 4.15 I/Os per second

Finding the total system I/O rate

Now we have to find the total system I/O rate, and subtract the page/swap I/O from it. Figure 6.9 shows the I/O queuing activity report, and at the top you can see the total I/O rate through all the DASD controllers; 668.081 I/Os per second (we will round this to 668). Each logical control unit (LCU), made up of two physical control unit directors on this system, supports a number of I/Os. It is possible to have four storage paths through two directors to a single device, with the IBM 3990 Model 2 or 3 DASD controller (see the LCUs 0CD and 0D5 on the I/O queuing activity report in Fig 6.9; they are the two directors of an IBM 3990 Model 3 (cached) DASD controller).

The I/Os are totalled for you, and the sum is placed at the top of this report. It is the same sum that you would arrive at if you added the total I/Os through each LCU on the same page (see column CHPID TAKEN which shows the absolute number of I/Os through each LCU; again it is highlighted. It is also the total you would arrive at if you summed the columns DEVICE ACTIVITY RATE on the DASD device activity reports in Fig. 6.10. Again, these columns are highlighted.

To arrive at our application I/O rate per second, we must subtract 4.15 from 668:

Total application I/O = 668 − 4.15 = 663.85 I/Os per second

The share of application I/O rate for period 3 of PG 42

In Fig. 6.11 you will see the WAR system summary, and the total number of SUs absorbed for the purpose of I/O is highlighted; IOC = 2 760 090. If we see what percentage of this figure applies to period 3 of PG 42, then we will have the percentage of the total I/Os issued by period 3 of PG 42. We can pick up the IOC value for the required period/PG from the WAR for PG 42 in Fig. 6.12. The value is highlighted; IOC = 96 205. Therefore, the percentage of I/Os 'belonging' to period 3 of PG 42 is:

(96 205/2 760 090) × 100 = 3.49%

I/O rate for period 3 of PG 42 is:

0.0349 × 663.85 = 23.17 I/Os per second

I/O QUEUING ACTIVITY

MVS/ESA SP/4.2.0			SYSTEM ID MAC1 RPT VERSION 4.2.1		DATE 28/06/93 TIME 09.00.00				INTERVAL 15.00.00 CYCLE 1 SECOND

TOTAL SAMPLES = 900   IOP 02   ACTIVITY RATE 668.081   AVE Q LNGTH 0.03   IODF = 99   NO CREATION DATE AVAILABLE   ACT: ACTIVATE

LCU	CONTENTION RATE	DELAY Q LNGTH	% ALL CH PATH BUSY	CONTROL UNITS	CHAN PATHS	CHPID TAKEN	% DP BUSY	% CU BUSY	
097	0.005	0.00	1.18	1C0	01				OFFLINE
					81	43.842		0.39	
				1C1	25	43.858		0.48	
					A5				OFFLINE
0CD	0.094	0.55	3.57	560	05				OFFLINE
				561	85	58.598		1.51	
				562	21	58.530		1.46	
				563	A1				OFFLINE
0D5	0.000	0.00	12.54	620	06				OFFLINE
				621	86	92.761		0.04	
				622	22	92.747		0.03	
				623	A2				OFFLINE
0F0	0.710	0.27	5.53	780	07				OFFLINE
					87	44.458		5.06	
				781	23	44.254		5.12	
					A3				OFFLINE
15C	0.025	0.13	2.65	A90	0A				OFFLINE
					8A	53.623		0.64	
				A91	2E	53.421		0.63	
					AE				OFFLINE
173	0.000	0.00	1.30	C10	19				OFFLINE
					99	41.051		0.01	
				C11	1D	40.938		0.00	
					9D				OFFLINE

Figure 6.9. I/O DASD controller queuing activity report.

DIRECT ACCESS DEVICE ACTIVITY

PAGE 1

MVS/ESA SP/4.2.0				SYSTEM ID MAC1 RPT VERSION 4.2.1				DATE 28/06/93 TIME 09.00.00								INTERVAL 15.00.00 CYCLE 1 SECOND		

TOTAL SAMPLES = 900   IODF = 99

STORAGE GROUP	DEV NUM	DEVICE TYPE	VOLUME SERIAL	IOP	LCU	DEVICE ACTIVITY RATE	AVE RESP TIME	AVE IOSQ TIME	AVE Q LNGTH AVE DPB DLY	AVE CUB DLY	AVE DB DLY	AVE PEND TIME	AVE DISC TIME	AVE CONN TIME	% DEV CONN	% DEV UTIL	% DEV RESV	AVE NUMBER ALLOC	% ANY ALLOC	% MT PEND
	1C0	3380D	CACHE1		097	18.794	3	0		0.0	0.1	0.2	0.7	2.2	4.05	5.51	2.6	7.7	100.0	0.0
	1C1	3380D	CACHE2		097	3.127	11	1		0.0	1.2	1.4	5.8	2.9	0.90	3.37	1.2	61.5	100.0	0.0
	1C2	3380D	CACHE3		097	26.931	3	0		0.0	0.1	0.2	0.0	2.8	7.52	7.60	0.0	1282	100.0	0.0
	1C3	3380D	CACHE4		097	25.537	2	0		0.0	0.1	0.2	0.0	2.2	5.55	5.68	0.0	241	100.0	0.0
	1C4	3380D	TSO1C4		097	6.758	9	1		0.0	1.3	1.5	3.5	3.6	2.43	7.06	3.5	127	100.0	0.0
	1C5	3380D	TSO1C5		097	6.554	8	1		0.0	1.5	1.6	2.7	3.2	2.09	4.60	2.7	173	100.0	0.0
			LCU		097	87.701	4	0		0.0	0.3	0.4	0.8	2.6	3.76	5.64	1.6	1892	100.0	0.0
	564	3380J	BAT564		OCD	20.039	4	1		0.0	0.0	0.3	0.4	3.0	6.08	19.37	13.9	5.6	100.0	0.0
	565	3380J	BAT565		OCD	10.908	5	0		0.0	0.0	0.3	0.5	3.5	3.85	10.69	6.7	2.7	100.0	0.0
	566	3380J	IDAVOL		OCD	15.489	2	0		0.0	0.0	0.1	0.0	1.7	2.66	2.71	0.0	7.2	100.0	0.0
	567	3380J	CB84LB		OCD	0.967	25	1		0.0	0.0	0.2	18.0	5.6	0.54	2.29	0.0	1.9	100.0	0.0
	570	3380J	CIC570		OCD	0.043	24	0		0.0	0.0	0.5	12.2	11.2	0.05	0.32	0.3	1.1	100.0	0.0
	571	3380J	WRK571		OCD	0.284	4	0		0.0	0.0	0.8	0.5	2.8	0.08	0.09	0.0	3.3	100.0	0.0
	572	3380J	BAT572		OCD	16.357	5	1		0.0	0.0	0.2	0.4	3.5	5.65	10.44	4.7	3.5	100.0	0.0
	573	3380J	BAT573		OCD	13.686	6	0		0.0	0.0	0.2	0.7	4.2	5.80	57.97	52.9	3.7	100.0	0.0
	574	3380J	BAT574		OCD	6.857	7	1		0.0	0.0	0.2	1.3	4.9	3.33	5.03	1.3	3.8	100.0	0.0
	575	3380J	BAT575		OCD	12.697	5	0		0.0	0.0	0.3	0.6	3.5	4.41	5.16	0.0	3.3	100.0	0.0
	576	3380J	MVS576		OCD	0.583	24	0		0.0	0.0	0.1	18.6	5.3	0.31	1.39	0.0	1.0	100.0	0.0
	577	3380J	MVS577		OCD	19.220	3	0		0.0	0.0	0.2	0.5	1.8	3.54	4.50	0.0	2674	100.0	0.0
			LCU		OCD	117.129	4	0		0.0	0.0	0.2	0.7	3.1	3.03	10.00	6.6	2711	100.0	0.0

NO CREATION DATE AVAILABLE   ACT: ACTIVATE

Figure 6.10(a). Direct Access Device Activity report (*Continues*).

DIRECT ACCESS DEVICE ACTIVITY

PAGE 1

MVS/ESA SP/4.2.0

SYSTEM ID MAC1
RPT VERSION 4.2.1

DATE 28/06/93
TIME 09.00.00

INTERVAL 15.00.00
CYCLE 1 SECOND

TOTAL SAMPLES = 900   IODF = 99   ACT: ACTIVATE

STORAGE GROUP	DEV NUM	DEVICE TYPE	IOP	VOLUME SERIAL	LCU	DEVICE ACTIVITY RATE	AVE RESP TIME	AVE Q LNGTH / AVE IOSQ TIME	AVE DPB DLY	AVE CUB DLY	AVE DB DLY	AVE PEND TIME	NO CREATION DATE AVAILABLE / AVE DISC TIME	AVE CONN TIME	% DEV CONN	% DEV UTIL	% DEV RESV	AVE NUMBER ALLOC	% ANY ALLOC	% MT PEND
	630	3380J		BAT630	0D5	27.962	69	44		0.0	0.1	0.2	21.2	3.6	10.08	69.47	9.6	9.1	100.0	0.0
	631	3380J		BAT631	0D5	21.071	58	35		0.0	0.1	0.2	20.2	3.4	7.27	64.11	29.3	7.3	100.0	0.0
	632	3380J		BAT632	0D5	25.570	59	34		0.0	0.1	0.2	21.4	3.5	8.95	63.96	2.6	7.4	100.0	0.0
	633	3380J		BAT633	0D5	23.764	69	44		0.0	0.1	0.2	21.0	3.4	8.13	58.75	5.3	7.5	100.0	0.0
	634	3380J		BAT634	0D5	26.511	58	34		0.0	0.1	0.2	20.3	3.2	8.50	64.35	10.9	8.6	100.0	0.0
	635	3380J		BAT635	0D5	18.199	46	21		0.0	0.1	0.2	19.9	4.0	7.30	48.37	12.9	6.2	100.0	0.0
	636	3380J		BAT636	0D5	20.493	45	22		0.0	0.1	0.2	19.5	3.4	6.87	66.43	33.2	6.6	100.0	0.0
	637	3380J		BAT637	0D5	21.946	74	46		0.0	0.1	0.2	23.3	4.3	9.54	76.82	51.5	7.9	100.0	0.0
				LCU	0D5	185.517	60	36		0.0	0.1	0.2	20.9	3.6	8.33	64.03	19.4	60.6	100.0	0.0
	780	3380E		RS189A	0F0	21.638	33	14		0.0	2.0	2.3	10.8	6.0	12.93	40.85	31.3	16.2	100.0	0.0
	781	3380E		RS289A	0F0	21.848	28	10		0.0	1.2	1.4	10.9	5.3	11.57	41.21	30.5	36.6	100.0	0.0
	782	3380E		CAT89A	0F0	4.999	18	2		0.0	2.7	3.1	10.1	3.5	1.76	7.66	2.5	115	100.0	0.0
	783	3380E		SPL89A	0F0	4.822	19	2		0.0	2.6	3.0	11.1	3.5	1.67	7.62	2.4	125	100.0	0.0
	784	3380E		SC189A	0F0	5.332	20	3		0.0	2.8	3.2	11.1	3.4	1.81	8.34	2.7	123	100.0	0.0
	785	3380E		DL189A	0F0	4.547	19	1		0.0	2.5	2.9	11.6	3.3	1.49	7.61	2.6	123	100.0	0.0
	786	3380E		DL289A	0F0	19.243	30	11		0.0	1.3	1.6	11.8	5.6	10.79	37.45	29.3	27.1	100.0	0.0
	787	3380E		MVSTS3	0F0	0.000	0	0		0.0	0.0	0.0	0.0	0.0	0.00	0.00	0.0	0.0	100.0	0.0
	788	3380E		SMP89A	0F0	6.284	22	4		0.0	3.1	3.5	10.7	3.3	2.05	9.35	3.1	121	100.0	0.0
				LCU	0F0	88.713	27	9		0.0	1.9	2.2	11.1	5.0	4.90	17.79	11.6	686	100.0	0.0

Figure 6.10(a). Direct Access Device Activity report (*Concluded*).

DIRECT ACCESS DEVICE ACTIVITY

PAGE 2

MVS/ESA SP/4.2.0
SYSTEM ID MAC1
RPT VERSION 4.2.1
DATE 28/06/93
TIME 09.00.00
INTERVAL 15.00.00
CYCLE 1 SECOND

TOTAL SAMPLES = 900   IODF = 99   ACT: ACTIVATE

STORAGE GROUP	DEV NUM	DEVICE TYPE	IOP	VOLUME SERIAL	LCU	DEVICE ACTIVITY RATE	AVE RESP TIME	AVE IOSQ TIME	AVE DPB DLY	AVE CUB DLY	AVE DB DLY	AVE PEND TIME	AVE DISC TIME	AVE CONN TIME	% DEV CONN	% DEV UTIL	% DEV RESV	AVE NUMBER ALLOC	% ANY ALLOC	% MT PEND
	A90	3380D		TSOA90	15C	8.906	28	7		0.0	0.1	0.2	17.6	3.0	2.65	19.93	5.8	137	100.0	0.0
	A91	3380D		TSOA91	15C	20.838	28	11		0.0	0.2	0.2	13.7	2.7	5.66	34.93	7.6	153	100.0	0.0
	A92	3380D		TSOA92	15C	12.107	25	8		0.0	0.2	0.2	13.8	3.0	3.64	21.97	5.8	139	100.0	0.0
	A93	3380D		TSOA93	15C	6.753	23	3		0.0	0.1	0.2	16.9	2.9	1.97	15.56	5.1	151	100.0	0.0
	A94	3380D		TSOA94	15C	6.622	28	7		0.0	0.1	0.2	17.9	3.0	2.01	15.34	4.2	122	100.0	0.0
	A95	3380D		TSOA95	15C	4.586	25	4		0.0	0.2	0.2	17.7	2.8	1.28	9.92	2.9	121	100.0	0.0
	A96	3380D		TSOA96	15C	9.090	32	10		0.0	0.1	0.2	19.8	2.4	2.15	22.46	8.4	163	100.0	0.0
	A97	3380D		TSOA97	15C	7.821	24	4		0.0	0.1	0.2	17.0	2.8	2.22	17.66	6.8	125	100.0	0.0
	A98	3380D		TSOA98	15C	8.099	24	4		0.0	0.1	0.2	16.9	3.0	2.47	17.57	5.4	177	100.0	0.0
	A99	3380D		TSOA99	15C	6.767	25	4		0.0	0.1	0.2	17.2	3.6	2.42	15.48	4.8	145	100.0	0.0
	A9A	3380D		TSOA9A	15C	7.977	27	6		0.0	0.1	0.2	17.8	2.9	2.30	18.87	7.1	163	100.0	0.0
	A9B	3380D		TSOA9B	15C	7.476	23	3		0.0	0.1	0.2	17.2	2.7	2.04	16.48	3.7	134	100.0	0.0
				LCU	15C	107.040	26	7		0.0	0.1	0.2	16.4	2.9	2.57	18.85	5.6	1729	100.0	0.0
	C10	3380E		MVSDLB	173	17.546	19	2		0.0	0.0	0.1	14.7	1.8	3.10	29.01	0.3	115	100.0	0.0
	C11	3380E		CICIPO	173	2.750	19	1		0.0	0.1	0.2	14.9	2.9	0.80	4.89	0.0	3.0	100.0	0.0
	C12	3380E		AKESM1	173	0.623	21	0		0.0	0.3	0.3	15.3	5.2	0.32	1.28	0.0	5.4	100.0	0.0
	C13	3380E		MVSRES	173	28.394	115	90		0.0	0.4	0.5	20.3	4.3	12.24	69.99	3.6	7903	100.0	0.0
	C14	3380E		ESCDLB	173	0.000	0	0		0.0	0.0	0.0	0.0	0.0	0.00	0.00	0.0	0.0	100.0	0.0
	C15	3380E		MVSCAT	173	32.017	10	1		0.0	0.0	0.1	6.6	1.9	6.06	28.42	7.2	734	100.0	0.0
	C16	3380E		ESCRES	173	0.000	0	0		0.0	0.0	0.0	0.0	0.0	0.00	0.00	0.0	4.0	100.0	0.0
	C17	3380E		ESCCAT	173	0.662	21	0		0.0	0.2	0.2	14.9	5.6	0.37	1.36	0.0	1.0	100.0	0.0
				LCU	173	81.992	49	32		0.0	0.2	0.2	13.5	2.8	2.86	16.87	1.4	8765	100.0	0.0

Figure 6.10(b). Direct Access Device Activity report.

WORKLOAD ACTIVITY

MVS/ESA SP4.2.0				SYSTEM ID MAC1 RPT VERSION 4.2.1			DATE 28/06/93 TIME 09.00.000			INTERVAL 15.00.000 IPS = IEAIPS00

SYSTEM SUMMARY

OPT = IEAPT00
ICS = IEAICS00

SERVICE DEFINITION COEFFICIENTS
IOC = 5.0   CPU = 10.0   SRB = 10.0   SU/SEC = 1162.3   MSO = 0.1000

PGN	PGP	DMN	TIME SLICE GROUP	INTERVAL SERVICE		AVERAGE AVE TRX TCB + SRB	ABSORPTION SERV RATE SECONDS, %	PAGE-IN RATES	RATES	STORAGE		TRANSACTIONS		AVE TRANS TIME, STD DEVIATION HHH.MM.SS.TTT	
ALL	ALL	ALL	ALL	IOC	**2 760 090**	ABSRPTN	247	SINGLE	0.05	AVERAGE	982.41	AVE	50.59	TRX	000.00.01.688
				CPU	6 638 865	TRX SERV	226	BLOCK	0.04			MPL	46.20	SD	000.00.12.340
				MSO	305 398	TCB	571.1	HSP	0.00	TOTAL	45 396	ENDED	15 815		
				SRB	600 186	SRB	51.6	HSP MISS	0.00	CENTRAL	13 844	END/SEC	17.57	QUE	000.21.16.965
				TOT	10 304 539	TCB + SRB%	69.1	EXP SINGL	14.78	EXPAND	31 552	#SWAPS	16 288		
				PER SEC	11 449			EXP BLK	0.38					TOT	000.21.18.654

Figure 6.11. Workload Activity report—system summary.

WORKLOAD ACTIVITY

```
MVS/ESA                SYSTEM ID MAC1              DATE 28/06/93                              INTERVAL 15.00.000
SP4.2.0                RPT VERSION 4.2.1           TIME 09.00.000                             IPS = IEAIPS00

  OPT = IEAPT00        REPORT BY PERFORMANCE GROUP        SERVICE DEFINITION COEFFICIENTS     SU/SEC = 1162.3
  ICS = IEAICS00              PERIOD                 IOC = 5.0   CPU = 10.0   SRB = 10.0      MSO = 0.1000
```

					AVERAGE	ABSORPTION						AVE TRANS TIME,
			TIME SLICE	INTERVAL	AVE TRX	SERV RATE	PAGE-IN					STD DEVIATION
PGN	PGP	DMN	GROUP	SERVICE	TCB + SRB	SECONDS, %	RATES	RATES	STORAGE		TRANSACTIONS	HHH.MM.SS.TTT

SUBSYS = TSO
USERID =   TRXCLASS =   ACCTINFO = NO
                    TRXNAME =

PGN	PGP	DMN	GROUP	INTERVAL SERVICE		AVE TRX TCB+SRB	ABSORPTION SERV RATE SECONDS,%	PAGE-IN RATES	RATES	STORAGE		TRANSACTIONS		AVE TRANS TIME STD DEVIATION
0042	1	031	**	IOC =	58 875	ABSRPTN	1059	SINGLE	0.74	AVERAGE	470.88	AVE	0.39	TRX 000.00.00.049
				CPU =	276 936	TRX SERV	1024	BLOCK	0.77			MPL	0.38	SD 000.00.00.225
				MSO =	12 696	TCB	23.8	HSP	0.00	TOTAL	180.69	ENDED	2564	
				SRB =	17 391	SRB	1.4	HSP MISS	0.00	CENTRAL	91.06	END/SEC	2.84	QUE 000.00.00.000
				TOT =	365 898	TCB + SRB%	2.8	EXP SNGL	304.67	EXPAND	89.63	#SWAPS	2554	
				PER SEC =	406			EXP BLK	0.00					TOT 000.00.00.049
0042	2	032	**	IOC =	134 290	ABSRPTN	724	SINGLE	0.20	AVERAGE	479.25	AVE	0.91	TRX 000.00.01.217
				CPU =	407 099	TRX SERV	699	BLOCK	0.11			MPL	0.88	SD 000.00.01.087
				MSO =	21 769	TCB	35.0	HSP	0.00	TOTAL	424.72	ENDED	573	
				SRB =	14 934	SRB	1.2	HSP MISS	0.00	CENTRAL	252.38	END/SEC	0.63	QUE 001.15.14.522
				TOT =	578 092	TCB + SRB%	4.0	EXP SNGL	19.33	EXPAND	172.34	#SWAPS	609	
				PER SEC =	642			EXP BLK	0.01					TOT 001.15.15.739
0042	3	033	**	IOC =	96 205	ABSRPTN	605	SINGLE	0.01	AVERAGE	513.31	AVE	0.60	TRX 000.00.06.913
				CPU =	204 427	TRX SERV	589	BLOCK	0.00			MPL	0.59	SD 000.00.05.150
				MSO =	12 502	TCB	17.5	HSP	0.00	TOTAL	304.19	ENDED	131	
				SRB =	9 643	SRB	0.8	HSP MISS	0.00	CENTRAL	198.22	END/SEC	0.14	QUE 000.00.00.000
				TOT =	322 777	TCB + SRB%	2.0	EXP SNGL	6.24	EXPAND	105.97	#SWAPS	137	
				PER SEC =	358			EXP BLK	0.00					TOT 000.00.06.913
0042	ALL	ALL	ALL	IOC =	289 370	ABSRPTN	755	SINGLE	0.25	AVERAGE	488.36	AVE	1.92	TRX 000.00.00.529
				CPU =	888 462	TRX SERV	731	BLOCK	0.21			MPL	1.86	SD 000.00.01.789
				MSO =	46 967	TCB	76.4	HSP	0.00	TOTAL	909.61	ENDED	3268	
				SRB =	41 968	SRB	3.6	HSP MISS	0.00	CENTRAL	541.66	END/SEC	3.63	QUE 000.13.11.560
				TOT =	1 266 767	TCB + SRB%	8.9	EXP SNGL	73.95	EXPAND	367.95	#SWAPS	3300	
				PER SEC =	1407			EXP BLK	0.00					TOT 000.13.12.090

Figure 6.12. RMF Monitor I report for performance group 42.

Calculating the ETR for period 3 of PG 42

Now that we have the I/O rate for the period in question, we have to find the ETR. We need this figure in order to arrive at the I/Os per transaction. Once we have the I/Os per transaction we can calculate the average response time per I/O, and see how this compares with the overall system average. If it is high, then we may have to look at the placing of the data sets used by TSO in general and period 3 of PG 42 in particular. The ETR is the total number of completed transactions divided by the measured elapsed interval (900 seconds). The number of completed transactions is from the WAR for period 3 of PG 42 in Figure 6.12; again, the figure is highlighted (131).

$$ETR = 131/900 = 0.15 \text{ transactions per second (rounded)}$$

Therefore, the I/Os per transaction for period 3 of PG 42 are:

$$\text{I/Os per second}/ETR = 23.17/0.15 = 154.5 \text{ I/Os per transaction}$$

Now we can see what the average I/O response time is. The total amount of residency time still unaccounted for is 6.5 seconds, which seems a long time. The average I/O response time is:

Unaccounted residency time/I/Os per transaction

$$= 6.5/154.5 = 0.042 \text{ (42 milliseconds)}$$

I/O response time for period 3 of PG 42

So we see that the average DASD response time for period 3 of PG 42 is 42 milliseconds. This is quite high for an I/O response time today. A lot of these I/Os are probably going to LCUs 0D5 or 15C, but only an examination of the application documentation will confirm this. Possibly the data sets are spread widely across the volume(s), hence giving long SEEK times. We will be dealing with the analysis of the I/O subsystem in greater detail in Chapter 7.

Finally, we now know that there appears to be a lot of explaining to do for this period/PG in terms of the I/O, but how does 42 milliseconds compare against the system average I/O response time? The weighted system average response time can be calculated from Fig. 6.10 by finding the weighted average of the average response time for each LCU.

The weighted average is calculated from the DEVICE ACTIVITY RATE column and the AVG RESP TIME column from Fig. 6.10, and the value is 31.65 milliseconds (0.03165 seconds). TSO period 3 of PG 42 seems to be unfavoured.

6.10 Summary

In this chapter, you have seen how to arrive at a breakdown of the transaction time into two major parts; the WTST and the residency time (RT). The RT in turn has been split into its own component parts, in order to see which part is giving pain to the system. In fact, we see that further examination of the I/O is required for period 3 of PG 42, unless of course, you are happy to accept an average I/O response time of 42 milliseconds. So you now know how to arrive at the analysis on your own systems.

7
Analysis of the I/O subsystem

7.1 Introduction

This chapter will deal with the I/O subsystem of the central electronic complex (CEC). We will be obtaining the answers to the type of questions you should be asking in order to find the optimum I/O configuration. For example: 'Is the I/O subsystem installed adequate for my current purposes?', 'Do I need swap data sets?', 'If so, how many?' These and many other questions will be encountered. At the end of the chapter, you will be able to analyse your own CEC with confidence, and derive meaningful information regarding your current and future I/O subsystem requirements. This chapter will also cover a review of the I/O terms, and an overview of the I/O operation.

The best I/O is no I/O at all, and this is best achieved by using processor-storage to processor-storage I/O. MVS/ESA provides many new and advanced functions to assist in this area, for example, Library Lookaside (LLA), Virtual Lookaside Facility (VLF), Data Lookaside Facility (DLF, used by HIPERBATCH), data spaces, and hiperspaces. All these features embody the principle of data-in-memory (DIM). If you decide to use them, then remember to take this into account when you analyse your storage requirements. This will be addressed in Chapter 8.

In addition, Data Facility Systems Managed Storage (DFSMS) assists in managing data in the most efficient manner, by allowing the users to concentrate on the data and its relative importance, rather than data set placement, record lengths and physical block sizes, etc.

7.2 The balanced system

Recall that in Chapter 3 we talked about the internal throughput rate (ITR), and how it defined the service rate of the engine(s). In other words, it refers to the optimum speed of the CEC if it is unencumbered by any I/O, and there is an infinite amount of central storage high-speed cache. Unfortunately, this is not the case. Most installations compromise by having an adequate I/O subsystem, allied

Analysis of the I/O subsystem

to 'sufficient' storage. The effect of this is that the engines have an in-built limiting factor placed upon their performance, by having to be held up while I/O is effected, or while movement of data and code takes place between central and expanded storage, or central and auxiliary storage.

The idea, therefore, is to have a 'balanced system'. This means that we have a system that is a best fit for our purposes, the system being adequate to achieve the company's business objectives at the minimum cost. The overall system is made up of the engine(s), the I/O subsystem that gives us the DASD response times that we need, and the amount of central/expanded storage that ensures that we can meet the terminal response times of our CICS/IMS/TSO community, and turn round the batch jobs in times that meet our service-level agreements. In effect, we are looking for a balanced system; the one that has the minimum impact on the performance of the engine(s), and hence optimizes the throughput of the system. IT equipment suppliers will always state throughput figures for various types of transactions, and these will be based on the principle of the balanced system.

7.2.1 Typical I/O subsystem designers' questions

As a designer of the potential IT configuration required, you will need satisfactory answers to the following questions in order to recommend the I/O subsystem to be installed:

- What is the maximum rate of total I/O that my I/O subsystem will sustain?
- Is my I/O subsystem adequate to achieve my objectives?
- How many DASD volumes do I need to meet my performance objectives?
- What is the maximum I/O rate to allow to all DASD?
- What is the maximum utilization for a DASD?
- What is the upper bound of I/O rate to any individual DASD?
- Do I need DASD cached controllers?
- How many channel paths do I need?
- What is the upper bound of I/O rate through the channel paths?
- What should be my page/swap data set configuration?
- How many page data sets do I need and what size should they be?
- Do I need swap data sets? If so, what size should they be?

7.3 The anatomy of an I/O

Before we go into the calculation side of I/O response times, let us review the component parts of an I/O operation. By doing this, we will ensure that there is the required fundamental understanding to carry out the I/O study. We will use Fig. 7.1 to explain the individual parts of the I/O operation, and define our terms. Refer to this figure whenever you need clarification of the definition of any term that is used throughout this study.

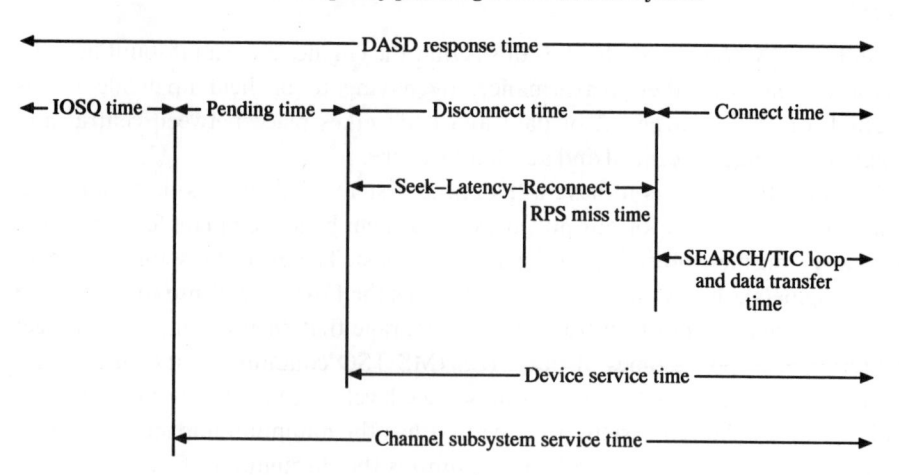

Figure 7.1. The component parts of an I/O operation.

7.3.1 Definitions

DASD response time

The total time taken to effect an I/O operation, from STARTIO macro time in the I/O supervisor (IOS), to IOS receiving channel-end/device-end for the I/O.

IOSQ time

The time that the I/O operation is queued on the I/O supervisor's unit control block (UCB) queue, because there is already an I/O operation to the selected DASD. A DASD can only sustain *one* I/O operation at a time from the same system. This is sometimes referred to as 'software queuing', as opposed to the 'hardware queuing' incorporated in pending time.

Pending time

The time the I/O operation is queued within the channel subsystem on a unit control word (UCW), because either there is already an I/O operation to the selected DASD from another system, or the paths through to the head-of-string/controller/channel are busy with other I/O operations for the same system. Longer times are usually caused by SHARED DASD. This time should be very small on a balanced I/O subsystem (circa 2 milliseconds at most). Pending time is sometimes referred to as 'hardware queuing', or 'channel subsystem queuing'.

Seek time

The time for the actuator arm physically to move across the disk to the correct cylinder, and select the track within that cylinder, within which the physical block incorporating the logical record will be found.

Analysis of the I/O subsystem 79

Latency time

The time that elapses before that sector on the track, which is about three before the sector in which the physical block containing the required logical record, lies under the read/write head of the actuator (the number depends upon the DASD type). For example, on an IBM 3380 DASD which has 222 sectors, the latency tries to complete three sectors before the one containing the start of the physical block.

At this point reconnect time starts. Latency is only apparent on rotational position sensing (RPS) devices, and is sometimes referred to as 'rotational delay time'. Latency is normally taken to be the time to complete half a revolution of the DASD, for performance and capacity planning purposes. Figure 7.2 includes an illustration of latency.

Reconnect time

The time to connect the DASD to the channel subsystem, once the sector defined in latency is under the read/write head. This is referred to as 'RPS miss time', and

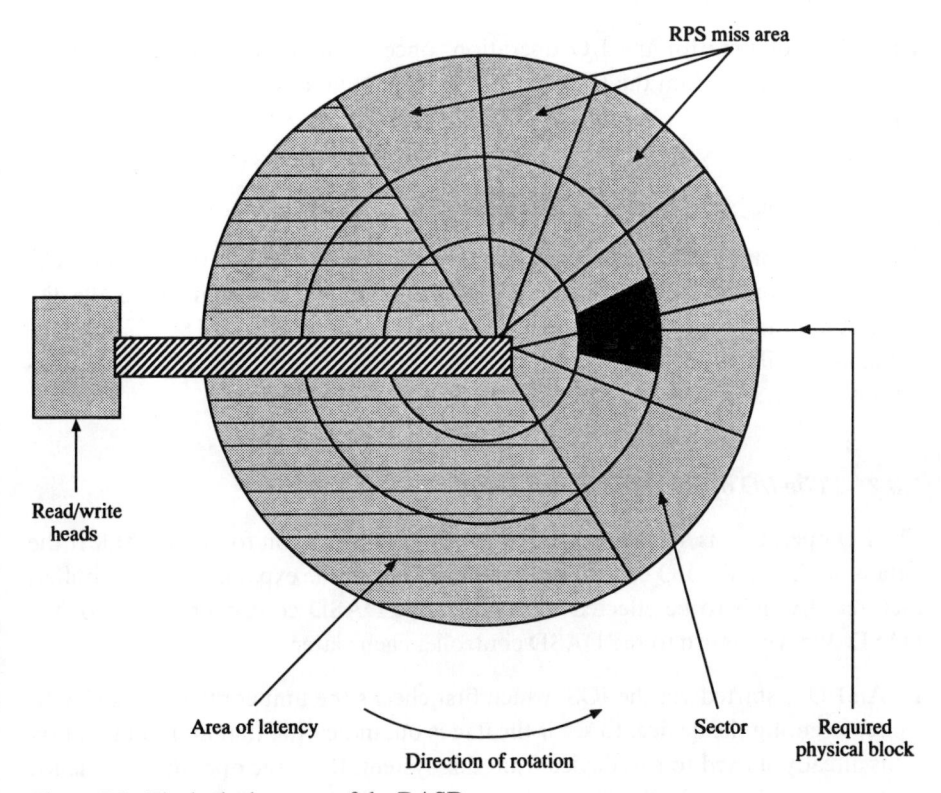

Figure 7.2. The logical aspects of the DASD.

Disconnect time

is a function of how busy the paths back to the processor are (which represents the probability of *not* reconnecting within one complete revolution of the DASD), allied to the rotation speed of the DASD. It is a very important component part of response time, as you will see.

Disconnect time

The total of seek, latency and reconnect times.

Connect time

The time taken to skip through the SEARCH/TIC channel command words (CCWs) loop, in order to find the start of the physical block containing the logical record, after reconnect has completed, and transfer the block(s) from the DASD to the buffer in storage (or vice versa). During this period, the channel path from the DASD to the buffer is busy and dedicated to the I/O operation. The number of blocks transferred is a function of the BUFNO parameter.

Device service time

The subset of time for the I/O operation, once it has been selected within the channel subsystem from the UCW queue. It is the total of connect and disconnect times.

Channel subsystem service time

The time to complete the I/O operation, once it is received into the channel subsystem, and possibly queued on a UCW. It is the total of the pending time, the disconnect time and the connect time.

Figure 7.2 illustrates the logical aspects of a DASD referred to in these definitions.

7.3.2 The I/O operation—more detail

The I/O operation is started at the request of an application for some data. If the data is neither in the I/O central storage buffer nor in the expanded storage buffer, then real I/O has to be effected from either the DASD controller's cache or the DASD. We will return to the DASD controller cache later.

1 An I/O is started via the IOS, which first checks the unit control block (UCB) representing the device, to see if the flag is on, indicating that an I/O operation is already started to this device from this system. If so, the operation is queued from the relevant UCB. This is the start of the IOSQ time defined earlier (soft-

ware queuing). Otherwise the STARTIO macro is issued (or possibly the RESUMIO macro for a page data set).

2 Once the I/O operation is passed to the channel subsystem upon the completion of the previous I/O, then it has started channel subsystem service time. If there is an I/O being effected on the DASD from another system, which would happen only for a SHARED DASD, the I/O will be queued within the channel subsystem on the UCW representing the device; this is the start of the pending time. The other occasion when pending time will occur is when the data paths from the DASD, through the directors and the channels, are already in use by other I/O operations from *this* system. This would be the case particularly if an IBM 3880 DASD controller were installed. This device has only one path per director, and so even if there were four paths from the DASD (IBM 3390 DASD), there will be a bottleneck at the director; hence the pending time. If an IBM 3990 Model 2 or 3 DASD controller is installed, allied to IBM 3390 DASD, then there could be four paths through the directors (two per director), and four paths to each DASD. Therefore, there will be less likelihood of pending times with these devices, and where there is some, it will probably be less than you would get with the IBM 3880 controllers.

3 Once the I/O operation is dequeued within the channel subsystem then disconnect time starts. Disconnect time is the time that the DASD is disconnected from the channel subsystem. The first part is seek time (described earlier), the time to select the cylinder and track. This is followed by latency, the time the sector a few before the required sector comes under the read/write head. The final part of disconnect time is the reconnect time. This is the time to reconnect the DASD to the channel subsystem, in order that the data transfer from the DASD to the I/O buffer (or vice versa) can commence. The reconnect time is usually referred to as the 'RPS miss time', and it is a function of how busy the paths through the controller are, allied to the rotational speed of the DASD as we have already mentioned. This will be expanded on later.

4 When disconnect time completes upon the DASD reconnecting to the channel path, connect time starts. This begins with the time to execute the SEARCH and transfer-in-channel (TIC) loop of instructions in order to arrive at the start of the correct physical block. Once this has completed then data transfer to or from the I/O buffer commences. More than one physical block can be read or written with one I/O; this is a function of the BUFNO parameter. The speed at which this occurs is a function of the DASD type and DASD controller. An IBM 3380 will transfer data through to the controller at 3 megabytes per second (3000 bytes per millisecond). An IBM 3390 will transfer data at 4.2 megabytes per second (4200 bytes per millisecond).

Now that we know the anatomy of the I/O operation, we have to see how the time associated with each part of the I/O compares to the accepted standard for this component. In order to do this, we need to find out what is the current rate of

I/Os through the channels and the controllers to the DASD—we need to know how busy they are.

The first components we will look at are the channels, after which we will look at the DASD. However, first let us review the function of the DASD controller.

7.4 Review of DASD controllers

Before we continue with our I/O analysis, it might be advisable to review the working of the DASD controller and its function in effecting any I/O. If you feel that your knowledge of the physical aspects of the I/O subsystem is now adequate (or it was already), then skip this section.

We will review the the mechanics of the IBM 3990 DASD storage controller, and the IBM 3880 DASD storage controller, and the major differences between them. This is not intended to be an in-depth study, merely a quick review, in order to ensure that you have sufficient understanding of both types of DASD controller that are installed on the analysed system, and possibly on your own. Other DASD controller manufacturers' equipment will operate in almost the same manner; the major differences will be in the speeds of operation that are claimed by all manufacturers.

With the introduction of the IBM 3990 DASD storage controller Models 2 and 3, there is now the full availability of *four* complete paths within a logical control unit (LCU), from each DASD in the string(s) within the LCU, through the channel subsystem. This is because there are two storage paths through each of the two directors, each path representing a unique data path. IBM calls this feature *device level selection extended* (DLSE). This is not to be confused with the ability to support 16 *physical* paths per LCU; 8 per control unit director, on the 520-based IBM ES/9021 processors.

An LCU is made up of the control unit directors (up to four) attached to the string(s) of DASD. Normally two directors are attached from any one system, and the directors are normally within the same physical IBM 3990, unless the dual configuration option is installed, whereby two IBM 3990 controllers are used. If IBM 3880 controllers are installed, then usually the two directors are in different physical IBM 3880s.

The DASD that can be connected to the IBM 3990 controllers in full DLSE mode are the IBM 3390 DASD Models A and B and the IBM 3380 DASD Models J and K. The effect of this is that there can be four concurrent I/O operations to and from channel and DASD through an IBM 3990 Model 2, and eight concurrent I/O operations through the IBM 3990 Model 3 (cached controller).

The IBM 3880 Model 3 storage controller can sustain only two concurrent I/O operations, through two directors and two DASD paths, even if four path DASD are attached. This is because there is only one path per director. The IBM 3880 Model 23 cached controller can sustain four concurrent I/O operations to and from the DASD. Figure 7.3 illustrates the mechanics of the IBM 3990 model 3 cached DASD controller.

Analysis of the I/O subsystem

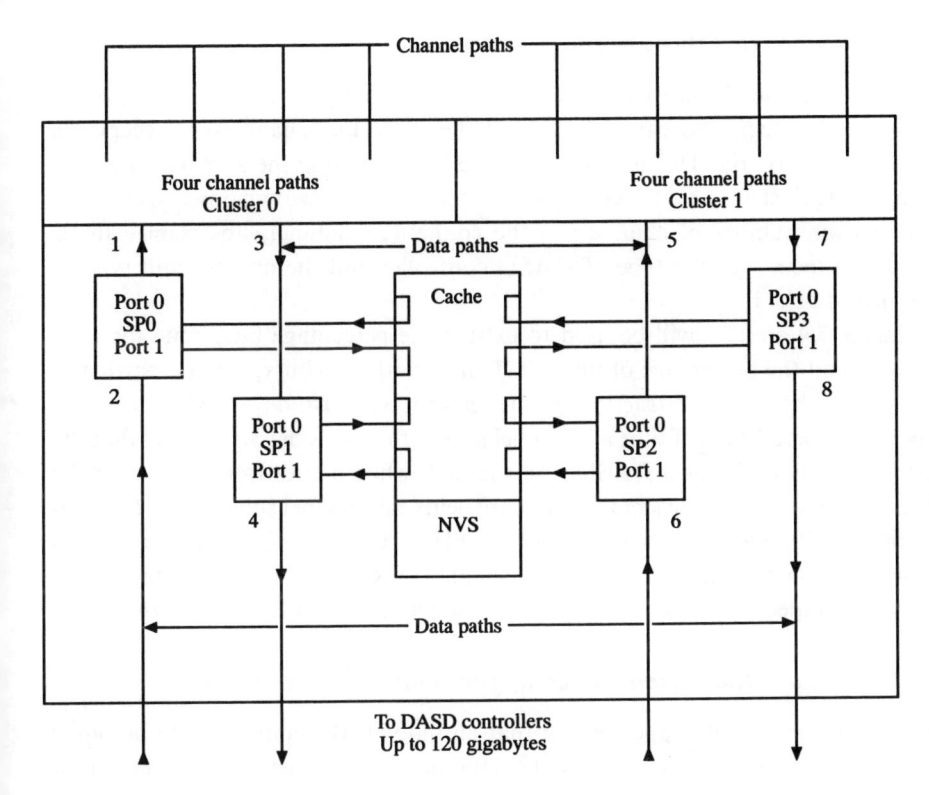

Figure 7.3. Eight I/O operations within the IBM 3990 Model 3 DASD controller.

Key:
CLUSTERn   Storage director
SPn   Storage path
NVS   Non-volatile storage

The eight I/O operations:

SP0 port 0	READ HIT from logical DASD in the cache
SP0 port 1	Stage from physical DASD
SP1 port 0	WRITE HIT to logical DASD in the cache
SP1 port 1	Destage to physical DASD
SP2 port 0	READ HIT from logical DASD in the cache
SP2 port 1	Stage from physical DASD
SP3 port 0	WRITE HIT to logical DASD in the cache
SP3 port 1	Destage to physical DASD

Paths connections:

Storage paths 0 and 1 connect to CLUSTER 0
Storage paths 2 and 3 connect to CLUSTER 1

On the system we are monitoring, there are in fact four physical control unit directors associated with two of the LCUs; LCU 0CD and LCU 0D5. Only two of them are online, therefore we are left with the normal configuration for any one system; two control unit directors linked to form one LCU. As will be seen, none of the LCUs is using the full capability of four paths per LCU.

7.5 The I/O rate through the channels

The first thing we have to ascertain is that the total rate of I/Os through the channel subsystem, and through each of the individual channels, is acceptable within stated criteria. This is normally done by comparing the activity on all the channels, against an accepted criterion of maximum rate through any one channel, allied to the number of channels in the configured channel subsystem. This is mainly a function of the type of DASD controller and the number and type of channels attached.

Figures 7.4 and 7.5 will be used to extract the percentage busy time for each channel, and the percentage of time all channel paths are busy, for any particular LCU. These figures are extractions of the relevant pages from the RMF Monitor I report. The percentage of time all channel paths are busy is the probability that the system is busy as far as a DASD is concerned, when it tries to reconnect to the channel subsystem (the 'system' in this case being the channel subsystem). It is also the probability that the DASD will *not* be able to reconnect to the controller; this is one of the factors that allows us to calculate the RPS miss time, the other being the rotation speed of the device (e.g. 14.1 milliseconds for an IBM 3390 DASD).

7.5.1 What is the recommended upper bound of channel busy?

What is the acceptable upper bound that an individual channel should be busy? Using Erlang's tables, we can plot some data that will show us that there is a point on the curve showing a recommended upper bound for the utilization of an individual channel path. This utilization is plotted against the probability of the DASD not reconnecting to the channel paths at the end of RPS miss time. Figure 7.6 shows that beyond 30 per cent individual channel path busy for a two-path system, and 55 per cent individual channel path busy for a four-path system, there is a steep rise in the probability of *any* of the channels in the LCU not reconnecting at the end of RPS miss time. *The maximum recommended probability of any channel in the LCU not reconnecting is at 9 per cent.*

The y-axis of Fig. 7.6 indicates the probability of *none* of the channels in the LCU reconnecting, and the x-axis indicates the *individual* channel busy percentages. The two curves show the relationship between the 'busy-ness' of any individual channel, and the probability of none of these channels reconnecting during RPS miss time. One curve is for a two-channel LCU, and the other is for a four-channel LCU. The assumption is that all the channels in the LCU are equally busy. This may seem an unrealistic assumption, but in fact the channel subsystem does its best to ensure that this in fact does happen. See the values in Fig. 7.4; they are reasonably close.

The point on the y-axis where the value representing the probability of *not* reconnecting starts to rise quickly is 9 per cent. You will see that this corresponds to an *individual* channel busy of 30 per cent in the two-channel LCU, and 55 per cent for the four-channel LCU.

CHANNEL PATH ACTIVITY

MVS/ESA SP/4.2.0
SYSTEM ID MAC1 RPT VERSION 4.2.1
DATE 28/06/93 TIME 09.00.00
INTERVAL 15.00.00 CYCLE 1 SECOND

IODF = 99   NO CREATION DATE AVAILABLE   ACT: ACTIVATE

CHANNEL PATH ID	TYPE	PERCENT CH PATH BUSY	CHANNEL PATH ID	TYPE	PERCENT CH PATH BUSY	CHANNEL PATH ID	TYPE	PERCENT CH PATH BUSY	CHANNEL PATH ID	TYPE	PERCENT CH PATH BUSY
60		OFFLINE	68		OFFLINE	80	BY	0.00	88	BL	0.05
61		OFFLINE	69		OFFLINE	**81**	**BL**	**11.55**	89	BL	0.00
62		OFFLINE	6A		OFFLINE	82	BL	0.00	8A	BL	16.31
63		OFFLINE	6B		OFFLINE	83	BL	0.00	8B	BL	0.00
64		OFFLINE	6C		OFFLINE	84	BL	0.00	8C	BL	0.00
65		OFFLINE	6D		OFFLINE	85	BL	18.61	8D	BL	0.00
66		OFFLINE	6E		OFFLINE	**86**	**BL**	**34.65**	8E	BL	0.00
67		OFFLINE	6F		OFFLINE	87	BL	23.49	8F	BL	0.00
90	BL	0.00	98	BL	0.00	A0	BL	0.00	A8	BL	0.00
91	BL	0.00	99	BL	11.13	A1	BL	19.20	A9	BL	0.00
92	BL	0.00	9A	BL	0.00	**A2**	**BL**	**36.20**	AA	BL	0.00
93	BL	0.00	9B	BL	0.00	A3	BL	23.52	AB	BL	0.00
94	BL	0.00	9C	BL	0.00	A4	BL	0.00	AC	BL	1.28
95	BL	0.00	9D	BL	11.65	**A5**	**BL**	**10.19**	AD	BL	0.00
96	BL	0.00	9E	BL	0.00	A6	BL	0.00	AE	BL	16.24
97	BL	0.00	9F	BL	0.00	A7	BL	0.00	AF	BL	0.00

All channel paths 00–5F are OFFLINE.
All channel paths B0–FF are OFFLINE.

Figure 7.4. The Channel Path Activity report.

I/O QUEUEING ACTIVITY

MVS/ESA SP/4.2.0
SYSTEM ID MAC1 RPT VERSION 4.2.1
DATE 28/06/93 TIME 09.00.00
INTERVAL 15.00.00 CYCLE 1 SECOND

TOTAL SAMPLES = 900   IOP 02   ACTIVITY RATE 668.081   AVE Q LNGTH 0.03   IODF = 99   NO CREATION DATE AVAILABLE   ACT: ACTIVATE

LCU	CONTENTION RATE	DELAY Q LNGTH	% ALL CH PATH BUSY	CONTROL UNITS	CHAN PATHS	CHPID TAKEN	% DP BUSY	% CU BUSY
097	0.005	0.00	**1.18**	1C0	01			OFFLINE
					81	43.842	0.39	OFFLINE
					25	43.858	0.48	
				1C1	**A5**			
0CD	0.094	0.55	3.57	560	05			OFFLINE
				561	85	58.598	1.51	OFFLINE
				562	21			
				563	A1	58.530	1.46	
0D5	0.000	0.00	**12.54**	620	06			OFFLINE
				621	**86**	92.761	0.04	OFFLINE
				622	22			
				623	**A2**	92.747	0.03	
0F0	0.710	0.27	5.53	780	07			OFFLINE
					87	44.458	5.06	OFFLINE
				781	23			
					A3	44.254	5.12	
15C	0.025	0.13	2.65	A90	0A			OFFLINE
					8A	53.623	0.64	OFFLINE
				A91	2E			
					AE	53.421	0.63	
173	0.000	0.00	1.30	C10	19			OFFLINE
					99	41.051	0.01	OFFLINE
				C11	1D			
					9D	40.938	0.00	

Figure 7.5. The I/O Queueing Activity report.

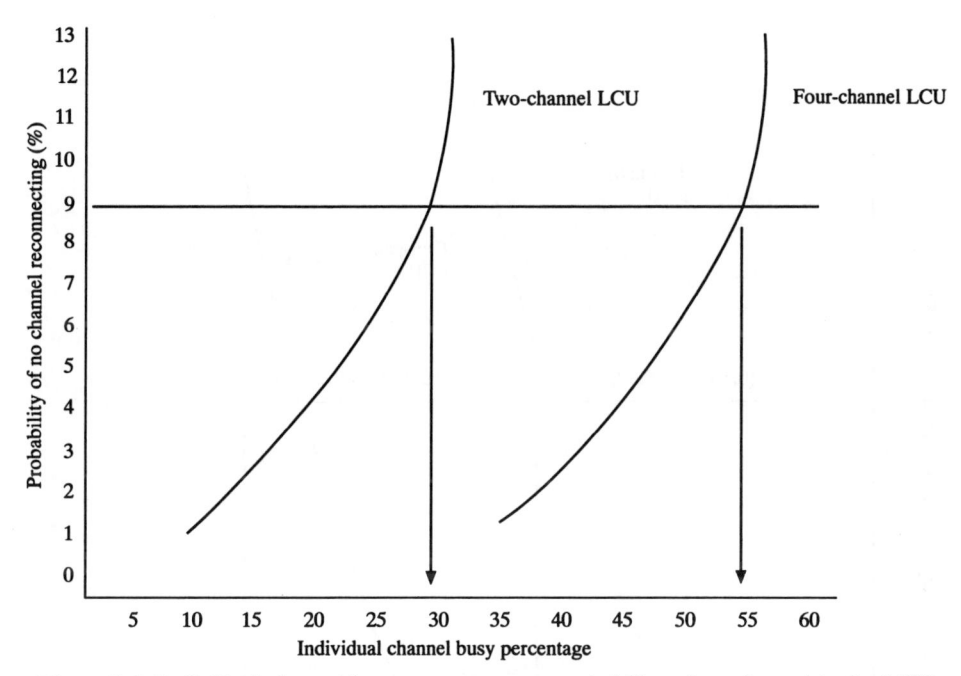

Figure 7.6. Individual channel busy percentage vs. probability of no channel in the LCU reconnecting.

The probability of any or all channels in the LCU not reconnecting for a two-path system is the busy percentage of the first channel path multiplied by the busy percentage of the second channel path. In our case this will be $0.3 \times 0.3 = 0.09 = 9$ per cent. For a four-path system, it will be the product arrived at by multiplying all four channel busy percentages in the LCU: $0.55 \times 0.55 \times 0.55 \times 0.55 = 0.0915 = 9$ per cent (rounded). The plots on each line in Fig. 7.6 are arrived at in this manner for every value.

So, reversing the statements, we can say that because 9 per cent probability of any or all channels in the LCU not reconnecting should be the maximum, then 30 per cent individual channel busy is the maximum busy percentage for a two-channel LCU. Similarly, because 9 per cent probability of any or all channels in the LCU not reconnecting should be the maximum, then 55% individual channel busy is the maximum busy percentage for a four-channel LCU.

Figure 7.7 is a similar illustration, but with a little more detail included.

Erlang's table (Fig. 6.4) can be used here and the assumption is made that all channel paths are equally busy. As previously stated, this is not always the case, although MVS/ESA in alliance with the channel subsystem tries to ensure this. None the less, we can use Erlang's table to arrive at the maximum value for the probability of no channel reconnecting, for practicality (0.09 or 9 per cent).

With the IBM 3880 DASD controllers, there could only be two paths concurrently to any DASD in the supported string(s), and this requires MVS/XA to

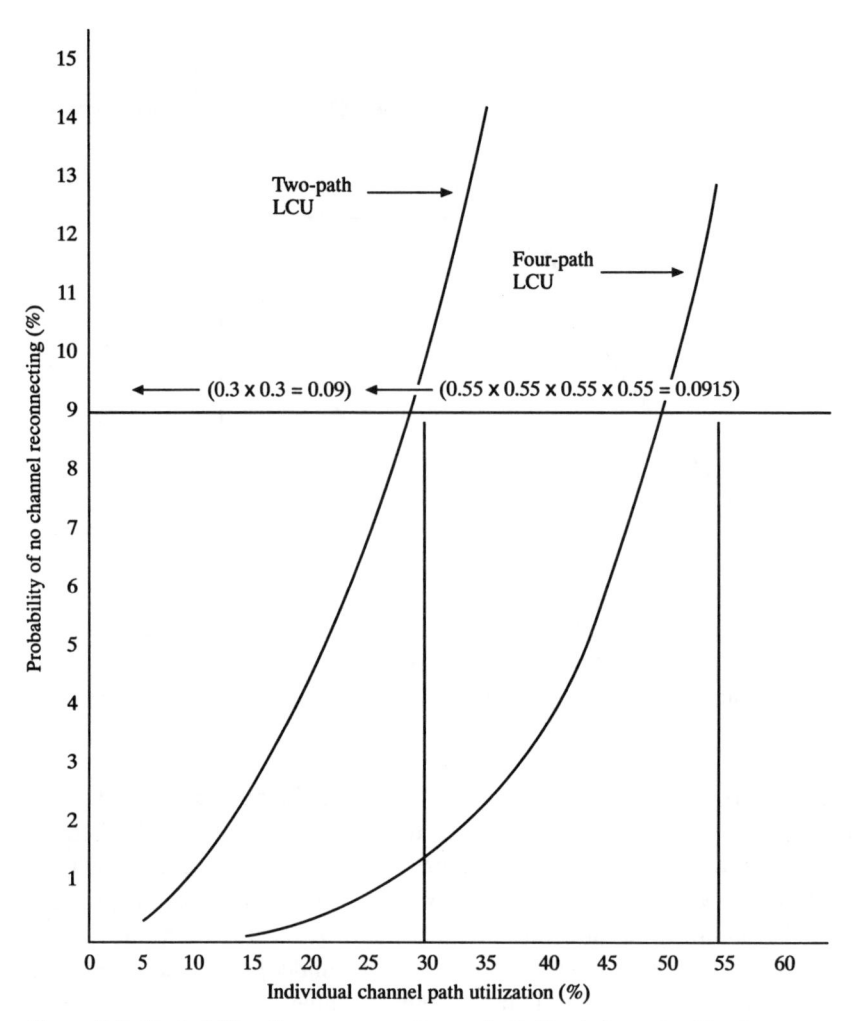

Figure 7.7. Probability of not reconnecting vs. individual channel utilization.

be installed. Recall that this is because each of the two directors from the same system making up the LCU has only *one* path per director. With the introduction of the IBM 3990 Models 2 and 3, this limitation disappeared, because each of the two directors making up the LCU has two storage paths, thus allowing four paths (and hence four concurrent I/Os within an IBM 3990 Model 2, and eight to an IBM 3990 Model 3) to the supported string(s) from the same system.

7.5.2 How do we calculate the probability that all channel paths are busy?

As previously stated, the probability that all channel paths are busy for a two-path system (IBM 3880) is the product of the busy percentage of one channel, multi-

Analysis of the I/O subsystem

plied by the busy percentage of the other. For four channel paths, it is the product of the four individual channel paths busy. This is in fact the method used by RMF. It is not exactly as Erlang would do it, but practicality is our (and RMF's) guiding principle, and even if the two (or four) channel paths have slightly different utilizations, it makes such a small difference that it does not matter for our purposes. The designers of RMF accepted this rationale, but you also now have the theoretical understanding, courtesy of Erlang's table reproduced in Fig. 6.4.

RMF calls the probability of not reconnecting % ALL CHANNEL PATHS ARE BUSY. This is the heading highlighted in Fig. 7.5. It is arrived at by multiplying together the busy times of the two channel paths making up the LCU.

7.5.3 Extracting the channel data from the RMF Monitor 1 report

Now that we know the theory, let us extract the data from the RMF Monitor I report, using Figs 7.4 and 7.5. We will extract the data for two LCUs; 097 and 0D5. These are two-path LCUs. IBM 3990 Model 3 controllers are installed on the test system, but only two of the possible paths are in use.

LCU 097

- Channel paths in the LCU are 81 and A5 (from Fig. 7.5).
- Percentage channel path 81 busy = 11.55 (from Fig. 7.4).
- Percentage channel path A5 busy = 10.19 (from Fig. 7.4). Note how close they are.
- Probability of not reconnecting = $0.1155 \times 0.1019 = 0.0118$ (1.18 per cent).
- % ALL CHANNEL PATHS ARE BUSY = 1.18 per cent (from Fig. 7.5).

LCU 0D5

- Channel paths in the LCU are 86 and A2 (from Fig. 7.5).
- Percentage channel path 86 busy = 34.65 (from Fig. 7.4).
- Percentage channel path A2 busy = 36.20 (from Fig. 7.4). Note how close they are.
- Probability of not reconnecting = $0.3465 \times 0.3620 = 0.1254$ (12.54 per cent).
- % ALL CHANNEL PATHS ARE BUSY = 12.54 per cent (from Fig. 7.5).

So, how do our channel paths look? According to our theory of what represents the upper bound of accepted busy time on a channel, LCU 097 is within limits and LCU 0D5 is not. LCU 097 % ALL CHANNEL PATHS ARE BUSY is less than 9 per cent and LCU 0D5 is greater than 9 per cent (12.54 per cent), our maximum recommended percentage. Or to look at it another way, the individual channel busy times are less than 30 per cent for LCU 097, and greater than 30 per cent for LCU 0D5 (34.65 and 36.20 per cent).

LCU 0D5 in more detail

Using our 30 per cent individual channel path busy, and 9 per cent all channel paths busy rule, we have seen that LCU 0D5 is not looking good. But is this rule always to be used? If the DASD incorporated within the LCU were page data sets (and there should be one of these per LCU), then the busy times could possibly be accepted, providing that the users are not complaining of bad transaction response times.

Do not make a problem where none exists, merely because the the criteria we lay down for 'good' I/O response times are not being met. The real test is 'Is the total *transaction* response time acceptable to the user?' If so, then leave the system alone. 'Don't fix it if it ain't broke!' Remember, what are acceptable times and busy percentages are always *guidelines*, not *rules*. On the other hand, if complaints are forthcoming, then LCU 0D5 is probably a good place to start!

Figure 7.8, the direct access device activity report, shows the individual DASD in the LCU 0D5 highlighted. Look at the device activity rates. They range from a low of 18.199 (device 635) to a high of 27.962 (device 630). Are these acceptable? Well, we do not know yet what 'acceptable' is, but we will in a short while. Look also at the average response times; are they 'acceptable'? Finally, look at the average IOSQ times. Well, enough said! We will arrive at answers to our 'What is acceptable?' questions now.

7.6 Acceptable utilization, I/O activity rate and response time for a DASD

The normal acceptable maximum utilization for an individual DASD is a function of the I/O rate and the DASD response time. Arriving at it is no different to the reasoning we have already been through. For 0.30 (30 per cent busy):

Utilization = Rate of arrival × Service time

Where rate of arrival is the I/O rate to the device. Therefore:

Utilization = I/O rate × Device response time

Device 'service time' in this instance is not the true service time of connect time plus disconnect time, as we have to include the times the I/O is waiting in the queue, pending time in the channel subsystem, and IOSQ time before the I/O is passed to the channel subsystem. Therefore we take the I/O response time for the 'service time' in order to arrive at our upper bound of utilization.

As you can see, the utilization can remain constant while the I/O rate and the response time vary inversely. In other words, as the I/O rate drops, we could allow the response time to rise, although we should aim at keeping it within an acceptable limit; but what is this limit? The normal absolute upper bound for a device response time for an uncached I/O is 25 milliseconds (0.025 s). An acceptable upper bound for a cached I/O is 7 milliseconds. Remember, with a cached I/O, the seek, latency and reconnect times are all eliminated, i.e. there is no disconnect time for a cached I/O.

7.6.1 How busy are the DASD in LCU 0D5?

Using our accepted criteria of 30 per cent busy and 25 milliseconds response time for an individual DASD, we can derive a maximum I/O rate to an individual (uncached DASD):

$$\text{Utilization} = \text{I/O rate} \times \text{Device response time}$$

Therefore:

$$\text{I/O rate} = \text{Utilization}/\text{Device response time}$$

Thus

$$\text{Maximum I/O rate} = 0.3/0.025 = 12 \text{ I/Os per second}$$

If you look again at Fig. 7.8, you will see that all the DASD in LCU 0D5 have activity rates greater than 12. We will break the response time into its component parts later, but you will also see in Fig. 7.8 that the IOSQ times are long; but what is 'long'? IOSQ times greater than three milliseconds are long, and so this is an indication that the I/O rates to the DASD in this LCU are too high.

The IOSQ times show that the rate at which I/Os are being sent to the DASD is such that they are being queued by the I/O supervisor (IOS). Remember that only one I/O per device per system can be passed to the channel subsystem by the IOS. The fact that there is a long time on the queue for each I/O shows that the arrival rate (activity—ranging from 18 to 28) is too high for the rate at which the DASD can service the I/Os (12 I/Os per second).

Let us now break the response time into its component parts, and identify other 'problems' with LCU 0D5.

7.7 Breaking down the response time

We know why the IOSQ queue time and pending time occur, and so we will now break down the true service time (connect time + disconnect time) into its component parts.

DIRECT ACCESS DEVICE ACTIVITY

PAGE 1

MVS/ESA SP/4.2.0
SYSTEM ID MAC1
RPT VERSION 4.2.1
DATE 28/06/93
TIME 09.00.00
INTERVAL 15.00.00CTI
CYCLE 1 SECOND

TOTAL SAMPLES = 900   IODF = 99

STORAGE GROUP	DEV NUM	DEVICE TYPE	VOLUME SERIAL	IOP	LCU	DEVICE ACTIVITY RATE	AVE RESP TIME	AVE IOSQ TIME	AVE Q LNGTH		AVE CUB DLY	AVE DB DLY	AVE PEND TIME	NO CREATION DATE AVAILABLE					ACT: ACTIVATE		
									AVE DPB DLY					AVE DISC TIME	AVE CONN TIME	% DEV CONN	% DEV UTIL	% DEV RESV	AVE NUMBER ALLOC	% ANY ALLOC	% MT PEND
	1C0	3380D	CACHE1		097	18.794	3	0			0.0	0.1	0.2	0.7	2.2	4.05	5.51	2.6	7.7	100.0	0.0
	1C1	3380D	CACHE2		097	3.127	11	1			0.0	1.2	1.4	5.8	2.9	0.90	3.37	1.2	61.5	100.0	0.0
	1C2	3380D	CACHE3		097	26.931	3	0			0.0	0.1	0.2	0.0	2.8	7.52	7.60	0.0	1282	100.0	0.0
	1C3	3380D	CACHE4		097	25.537	2	0			0.0	0.1	0.2	0.0	2.2	5.55	5.68	0.0	241	100.0	0.0
	1C4	3380D	TSO1C4		097	6.758	9	1			0.0	1.3	1.5	3.5	3.6	2.43	7.06	3.5	127	100.0	0.0
	1C5	3380D	TSO1C5		097	6.554	8	1			0.0	1.5	1.6	2.7	3.2	2.09	4.60	2.7	173	100.0	0.0
			LCU		097	87.701	4	0			0.0	0.3	0.4	0.8	2.6	3.76	5.64	1.6	1892	100.0	0.0
	564	3380J	BAT564		0CD	20.039	4	1			0.0	0.0	0.3	0.4	3.0	6.08	19.37	13.9	5.6	100.0	0.0
	565	3380J	BAT565		0CD	10.908	5	0			0.0	0.0	0.3	0.5	3.5	3.85	10.69	6.7	2.7	100.0	0.0
	566	3380J	IDAVOL		0CD	15.489	2	0			0.0	0.0	0.1	0.0	1.7	2.66	2.71	0.0	7.2	100.0	0.0
	567	3380J	CB84LB		0CD	0.967	25	1			0.0	0.0	0.2	18.0	5.6	0.54	2.29	0.0	1.9	100.0	0.0
	570	3380J	CIC570		0CD	0.043	24	0			0.0	0.0	0.5	12.2	11.2	0.05	0.32	0.3	1.1	100.0	0.0
	571	3380J	WRK571		0CD	0.284	4	1			0.0	0.0	0.8	0.5	2.8	0.08	0.09	0.0	3.3	100.0	0.0
	572	3380J	BAT572		0CD	16.357	5	1			0.0	0.0	0.2	0.4	3.5	5.65	10.44	4.7	3.5	100.0	0.0
	573	3380J	BAT573		0CD	13.686	6	1			0.0	0.0	0.2	0.7	4.2	5.80	57.97	52.9	3.7	100.0	0.0
	574	3380J	BAT574		0CD	6.857	7	1			0.0	0.0	0.2	1.3	4.9	3.33	5.03	1.3	3.8	100.0	0.0
	575	3380J	BAT575		0CD	12.697	5	0			0.0	0.0	0.3	0.6	3.5	4.41	5.16	0.0	3.3	100.0	0.0
	576	3380J	MVS576		0CD	0.583	24	0			0.0	0.0	0.1	18.6	5.3	0.31	1.39	0.0	1.0	100.0	0.0
	577	3380J	MVS577		0CD	19.220	3	0			0.0	0.0	0.2	0.5	1.8	3.54	4.50	0.0	2674	100.0	0.0
			LCU		0CD	117.129	4	0			0.0	0.0	0.2	0.7	3.1	3.03	10.00	6.6	2711	100.0	0.0

Figure 7.8. The DASD incorporated within LCU 0D5. (*Continues.*)

DIRECT ACCESS DEVICE ACTIVITY

MVS/ESA SP/4.2.0
SYSTEM ID MAC1
RPT VERSION 4.2.1
DATE 28/06/93
TIME 09.00.00
IODF = 99
INTERVAL 15.00.00CTI
CYCLE 1 SECOND
PAGE 2

TOTAL SAMPLES = 900

STORAGE GROUP	DEV NUM	DEVICE TYPE	VOLUME SERIAL	IOP	LCU	ACTIVITY RATE DEVICE ACTIVITY RATE	AVE RESP TIME	AVE Q LNGTH AVE IOSQ TIME	AVE DPB DLY	AVE CUB DLY	AVE DB DLY	AVE PEND TIME	AVE DISC TIME	NO CREATION DATE AVAILABLE AVE CONN TIME	% DEV CONN	% DEV UTIL	% DEV RESV	ACT: ACTIVATE AVE NUMBER ALLOC	% ANY ALLOC	% MT PEND
	630	3380J	BAT630		0D5	27.962	69	44		0.0	0.1	0.2	21.2	3.6	10.08	69.47	9.6	9.1	100.0	0.0
	631	3380J	BAT631		0D5	21.071	58	35		0.0	0.1	0.2	20.2	3.4	7.27	64.11	29.3	7.3	100.0	0.0
	632	3380J	BAT632		0D5	25.570	59	34		0.0	0.1	0.2	21.4	3.5	8.95	63.96	2.6	7.4	100.0	0.0
	633	3380J	BAT633		0D5	23.764	69	44		0.0	0.1	0.2	21.0	3.4	8.13	58.75	5.3	7.5	100.0	0.0
	634	3380J	BAT634		0D5	26.511	58	34		0.0	0.1	0.2	20.3	3.2	8.50	64.35	10.9	8.6	100.0	0.0
	635	3380J	BAT635		0D5	18.199	46	21		0.0	0.1	0.2	19.9	4.0	7.30	48.37	12.9	6.2	100.0	0.0
	636	3380J	BAT636		0D5	20.493	45	22		0.0	0.1	0.2	19.5	3.4	6.87	66.43	33.2	6.6	100.0	0.0
	637	3380J	BAT637		0D5	21.946	74	46		0.0	0.1	0.2	23.3	4.3	9.54	76.82	51.5	7.9	100.0	0.0
			LCU		0D5	185.517	60	36		0.0	0.1	0.2	20.9	3.6	8.33	64.03	19.4	60.6	100.0	0.0
	780	3380E	RS189A		0F0	21.638	33	14		0.0	2.0	2.3	10.8	6.0	12.93	40.85	31.3	16.2	100.0	0.0
	781	3380E	RS289A		0F0	21.848	28	10		0.0	1.2	1.4	10.9	5.3	11.57	41.21	30.5	36.6	100.0	0.0
	782	3380E	CAT89A		0F0	4.999	18	2		0.0	2.7	3.1	10.1	3.5	1.76	7.66	2.5	11.5	100.0	0.0
	783	3380E	SPL89A		0F0	4.822	19	2		0.0	2.6	3.0	11.1	3.5	1.67	7.62	2.4	12.5	100.0	0.0
	784	3380E	SC189A		0F0	5.332	20	3		0.0	2.8	3.2	11.1	3.4	1.81	8.34	2.7	12.3	100.0	0.0
	785	3380E	DL189A		0F0	4.547	19	1		0.0	2.5	2.9	11.6	3.3	1.49	7.61	2.6	12.3	100.0	0.0
	786	3380E	DL289A		0F0	19.243	30	11		0.0	1.3	1.6	11.8	5.6	10.79	37.45	29.3	27.1	100.0	0.0
	787	3380E	MVSTS3		0F0	0.000	0	0		0.0	0.0	0.0	0.0	0.0	0.00	0.00	0.0	0.0	100.0	0.0
	788	3380E	SMP89A		0F0	6.284	22	4		0.0	3.1	3.5	10.7	3.3	2.05	9.35	3.1	121	100.0	0.0
			LCU		0F0	88.713	27	9		0.0	1.9	2.2	11.1	5.0	4.90	17.79	11.6	686	100.0	0.0

Figure 7.8. The DASD incorporated within LCU 0D5. *(Concluded.)*

7.7.1 Disconnect time

Disconnect time can be taken directly from the RMF Monitor I Direct Access Device Activity report. See Fig. 7.8; we will still be using LCU 0D5. The field AVE DISC TIME shows the total disconnect time. The times range from 19.5 milliseconds to 23.3 milliseconds. Let us look at device 637. This is clearly a device whose times need inspection; the disconnect time is 23.3 milliseconds, and it is made up of the following: seek time, latency time and reconnect time (RPS miss time). We can make an educated guess at latency; we can calculate RPS miss time; and hence we can force out seek time.

Let us consider latency time first, as this is the simplest to explain. Latency is the time to find the sector that is approximately three before the sector in which the required physical block containing the logical record starts (this depends upon the DASD type). On average, this will be the time to complete half a revolution. Therefore, if the DASD is an IBM 3390, the time to complete half a revolution is 7.1 milliseconds (14.2 milliseconds for a complete revolution). If the DASD is an IBM 3380, then the respective times are 8.3 milliseconds and 16.6 milliseconds. Device 637 is an IBM 3380 Model J, therefore the latency is taken as 8.3 milliseconds. This leaves 15 (23.3 − 8.3) milliseconds still to be explained.

Calculating the RPS miss time for device 637

RPS miss time is synonymous with 'time on the queue' (TQ). The formula for TQ is:

$$TQ = \text{Average queue length} \times \text{Service time}$$

or:

$$TQ = \text{Probability that the system is busy} \times \text{Service time}$$

The rationale does not change, but the terminology does. The formula for calculating the RPS miss time is:

$$\text{RPS miss time} = \text{Probability all channel paths are busy} \\ \times \text{DASD rotation time}$$

The probability that all channel paths are busy is the probability that the system is busy, and DASD rotation time is the service time in this instance. Therefore, as device 637 belongs to LCU 0D5, which has a probability that all channel paths are busy of 12.54 per cent (see earlier discussion) and a rotation time of 16.6 milliseconds:

$$\text{RPS miss time} = 0.1254 \times 0.0166 = 0.002\,08 \text{ (approx. 2.1 milliseconds)}$$

This time is above the accepted criterion of 1.5 milliseconds for this device type (0.09 × 0.0166 = 0.0015). The IBM 3390 DASD criterion is 1.3 milliseconds (0.09 × 0.0142 = 0.0013). It is another indication of the device being overworked.

Analysis of the I/O subsystem

Forcing out the seek time

If we subtract 2.1 milliseconds from our remaining time to be explained of 15 milliseconds, this leaves us with 12.9 milliseconds, which has to be the seek time. This is too long, and is explained by the placing of the data sets on the DASD. The read/write head is being pulled from one side of the DASD to the other. The remedy is either to cache the data sets on the DASD, or, if the read/write ratio is too low (less than 3:1), then to consider moving the data sets closer to any 'related' data sets on the same DASD. Related data sets are those used by the same application.

The high seek time is yet another indication of the high I/O rate to the device. Moving data sets that are related closer together will help to reduce the seek time, but, in addition, the I/O rate should be reduced. This can be done only by analysing which data sets are used by which applications, and by moving some related data sets to another DASD. Generalized trace facility (GTF), a function incorporated within MVS/ESA, can be used to find the 'high seekers', but an examination of the application documentation will be required to find related data sets for any particular application.

More caching for the DASD on this LCU should be considered, allied to the implementation of DFSMS, to assist in the placing of data sets according to user-stated criteria.

7.7.2 Connect time

The connect time is made up of the SEARCH/TIC loop, plus the actual transfer of data from and to the DASD from and to the storage buffer. The connect time is a function of the block size, allied to the speed of data transfer for the device type. Again, using Fig. 7.8, we take this value directly from the direct access device activity report, from the AVE CONN. TIME field. In our case, for device 637, this is 4.3 milliseconds. What does this tell us?

The device type is an IBM 3380 Model J, with a data transfer rate of 3000 bytes per millisecond. Assuming a SEARCH/TIC loop of up to 1 millisecond (reasonable), this leaves 3.3 milliseconds for the actual data transfer. At 3000 bytes per millisecond, this will be $3000 \times 3.3 = 9900$ bytes per data transfer. This could mean a block size of 9900 bytes, probably 10K, but it also assumes a BUFNO parameter value of 1. This is unlikely, as the default is normally 5, and in fact the BUFNO value in our case is 5. Therefore, the block size is 10K/5 = 2K. What is important, however, is the total data transferred; 10K bytes (rounded). Again, what does this tell us?

The question is really whether the block size is right for the type of work. If the workload is primarily TSO/CICS/IMS (i.e. response-time oriented), then the block size of 2K (data transfer of 10K) is about right. It is a balance between too little data being read or written in one EXCP, and response times for the total transaction, of which I/O is only one part. If the workload is primarily batch on the other hand, then a larger data transfer would be better. As the response time criterion is no longer applicable, it would be in order to have a large block size (full track blocking if possible), so that the greatest amount of data as possible is transferred in one EXCP.

7.7.3 EXCP or connect time for absorbing SUs

When setting up the SRM parameters, it is possible to state that the I/O SUs will be absorbed as a function of either EXCPs or the connect time of the DASD to the channel. The selection of which method is by the IOSRVC keyword in the IEAIPSxx member of SYS1.PARMLIB; one SU per EXCP, or SUs allocated by the length of connect time, up to half a revolution of connect time, representing a complete SU. Both methods have their advantages and disadvantages.

Using the EXCP count is good for a batch workload which does not have response time criteria. Therefore the block size should be large, and the total number of EXCPs will be minimized, with the result that SU absorption is lower. But if the workload is primarily TSO/CICS/IMS, then by using the EXCP count, you will be penalizing these users, as these types of user are response time oriented, and their response times will be extended by the longer times required for the I/O. In this instance, you should use connect time as the IOSRVC keyword, but of course, you are then penalizing the batch jobs! What to do?

Unfortunately it is not possible to mix and match, as the IOSRVC keyword will only allow either COUNT or TIME (EXCP count or connect time). Therefore you will have to work on the principle of the greatest good for the greatest number. If the workload is mainly response time oriented (TSO/CICS/IMS) then use connect time (TIME), otherwise use the EXCP count (COUNT). The default is EXCP count.

Also, use the DFSMS function of MVS/ESA to place data sets where they are most efficient. Let MVS/ESA take the strain of data set placement, dependent upon criteria stated by the users. DFSMS will allow you to state (via the data class) such criteria as record format (RECFM), logical record length (LRECL) and space requirements, I/O performance via the storage class, and backup and migration characteristics via the management class.

7.8 A few words on device utilization

The DASD has a maximum recommended utilization of around 30 per cent. As usual, the utilization is arrived at by multiplying the arrival rate by the service time; yes, in this case it really is the service time, not the response time that RMF uses! Except that the value placed into the % DEV UTIL field by RMF is not computed in this straightforward manner!

If we look at device 637 again in Fig. 7.8, we will see the following:

- Device activity rate   21.946
- Average disconnect time   23.3 milliseconds
- Average connect time   4.3 milliseconds
- % device utilization   76.82%
- % device reserved   51.50%

Let us examine this data. Multiplying the activity rate (21.946) by the sum of the disconnect and connect times (the DASD service time (23.3 + 4.3 ms)) will give us 0.6057. This represents 60.57 per cent utilization, but we can see that the utilization of the device is in fact 76.82 per cent. The difference is made up of the percentage of time that the device was *reserved*, but not involved in an I/O operation *from this system*. Subtracting 0.6057 from 0.7682 gives us 0.1625 (16.25 per cent), which means that for 16.25 per cent of the utilization, this device was RESERVED, but not by this system. To look at this another way, for 16.25 per cent of the time, the device was not usable by this system, because it was being used for an I/O operation from another system. The field that shows the total time reserved indicates a value of 51.5 per cent. This is the total percentage of utilization that the device was reserved by *this* system.

In summary, we can see that all the devices in LCU 0D5 are overused. Some of this is because the devices are SHARED, but the I/O rate from this system is too high. The fault is mainly from this system, as the pending time is not very high (0.2 milliseconds average). If the I/O rate from the other system were high, then the pending times on this system would be higher than they are.

7.8.1   What about the average number of allocations?

The field AVE NUMBER ALLOC indicates the number of OPEN DCBs or ACBs on the device, each DCB or ACB supposedly representing a data set according to the wording in the RMF manuals. Beware of this, and do not be worried by a high value in this field.

Take device number 577 in Fig. 7.8. You will see a value of 2674! Does this mean 2674 data sets OPENed on this device? No, it does not. The value of 2674 is made up of the *count* of OPENs against DCBs or ACBs for data sets on this device. This could mean 2674 OPENs against 2674 individual data sets, in which case you probably *do* have a problem, or it could mean 2674 OPENs against just *one* data set. If this is a TSO sign-on pack for example, then this number of OPENs is not a problem, as a lot of these OPENs are single occurrences for a single data set.

Look at the other data for the device. I/O rate of 19.22, average response time of 3 milliseconds, with no IOSQ time at all. Does this look like a problem device? Enough said.

7.9 What is the maximum I/O rate my system will sustain?

It has been established over many capacity planning studies that there is a relationship between the I/O rate that a system is supporting, and the utilized RPP (URPP) of the processor. This relationship is a function of the workload, and so if there is a change in emphasis of (say) CICS relative to the remainder of the workload, then this relationship would change. None the less, while the workload remains constant, then this link between I/O rate and URPP is very useful in allowing us to establish the upper bound of I/O rate that your system can sustain. The principle that links I/O rate to URPP is called the *relative I/O content* (RIOC).

7.9.1 Relative I/O content

The RIOC is calculated by extracting the total I/O rate at peak period (in our case 15 minutes) to the page data sets, subtracting the page/swap I/O, and dividing the result by the total URPP. The resulting value is the I/Os issued per URPP. As previously explained, the page/swap I/O is subtracted from the application I/O, as this is not part of the work of the application. It is the manner in which MVS/ESA handles its resources, and so no part of paging/swapping should be allocated to these applications.

$$\text{RIOC} = \frac{\text{Total application I/O}}{\text{Total URPP}}$$

7.9.2 Calculating the RIOC

Figure 7.9 shows the page/swap data set activity report from the RMF Monitor I report. The column headed NUMBER IO REQ has been highlighted. This column shows, for each page/swap data set, the total number of page/swap I/Os issued during the measured interval; in our case 15 minutes (900 seconds). The total number of I/Os to the page/swap data sets over the 15 minute period is 3737, therefore the page/swap I/O RATE is:

Page/swap I/O rate = 3737/900 = 4.15 per second

Figure 7.10 shows the device activity report. The total I/O rate is entered at the bottom of Fig. 7.10(b), and is 668 (rounded) for all LCUs. Subtracting the page/swap I/O rate (rounded to 4) from the total I/O rate will leave the application I/O rate:

Application I/O rate = 668 − 4 = 664 I/Os per second

The URPP was calculated and placed into the completed analysis worksheet (see Fig. 5.11); the value is 24.08 URPP. So now we can calculate our RIOC:

RIOC = 664/24.08 = 27.57 I/Os per URPP

PAGE DATA SET USAGE

MVS/ESA SP/4.2.0
SYSTEM ID MAC1
RPT VERSION 4.2.1
DATE 28/06/93
TIME 09.00.00
INTERVAL 15.00.00
CYCLE 1 SECOND

NUMBER OF SAMPLES = 900

PAGE SPACE TYPE	VOLUME SERIAL	DEV NUM	DEVICE TYPE	SLOTS ALLOC	SLOTS USED MIN	SLOTS USED MAX	SLOTS USED AVE	BAD SLOTS	% IN USE	PAGE TRANS TIME	NUMBER IO REQ	PAGES XFER'D	VIO	DATA SET NAME
PLPA	MVSCAT	C15	3380E	3000	2986	2986	2986	0	0.06	0.018	38	28		PAGE.VMVSCAT.PLPA.CYL20
COMMON	MVSCAT	C15	3380E	1950	520	525	521	0	0.06	0.062	8	8		PAGE.VMVSCAT.COMMON
LOCAL	MVS576	576	3380J	60 000	5998	6985	6333	0	1.50	0.010	525	1402	Y	PAGE.VMVS576.LOCAL
LOCAL	AKESM1	C12	3380E	42 000	6723	7747	7097	0	0.83	0.005	515	1417	Y	PAGE.VAKESM1.LOCAL
LOCAL	ESCCAT	C17	3380E	32 100	6827	7899	7276	0	2.06	0.011	596	1678	Y	PAGE.VESCCAT.LOCAL
LOCAL	MVS577	577	3380J	16 050	5469	6060	5693	0	1.33	0.011	687	1064	Y	PAGE.VMVS577.LOCAL
LOCAL	CB84LB	567	3380J	60 000	6189	7138	6568	0	1.83	0.012	518	1362	Y	PAGE.VCB84LB.LOCAL
LOCAL	CICIPO	C11	3380E	60 000	6460	7476	6876	0	1.89	0.011	850	1528	Y	PAGE.VCICIPO.LOCAL
			TOTAL LOCAL SLOTS	43 305					Average →	0.010	3737 ← Total			

Figure 7.9. Page/swap data set activity report.

DIRECT ACCESS DEVICE ACTIVITY

PAGE 1

MVS/ESA SP/4.2.0
SYSTEM ID MAC1
RPT VERSION 4.2.1
DATE 28/06/93
TIME 09.00.00
INTERVAL 15.00.00
CYCLE 1 SECOND

TOTAL SAMPLES = 900 IODF = 99 NO CREATION DATE AVAILABLE ACT: ACTIVATE

STORAGE GROUP	DEV NUM	DEVICE TYPE	VOLUME SERIAL	LCU	DEVICE ACTIVITY RATE	AVE RESP TIME	AVE IOSQ TIME	AVE DPB DLY	AVE CUB DLY	AVE DB DLY	AVE PEND TIME	AVE DISC TIME	AVE CONN TIME	% DEV CONN	% DEV UTIL	% DEV RESV	AVE NUMBER ALLOC	% ANY ALLOC	% MT PEND
	1C0	3380D	CACHE1	097	18.794	3	0		0.0	0.1	0.2	0.7	2.2	4.05	5.51	2.6	7.7	100.0	0.0
	1C1	3380D	CACHE2	097	3.127	11	1		0.0	1.2	1.4	5.8	2.9	0.90	3.37	1.2	61.5	100.0	0.0
	1C2	3380D	CACHE3	097	26.931	3	0		0.0	0.1	0.2	0.0	2.8	7.52	7.60	0.0	1282	100.0	0.0
	1C3	3380D	CACHE4	097	25.537	2	0		0.0	0.1	0.2	0.0	2.2	5.55	5.68	0.0	241	100.0	0.0
	1C4	3380D	TSOIC4	097	6.758	9	1		0.0	1.3	1.5	3.5	3.6	2.43	7.06	3.5	127	100.0	0.0
	1C5	3380D	TSOIC5	097	6.554	8	1		0.0	1.5	1.6	2.7	3.2	2.09	4.60	2.7	173	100.0	0.0
			LCU	097	**87.701**	4	0		0.0	0.3	0.4	**0.8**	**2.6**	3.76	5.64	1.6	1892	100.0	0.0
	564	3380J	BAT564	0CD	20.039	4	1		0.0	0.0	0.3	0.4	3.0	6.08	19.37	13.9	5.6	100.0	0.0
	565	3380J	BAT565	0CD	10.908	5	0		0.0	0.0	0.3	0.5	3.5	3.85	10.69	6.7	2.7	100.0	0.0
	566	3380J	IDAVOL	0CD	15.489	2	0		0.0	0.0	0.1	0.0	1.7	2.66	2.71	0.0	7.2	100.0	0.0
	567	3380J	CB84LB	0CD	0.967	25	1		0.0	0.0	0.2	18.0	5.6	0.54	2.29	0.0	1.9	100.0	0.0
	570	3380J	CIC570	0CD	0.043	24	0		0.0	0.0	0.5	12.2	11.2	0.05	0.32	0.3	1.1	100.0	0.0
	571	3380J	WRK571	0CD	0.284	4	0		0.0	0.0	0.8	0.5	2.8	0.08	0.09	0.0	3.3	100.0	0.0
	572	3380J	BAT572	0CD	16.357	5	1		0.0	0.0	0.2	0.4	3.5	5.65	10.44	4.7	3.5	100.0	0.0
	573	3380J	BAT573	0CD	13.686	6	0		0.0	0.0	0.2	0.7	4.2	5.80	57.97	52.9	3.7	100.0	0.0
	574	3380J	BAT574	0CD	6.857	7	1		0.0	0.0	0.2	1.3	4.9	3.33	5.03	1.3	3.8	100.0	0.0
	575	3380J	BAT575	0CD	12.697	5	0		0.0	0.0	0.3	0.6	3.5	4.41	5.16	0.0	3.3	100.0	0.0
	576	3380J	MVS576	0CD	0.583	24	0		0.0	0.0	0.1	18.6	5.3	0.31	1.39	0.0	1.0	100.0	0.0
	577	3380J	MVS577	0CD	19.220	3	0		0.0	0.0	0.2	0.5	1.8	3.54	4.50	0.0	2674	100.0	0.0
			LCU	0CD	**117.129**	4	0		0.0	0.0	0.2	**0.7**	**3.1**	3.03	10.0	6.6	2711	100.0	0.0

Figure 7.10(a). The DASD configuration. (*Continues.*)

DIRECT ACCESS DEVICE ACTIVITY

MVS/ESA
SP/4.2.0
SYSTEM ID MAC1
RPT VERSION 4.2.1
DATE 28/06/93
TIME 09.00.00
INTERVAL 15.00.00
CYCLE 1 SECOND
PAGE 2

TOTAL SAMPLES = 900 IOP ACTIVITY RATE AVE Q LNGTH IODF = 99 NO CREATION DATE AVAILABLE ACT: ACTIVATE

STORAGE GROUP	DEV NUM	DEVICE TYPE	VOLUME SERIAL	LCU	DEVICE ACTIVITY RATE	AVE RESP TIME	AVE IOSQ TIME	AVE DPB DLY	AVE CUB DLY	AVE DB DLY	AVE PEND TIME	AVE DISC TIME	AVE CONN TIME	% DEV CONN	% DEV UTIL	% DEV RESV	AVE NUMBER ALLOC	% ANY ALLOC	% MT PEND
	630	3380J	BAT630	0D5	27.962	69	44		0.0	0.1	0.2	21.2	3.6	10.08	69.47	9.6	9.1	100.0	0.0
	631	3380J	BAT631	0D5	21.071	58	35		0.0	0.1	0.2	20.2	3.4	7.27	64.11	29.3	7.3	100.0	0.0
	632	3380J	BAT632	0D5	25.570	59	34		0.0	0.1	0.2	21.4	3.5	8.95	63.96	2.6	7.4	100.0	0.0
	633	3380J	BAT633	0D5	23.764	69	44		0.0	0.1	0.2	21.0	3.4	8.13	58.75	5.3	7.5	100.0	0.0
	634	3380J	BAT634	0D5	26.511	58	34		0.0	0.1	0.2	20.3	3.2	8.50	64.35	10.9	8.6	100.0	0.0
	635	3380J	BAT635	0D5	18.199	46	21		0.0	0.1	0.2	19.9	4.0	7.30	48.37	12.9	6.2	100.0	0.0
	636	3380J	BAT636	0D5	20.493	45	22		0.0	0.1	0.2	19.5	3.4	6.87	66.43	33.2	6.6	100.0	0.0
	637	3380J	BAT637	0D5	21.946	74	46		0.0	0.1	0.2	23.3	4.3	9.54	76.82	51.5	7.9	100.0	0.0
			LCU	0D5	**185.517**	60	36		0.0	0.1	0.2	**20.9**	**3.6**	8.33	64.03	19.4	60.6	100.0	0.0
	780	3380E	RS189A	0F0	21.638	33	14		0.0	2.0	2.3	10.8	6.0	12.93	40.85	31.3	16.2	100.0	0.0
	781	3380E	RS289A	0F0	21.848	28	10		0.0	1.2	1.4	10.9	5.3	11.57	41.21	30.5	36.6	100.0	0.0
	782	3380E	CAT89A	0F0	4.999	18	2		0.0	2.7	3.1	10.1	3.5	1.76	7.66	2.5	115	100.0	0.0
	783	3380E	SPL89A	0F0	4.822	19	2		0.0	2.6	3.0	11.1	3.5	1.67	7.62	2.4	125	100.0	0.0
	784	3380E	SC189A	0F0	5.332	20	3		0.0	2.8	3.2	11.1	3.4	1.81	8.34	2.7	123	100.0	0.0
	785	3380E	DL189A	0F0	4.547	19	1		0.0	2.5	2.9	11.6	3.3	1.49	7.61	2.6	123	100.0	0.0
	786	3380E	DL289A	0F0	19.243	30	11		0.0	1.3	1.6	11.8	5.6	10.79	37.45	29.3	27.1	100.0	0.0
	787	3380E	MVSTS3	0F0	0.000	0	0		0.0	0.0	0.0	0.0	0.0	0.00	0.00	0.0	0.0	100.0	0.0
	788	3380E	SMP89A	0F0	6.284	22	4		0.0	3.1	3.5	10.7	3.3	2.05	9.35	3.1	121	100.0	0.0
			LCU	0F0	**88.713**	27	9		0.0	1.9	2.2	**11.1**	**5.0**	4.90	17.79	11.6	686	100.0	0.0

Figure 7.10(a). The DASD configuration. (*Concluded.*)

DIRECT ACCESS DEVICE ACTIVITY

MVS/ESA SP/4.2.0
SYSTEM ID MAC1
RPT VERSION 4.2.1
DATE 28/06/93
TIME 09.00.00
INTERVAL 15.00.00
CYCLE 1 SECOND

TOTAL SAMPLES = 900   IODF = 99   NO CREATION DATE AVAILABLE   ACT: ACTIVATE

STORAGE GROUP	DEV NUM	DEVICE TYPE	VOLUME SERIAL	LCU	DEVICE ACTIVITY RATE	AVE RESP TIME	AVE IOSQ TIME	AVE DPB DLY	AVE CUB DLY	AVE DB DLY	AVE PEND TIME	AVE DISC TIME	AVE CONN TIME	% DEV CONN	% DEV UTIL	% DEV RESV	AVE NUMBER ALLOC	% ANY ALLOC	% MT PEND
	A90	3380D	TSOA90	15C	8.906	28	7		0.0	0.1	0.2	17.6	3.0	2.65	19.93	5.8	137	100.0	0.0
	A91	3380D	TSOA91	15C	20.838	28	11		0.0	0.2	0.2	13.7	2.7	5.66	34.93	7.6	153	100.0	0.0
	A92	3380D	TSOA92	15C	12.107	25	8		0.0	0.2	0.2	13.8	3.0	3.64	21.97	5.8	139	100.0	0.0
	A93	3380D	TSOA93	15C	6.753	23	3		0.0	0.1	0.2	16.9	2.9	1.97	15.56	5.1	151	100.0	0.0
	A94	3380D	TSOA94	15C	6.622	28	7		0.0	0.1	0.2	17.9	3.0	2.01	15.34	4.2	122	100.0	0.0
	A95	3380D	TSOA95	15C	4.586	25	4		0.0	0.2	0.2	17.7	2.8	1.28	9.92	2.9	121	100.0	0.0
	A96	3380D	TSOA96	15C	9.090	32	10		0.0	0.1	0.2	19.8	2.4	2.15	22.46	8.4	163	100.0	0.0
	A97	3380D	TSOA97	15C	7.821	24	4		0.0	0.1	0.2	17.0	2.8	2.22	17.66	6.8	125	100.0	0.0
	A98	3380D	TSOA98	15C	8.099	24	4		0.0	0.1	0.2	16.9	3.0	2.47	17.57	5.4	177	100.0	0.0
	A99	3380D	TSOA99	15C	6.767	25	4		0.0	0.1	0.2	17.2	3.6	2.42	15.48	4.8	145	100.0	0.0
	A9A	3380D	TSOA9A	15C	7.977	27	6		0.0	0.1	0.2	17.8	2.9	2.30	18.87	7.1	163	100.0	0.0
	A9B	3380D	TSOA9B	15C	7.476	23	3		0.0	0.1	0.2	17.2	2.7	2.04	16.48	3.7	134	100.0	0.0
			LCU	15C	**107.040**	26	7		0.0	0.1	0.2	**16.4**	**2.9**	2.57	18.85	5.6	1729	100.0	0.0
	C10	3380E	MVSDLB	173	17.546	19	2		0.0	0.0	0.1	14.7	1.8	3.10	29.01	0.3	115	100.0	0.0
	C11	3380E	CICIPO	173	2.750	19	1		0.0	0.1	0.2	14.9	2.9	0.80	4.89	0.0	3.0	100.0	0.0
	C12	3380E	AKESM1	173	0.623	21	0		0.0	0.3	0.3	15.3	5.2	0.32	1.28	0.0	5.4	100.0	0.0
	C13	3380E	MVSRES	173	28.394	115	90		0.0	0.4	0.5	20.3	4.3	12.24	69.99	3.6	7903	100.0	0.0
	C14	3380E	ESCDLB	173	0.000	0	0		0.0	0.0	0.0	0.0	0.0	0.00	0.00	0.0	0.0	100.0	0.0
	C15	3380E	MVSCAT	173	32.017	10	1		0.0	0.0	0.1	6.6	1.9	6.06	28.42	7.2	734	100.0	0.0
	C16	3380E	ESCRES	173	0.000	0	0		0.0	0.0	0.0	0.0	0.0	0.00	0.00	0.0	4.0	100.0	0.0
	C17	3380E	ESCCAT	173	0.662	21	0		0.0	0.2	0.2	14.9	5.6	0.37	1.36	0.0	1.0	100.0	0.0
			LCU	173	**81.992**	49	32		0.0	0.2	0.2	**13.5**	**2.8**	2.86	16.87	1.4	8765	100.0	0.0

Total application I/O rate → 668.092

Figure 7.10(b). The DASD configuration.

Analysis of the I/O subsystem

This is exceptionally high, and is explained by the test workload on the system! A more normal RIOC on today's TSO/CICS/IMS/batch system would be 8–12. It should be noted though, that with the advent of data-in-memory (DIM) techniques featured within MVS/ESA, which exploit expanded storage (e.g. hiperspaces), that RIOCs will fall over the next few years. None the less, whether they fall or not, their use in arriving at the upper bound of I/Os that your system will sustain will not change. So let us now work out what the maximum I/O rate is for our system.

7.9.3 Calculating the upper bound I/O rate for the system

What we have calculated so far is the I/O rate per URPP (the RIOC), therefore what we need to find out is the I/O rate that will be sustained when the maximum allowable use of our 27 RPP machine is reached. We will take the upper bound of CPU percentage as 90 per cent, as this allows us a buffer of space (and time) before we reach the 100 per cent mark; once this is reached, then your workload will suffer.

$$\text{Maximum sustainable I/O rate} = \text{RIOC} \times \text{CPU \% upper bound} \\ \times \text{RPP of machine} \\ = 27 \times 0.90 \times 27 = 656 \text{ I/Os per second}$$

Remember, these are application I/Os; they exclude any page/swap I/Os. As you can see, this is very close to our current I/O rate through all the channels on line, as we would expect, because the machine is running at close to 90 per cent CPU utilization (89.19 per cent). In fact, the application I/O that we are sustaining is 664 I/Os per second; slightly above our recommended value, but nothing to worry about.

Remember also, that this RIOC is based upon the current workload. If it changes dramatically then the RIOC will change. A dramatic change would be if we added another 10 per cent of CICS or TSO users, or started another batch initiator.

7.9.4 Is my I/O system adequate for the current I/O rate?

In order to find out this information, we need to extract some more data from our RMF Monitor I report. The data we need is the average DASD service time (made up of the disconnect time and connect time), and the average path service time (which is really the connect time). We need to calculate this average over all the LCUs. The data we need has been highlighted in Fig. 7.10.

We need to calculate the weighted average of the DASD service times for each LCU. Table 7.1 shows the extracted data and the associated weighted average of the DASD service time. We can then arrive at the aggregated weighted average.

Table 7.1. Extracted data

LCU number	Device activity rate A	Disc. time plus conn. time (ms) B	Average DASD serv. time A × B	Connect time C	Average path time A × C
097	87.701	3.4	298.18	2.6	228.02
0CD	117.129	3.8	445.09	3.1	363.10
0D5	185.517	24.5	4545.52	3.6	667.86
0F0	88.713	16.1	1428.28	5.0	443.57
15C	107.040	19.3	2065.87	2.9	310.42
173	81.992	16.3	1336.47	2.8	229.58
Totals	668.09[1]		10 119.41		2242.55

Note:
1   668.09 has to be reduced to 664 to remove the page/swap I/O.

We will be using the true service time (connect time plus disconnect time), as it is the ability of the device to service the I/O request that we are after. We will make an allowance for both types of queuing (IOSQ and pending time) a little later.

Calculating the weighted averages

Aggregated weighted average DASD service time
$$= \text{Sum } (A \times B)/\text{Sum } A$$
$$= 10\,119/664 = 15.24 \text{ ms}$$

Aggregated weighted average path service time $= \text{Sum } (A \times C)/\text{Sum } A$
$$= 2243/664 = 3.38 \text{ ms}$$

Now that we have calculated the aggregated weighted average DASD service time and aggregated weighted average path service time, we can derive the optimum number of actuators (volumes) and paths to sustain the current I/O rate. First we will find the optimum number of volumes.

Optimum number of volumes to sustain the current I/O rate

We need first of all to accept some fundamental criteria:

1 The maximum DASD utilization is 30 per cent. This is no randomly selected value, but is the point at which the service time starts to rise dramatically, owing to the principles of queuing already stated.
2 Not all DASD in an LCU have the same type and number of I/Os started to them. There are different access patterns to different DASD, and the intensity of I/O rate varies due to the type of application using a particular DASD. Because of this, you will find that you do not have a full millisecond's worth of time from a volume. It is the effect of these factors which mainly gives us the queue times: pending time (for I/Os from this system) and IOSQ time.

Analysis of the I/O subsystem

This rationale allows us to say that in fact we will only get about 700 milliseconds' worth of I/O time, out of the full 1000 milliseconds of I/O time available to each DASD. All these factors will give us a 'discount' value of 0.7 (700/1000) that we can incorporate into our calculations.

So first we will calculate the maximum I/O rate that we should allow to the average DASD:

$$\text{I/O rate per volume} = (1/\text{Average service time}) \times 30\% \times \text{Discount factor}$$
$$= (1/0.01524) \times 0.30 \times 0.7$$
$$= 14 \text{ I/Os per second (rounded up)}$$

Calculating the number of volumes required

Now we will calculate the required number of actuators (volumes) required for our application I/O:

$$\text{Total I/O rate/Maximum I/Os per volume}$$
$$= 664/14$$
$$= 48 \text{ volumes (rounded to a multiple of 4)}$$

Note that the total I/O rate (664) does *not* include the page/swap I/O. The page/swap data sets will be dealt with separately.

A final check

The calculated weighted average response time from Fig. 7.10 is 31.65 milliseconds. Using this value instead of the calculated device service time of 15.24 milliseconds, allied to the discount factor of 0.7, gives us:

$$(1/0.03165) \times 0.30 = 9.5 \text{ I/Os per second (rounded)}$$

We have a calculated value, using the discount factor of 0.7, of 14 I/Os per second. We are in fact achieving much less than this (9.5 I/Os per second). This confirms what we already know; the IOSQ times are too long.

Optimum number of paths to sustain the current I/O rate

Again, we need to accept some basic criteria regarding the maximum rate that should be sustained on a channel path. This rate is a function of the type of DASD controller and the maximum number of paths through these controllers. We have already been through the rationale of how we arrive at the following values:

- IBM 3880 DASD controller (maximum of two paths per LCU):

    Maximum path I/O rate $= (1/\text{Average path time}) \times 0.3$

- IBM 3990 DASD controller (maximum of four paths per LCU):

    Maximum path I/O rate $= (1/\text{Average path time}) \times 0.55$

In the system currently being examined, there is in fact an IBM 3990 DASD controller installed, although only one path through each director is being used per system attached, therefore there are only two paths per LCU. We will derive the maximum path I/O rate for both two paths per LCU four paths per LCU configurations:

- For two-path LCUs:

    $(1/0.0038) \times 0.3 = 80$ I/Os per second (rounded up)

- For four-path LCUs:

    $(1/0.0038) \times 0.55 = 145$ I/Os per second (rounded up)

Now we calculate the required number of paths:

Optimum number of paths
$$= \text{Aggregated I/O rate}/\text{Maximum I/Os per path}$$

For two paths per LCU mode:

$664/80 = 8$ paths

For four paths per LCU mode:

$664/145 = 4$ paths

The four paths per LCU value of four has to be rounded to a multiple of four, and in fact we have rounded down. We could certainly get away with eight paths and four paths respectively, until there is a significant increase in the I/O rate, or there is a significant change in the workload.

Summary: calculated versus actual volumes/paths

We have calculated that we need 48 volumes and 4 paths (4 paths per LCU mode) or 8 paths (2 paths per LCU mode). In fact, we have 55 volumes installed and 12 paths on line. You can see that our DASD configuration is about right in terms of our derived values, but we could get away with fewer channels, particularly if we went over to 4 paths per LCU; using the IBM 3990s properly instead of emulating the IBM 3880s.

Of course, it is certainly better to be slightly overconfigured for DASD and channels, rather than underconfigured. This is all the more important as the LCUs are operating in two-path mode.

In addition, there is the requirement for low response times for some applications. This is reflected by the cached times for LCU 0CD (ranging from 2 to 7 milliseconds for all but three of the DASD in the LCU), and the DASD in LCU 097.

Using DFSMS would allow us to ensure that applications communicating with high-response data sets were allocated on the DASD associated with LCU 0CD or

097. This could be done without any input from users, other than stating their requirements in terms of response time and backup.

7.10 Page and swap data sets

The first question is 'Do you need swap data sets as well as page data sets?' There is a simple way of arriving at an answer to this query. If you have expanded storage installed, then you probably do *not* need swap data sets. If you do not have expanded storage installed, then look to see if your real swapping to the page/swap data sets is greater than 20 per cent of total swapping—total swapping consisting of real swaps (swaps to and from auxiliary storage) and processor storage swaps. Processor storage swaps are swaps to and from expanded storage, and logical swaps.

If real swapping is greater than 20 per cent of the total swapping, then you may need to have swap data sets. Real swapping should always be less than 20 per cent of total swapping, therefore if your system is set up correctly, it is unlikely that you need swap data sets. In case you either need swap data sets, or just like to have them (some people do!), then you need to know how to calculate the number and size of the swap data sets.

7.10.1 *The primary and secondary working sets*

On Fig. 7.11 you will see highlighted the AVERAGE PAGES PER SWAP OUT (105 pages). We need only this value, as opposed to AVERAGE PAGES PER SWAP IN (140 pages), because the swapped out pages are regarded as the *primary* working set, and it is only the primary working set that goes to the swap data sets. The primary working set is made up of the LSQA and the recently referenced changed and unchanged pages. 'Recently referenced' means referenced since the last check by the real storage manager (RSM). Remember, only the primary working set goes to the swap data sets if you have them.

The *secondary* working set goes to the page data sets even if you have both swap and page data sets. AVERAGE PAGES PER SWAP IN includes both the primary and secondary working sets, even though the secondary pages (unreferenced changed pages) will have come from the page data set(s).

Average pages per swap in includes the LSQA, referenced changed and unchanged (the primary working set), plus the unreferenced changed pages (secondary working set). The secondary working set pages *may* still be in storage. If they are not then they will be demand paged from the page data sets as required, as will the unreferenced unchanged pages, which were 'thrown away' at swap out time. There is no need to save these pages, as the RSM knows where to get a new copy of any page if it is required.

PAGING ACTIVITY

MVS/ESA SP/4.2.0
OPT = IEAOPT00
SYSTEM ID MAC1
RPT VERSION 4.2.1
DATE 28/06/93
TIME 09.00.00
PAGE 3
INTERVAL 15.00.00
CYCLE 1 SECOND

SWAP PLACEMENT ACTIVITY

			AUX STORAGE			LOGICAL SWAP		EXPANDED STORAGE				
		TOTAL	AUX STOR TOTAL	AUX STOR DIRECT	AUX STOR VIA TRANSITION	LOG SWAP	LOG SWAP EFFECTIVE	EXP STOR DIRECT	EXP STOR TOTAL	MIGRATED FROM EXP STOR	EXP STOR EFFECTIVE	LOG SWAP /EXP STOR EFFECTIVE
TERMINAL INPUT/OUTPUT WAIT	CT RT %	15556 17.28 94.4%	3 0.00 0.0%	0 0.00 0.0%	3 0.00 100.0%	15556 17.28 100.0%	12013 13.35 77.2%	0 0.00 0.0%	3540 3.93 22.8%	0 0.00 0.0%	3540 3.93 100.0%	15553 17.28 100.0%
LONG WAIT	CT RT %	7 0.01 0.0%	0 0.00 0.0%	0 0.00 0.0%	0 0.00 0.0%	7 0.01 100.0%	5 0.01 71.4%	0 0.00 0.0%	2 0.00 28.6%	0 0.00 0.0%	2 0.00 100.0%	7 0.01 100.0%
DETECTED WAIT	CT RT %	99 0.11 0.6%	0 0.00 0.0%	0 0.00 0.0%	0 0.00 0.0%	99 0.11 100.0%	54 0.06 54.5%	0 0.00 0.0%	45 0.05 45.5%	0 0.00 0.0%	45 0.05 100.0%	99 0.11 100.0%
UNILATERAL	CT RT %	776 0.86 4.7%	0 0.00 0.0%	0 0.00 0.0%	0 0.00 0.0%	755 0.84 97.3%	189 0.21 25.0%	21 0.02 2.7%	587 0.65 75.6%	0 0.00 0.0%	587 0.65 100.0%	776 0.86 100.0%
EXCHANGE ON RECOMMENDATION VALUE	CT RT %	14 0.02 0.1%	0 0.00 0.0%	0 0.00 0.0%	0 0.00 0.0%	13 0.01 92.9%	0 0.00 0.0%	1 0.00 7.1%	14 0.02 100.0%	0 0.00 0.0%	14 0.02 100.0%	14 0.02 100.0%
TRANSITION TO NON-SWAPPABLE	CT RT %	1 0.00 0.0%	0 0.00 0.0%	0 0.00 0.0%	0 0.00 0.0%	0 0.00 0.0%	0 0.00 0.0%	0 0.00 100.0%	0 0.00 100.0%	0 0.00 0.0%	0 0.00 100.0%	1 0.00 100.0%
IMPROVE CENTRAL STORAGE	CT RT %	30 0.03 0.2%	0 0.00 0.0%	0 0.00 0.0%	0 0.00 0.0%	30 0.03 100.0%	1 0.00 3.3%	0 0.00 0.0%	29 0.03 96.7%	0 0.00 0.0%	29 0.03 100.0%	30 0.03 100.0%
TOTAL	CT RT %	16483 18.31 100.0%	3 0.00 0.0%	0 0.00 0.0%	3 0.00 100.0%	16460 18.29 99.9%	12262 13.62 74.5%	23 0.03 0.1%	4218 4.69 25.6%	0 0.00 0.0%	4218 4.69 100.0%	16480 18.31 100.0%

AUXILIARY STORAGE – AVERAGE PAGES PER SWAP OUT – 105   AVERAGE PAGES PER SWAP IN – 140
OCCURRENCES OF TERMINAL OUTPUT WAIT – 1079

Figure 7.11. Swap placement activity report.

Analysis of the I/O subsystem

Pages are swapped to the swap data sets in what are termed 'swap sets'. There are 12 pages in a swap set (48K), therefore there are:

$$105/12 = 9 \text{ (rounded) swap sets required per swap out}$$

All of the 9 swap sets are sent to the swap data sets *in parallel*, therefore we would need 9 swap data sets, with each swap data set on a separate path. We have 12 paths online in this system, so we could implement this if we wish; but of course we do not. Why? Because we have expanded storage installed.

An explanation of whether a swapped address space goes to auxiliary storage (a page/swap data set), expanded storage, or stays in central storage (logically swapped), is dealt with in Chapter 8.

7.10.2 What size should our swap data sets be?

If, for whatever reason, you decide to have swap data sets, then you need to ask the following questions in order to arrive at the correct size of the swap (and page) data sets:

- Maximum number of production TSO users during the peak period?
- Maximum number of development TSO users during the peak period?
- Maximum rate of production batch jobs per hour during the peak period?
- Average turnaround time per production batch job?
- Maximum rate of development batch jobs per hour?
- Average turnaround time per development batch job?

The answers to these questions are:

- Maximum production TSO users = 70
- Maximum development TSO users = 200
- Maximum rate of production batch jobs per hour = 400 per hour
- Average turnaround time per production batch job = 30 seconds
- Maximum rate of development batch jobs per hour = 900 per hour
- Average turnaround time per development batch job = 1 minute

We can complete 3600/30 = 120 batch production jobs in 1 hour, therefore we need 400/120 = 4 (rounded) batch initiators started for the correct job classes.

We can complete 3600/60 = 60 batch development jobs in 1 hour, therefore we need 900/60 = 15 batch initiators started for the correct job classes.

This means a total of 19 initiators (19 initiator address spaces) for the batch, plus 270 address spaces for TSO, making a total of 289 address spaces that *could* require swapping at any one time.

We have calculated that we needed 9 swap sets per address space, therefore the total number of swap sets required is:

$$\text{Total swap sets} = 289 \times 9 = 2601$$

Each swap set consists of 12 pages, therefore the total 4K slots required are:

Total 4K slots required $= 2601 \times 12 = 31\,212$

Each swap data set should be no more than 20 per cent full, as this allows the auxiliary storage manager's (ASM) algorithms to work most effectively, and ensures the best performance of the swap configuration. Therefore, allowing 150 slots per cylinder on an IBM 3380 DASD, and 180 slots per cylinder on an IBM 3390 DASD, we will need

$(31\,212/150)/0.2 = 1040$ cylinders on IBM 3380 DASD

and we will need

$(31\,212/180)/0.2 = 867$ cylinders on IBM 3390 DASD

We need 9 swap data sets, therefore:

$1040/9 = 116$ cylinders per swap data set on IBM 3380 DASD

and

$867/9 = 97$ cylinders per swap data set on IBM 3390 DASD

We need to go through this tiresome calculation only if we have no expanded storage installed. This system does, therefore we do not need swap data sets.

7.10.3 Page data sets—how many and what size?

Swap sets go only onto the swap data sets, and so if you do not have swap data sets, all page/swap I/O that has to suffer real movement will go to and from the page data sets, utilizing what is called the ASM 'contiguous slot algorithm'. This algorithm calculates the most efficient 'burst size' for a number of contiguous pages in storage, and places them on contiguous slots on the page data sets. The size of the burst is a function of the device type. For example, the burst size for an IBM 3390 DASD is 32 pages, and for an IBM 3380 DASD it is 30 pages.

For the contiguous slot algorithm to work most effectively, the page data sets should not be more than 20 per cent full. We will use this value in arriving at the optimum number of page data sets. If the page data sets are used for both paging and swapping, the two types of data are kept separate on the data sets. This is essential otherwise the contiguous slot algorithm would not work very efficiently.

The function of seldom ending channel program (SECP) means that only one page data set should be on a volume; indeed, only one reasonably active data set should be on the volume. Setting the USE attribute to PRIVATE will ensure that only *specific* requests will allocate data sets on the volume. If this rule is not followed, then I/O to page data sets will be started by the IOS using the normal STARTIO macro, instead of the RESUMIO macro which is much more efficient.

RESUMIO 'resumes' a 'suspended' channel program; whereas STARTIO starts the I/O process from the beginning of the channel program.

MVS version 2 (MVS/XA) allows only a maximum of 65 400 slots per page data set. If you maintain the SECP rule of one page data set per volume, then a lot of space is wasted on the device. Most users understandably have found it difficult to justify putting only one page data set on a volume, or even putting only one reasonably active data set on the volume.

A channel end/device end presented for any data set on the volume (page data set or not) means that the RESUMIO macro can no longer be used to restart an I/O operation to the page data set, therefore the benefits of SECP are hard to maintain under MVS/XA. RESUMIO applies only to the page data sets, not to the swap data sets.

65 400 slots represents about 268 megabytes; only about 14 per cent of an IBM 3380 Model K—quite a waste. MVS version 3 (MVS/ESA) allows 16 777 000 slots to be defined for a page data set, therefore the restriction incorporated within MVS/XA is removed. It is now possible to use a complete IBM 3380 Model K or IBM 3390 Model 2 for a page data set.

7.10.4 Calculating the number and size of the page data sets

Figure 7.12 shows the page data set usage report; the maximum slots used column has been highlighted. We will use the total of slots used for local page data sets for our calculations, which is 43 305. This total includes those slots used for swapping address spaces using the contiguous slot algorithm (no swap data sets on this system). The primary and common page data sets will be dealt with later.

Let us first of all look at a method of arriving at the number of page data sets which is general in nature, and is based upon accepted criteria for page data set calculations. This will be followed by a more sophisticated method, which was in fact used to establish the number of local page data sets on the system used for analysis.

Number and size of page data sets—MVS version 3 or 4 (MVS/ESA): general method

The limiting factor of maximum slots per page data set has been effectively removed, and so we can concentrate on the required number of volumes without having to take this constraint into account, as we will with MVS version 2 (MVS/XA).

We know that the maximum number of slots used should be no greater than 20 per cent of the total slots available. In addition, there should be at least two local page data sets for availability:

$$43\,305/0.2 = 216\,525 \text{ total slots required (at least)}$$

PAGE DATA SET USAGE

MVS/ESA SP/4.2.0
SYSTEM ID MAC1
RPT VERSION 4.2.1
DATE 28/06/93
TIME 09.00.00
INTERVAL 15.00.00
CYCLE 1 SECOND

NUMBER OF SAMPLES = 900

PAGE SPACE TYPE	VOLUME SERIAL	DEV NUM	DEVICE TYPE	SLOTS ALLOC	SLOTS USED MIN	SLOTS USED MAX	SLOTS USED AVE	BAD SLOTS	% IN USE	PAGE TRANS TIME	NUMBER IO REQ	PAGES XFER'D	V I O	DATASET NAME
PLPA	MVSCAT	C15	3380E	3000	2986	2986	2986	0	0.06	0.018	38	28		PAGE.VMVSCAT.PLPA.CYL20
COMMON	MVSCAT	C15	3380E	1950	520	525	521	0	0.06	0.062	8	8		PAGE.VMVSCAT.COMMON
LOCAL	MVS576	576	3380J	60 000	5998	6985	6333	0	1.50	0.010	525	1402	Y	PAGE.VMVS576.LOCAL
LOCAL	AKESM1	C12	3380E	42 000	6723	7747	7097	0	0.83	0.005	515	1417	Y	PAGE.VAKESM1.LOCAL
LOCAL	ESCCAT	C17	3380E	32 100	6827	7899	7276	0	2.06	0.011	596	1678	Y	PAGE.VESCCAT.LOCAL
LOCAL	MVS577	577	3380J	16 050	5469	6060	5693	0	1.33	0.011	687	1064	Y	PAGE.VMVS577.LOCAL
LOCAL	CB84LB	567	3380J	60 000	6189	7138	6568	0	1.83	0.012	518	1362	Y	PAGE.VCB84LB.LOCAL
LOCAL	CICIPO	C11	3380E	60 000	6460	7476	6876	0	1.89	0.011	850	1528	Y	PAGE.VCICIPO.LOCAL

Total slots used 43 305

Figure 7.12. Page data set usage report.

Analysis of the I/O subsystem

Therefore, with MVS/ESA, there should be a minimum of two page data sets, and each page data set should be a minimum size of:

$$216\,525/2 = 108\,263 \text{ slots per local page data set}$$

If you have IBM 3390 DASD installed, at 180 slots per cylinder:

$$108\,263/180 = 602 \text{ cylinders for each local page data set}$$

If you have IBM 3380 DASD installed, at 150 slots per cylinder:

$$108\,263/150 = 722 \text{ cylinders for each local page data set}$$

Number and size of page data sets—MVS version 2 (MVS/XA)

MVS/XA has the limitation of 65 400 slots per page data set, therefore our calculations will be slightly different. The minimum number of slots required is derived as before:

$$43\,305/0.2 = 216\,525 \text{ total slots (at least)}$$

The number of page data sets required is:

$$216\,525/65\,400 = 4 \text{ local page data sets required}$$

For IBM 3380 DASD installed:

$$65\,400/150 = 436 \text{ cylinders per local page data set}$$

Number and size of page data sets—MVS version 3 or 4 (MVS/ESA): sophisticated

The following method uses the RMF Monitor I Paging Activity reports and the Device Activity report. The easiest way to show this method is to use the following 'fill in the blanks' approach. Only the TSO address spaces have been used: as the batch rate is very low it has been ignored. This may not be the case in your installation. DIM allowance has also been made for more hiperspace use.

1. Actual TSO transactions per second = 17
   (from PGs 2 and 42)
2. % of item 1 to be processor storage swapped = 99%
   (logically or expanded storage swapped)
3. % of item 1 to be auxiliary storage swapped = 1%
   (100 − 99)
4. Actual number of auxiliary storage swaps/second) = 1
   (1% of 17 to nearest integer rounded up)
5. Item 4 × 2 (swaps in and out) = 2
6. Item 5 × Average pages per swap in = 280
   (see Fig. 7.13—highlighted value of 140)

PAGING ACTIVITY

MVS/ESA SP/4.2.0
OPT = IEAOPT00
SYSTEM ID MAC1
RPT VERSION 4.2.1
DATE 28/06/93
TIME 09.00.00
INTERVAL 15.00.00
CYCLE 1 SECOND

SWAP PLACEMENT ACTIVITY

		TOTAL	AUX STORAGE — AUX STOR TOTAL	AUX STOR DIRECT	AUX STOR VIA TRANSITION	LOGICAL SWAP — LOG SWAP	LOG SWAP EFFECTIVE	EXP STOR DIRECT	EXP STOR TOTAL	EXPANDED STORAGE — MIGRATED FROM EXP STOR	EXP STOR EFFECTIVE	LOG SWAP /EXP STOR EFFECTIVE
TERMINAL INPUT/OUTPUT WAIT	CT RT %	15556 17.28 94.4%	3 0.00 0.0%	0 0.00 0.0%	3 0.00 100.0%	15556 17.28 100.0%	12013 13.35 77.2%	0 0.00 0.0%	3540 3.93 22.8%	0 0.00 0.0%	3540 3.93 100.0%	15553 17.28 100.0%
LONG WAIT	CT RT %	7 0.01 0.0%	0 0.00 0.0%	0 0.00 0.0%	0 0.00 0.0%	7 0.01 100.0%	5 0.01 71.4%	0 0.00 0.0%	2 0.00 28.6%	0 0.00 0.0%	2 0.00 100.0%	7 0.01 100.0%
DETECTED WAIT	CT RT %	99 0.11 0.6%	0 0.00 0.0%	0 0.00 0.0%	0 0.00 0.0%	99 0.11 100.0%	54 0.06 54.5%	0 0.00 0.0%	45 0.05 45.5%	0 0.00 0.0%	45 0.05 100.0%	99 0.11 100.0%
UNILATERAL	CT RT %	776 0.86 4.7%	0 0.00 0.0%	0 0.00 0.0%	0 0.00 0.0%	755 0.84 97.3%	189 0.21 25.0%	21 0.02 2.7%	587 0.65 75.6%	0 0.00 0.0%	587 0.65 100.0%	776 0.86 100.0%
EXCHANGE ON RECOMMENDATION VALUE	CT RT %	14 0.02 0.1%	0 0.00 0.0%	0 0.00 0.0%	0 0.00 0.0%	13 0.01 92.9%	0 0.00 0.0%	1 0.00 7.1%	14 0.02 100.0%	0 0.00 0.0%	14 0.02 100.0%	14 0.02 100.0%
TRANSITION TO NON-SWAPPABLE	CT RT %	1 0.00 0.0%	0 0.00 0.0%	0 0.00 0.0%	0 0.00 0.0%	0 0.00 0.0%	0 0.00 0.0%	1 0.00 100.0%	1 0.00 100.0%	0 0.00 0.0%	1 0.00 100.0%	1 0.00 100.0%
IMPROVE CENTRAL STORAGE	CT RT %	30 0.03 0.2%	0 0.00 0.0%	0 0.00 0.0%	0 0.00 0.0%	30 0.03 100.0%	1 0.00 3.3%	0 0.00 0.0%	29 0.03 96.7%	0 0.00 0.0%	29 0.03 100.0%	30 0.03 100.0%
TOTAL	CT RT %	16483 18.31 100.0%	3 0.00 0.0%	0 0.00 0.0%	3 0.00 100.0%	16460 18.29 99.9%	12262 13.62 74.5%	23 0.03 0.1%	4218 4.69 25.6%	0 0.00 0.0%	4218 4.69 100.0%	16480 18.31 100.0%

AUXILIARY STORAGE — AVERAGE PAGES PER SWAP OUT – 105   AVERAGE PAGES PER SWAP IN – 140
OCCURRENCES OF TERMINAL OUTPUT WAIT – 1079

Figure 7.13. Analysis of where the swapped address spaces go.

Analysis of the I/O subsystem

7 Possible VIO page rate = 100
   (possible future use)
8 Possible hiperspace page rate = 100
   (possible future use)
9 Total page rate to auxiliary = 480
   (by adding items 6–8)
10 *Estimated number of local page data sets* = 6
   (480/80) (rounded)
   See following calculations to arrive at divisor of 80

Arriving at the divisor of 80

How did we arrive at a divisor of 80 on our calculations? Table 7.2 shows the activity rate and response times for each of the six local page data sets installed on this system. A weighted average response time has been calculated from this information, and then used to arrive at an upper bound of I/Os per second that should be allowed to the local page data sets. The principles used have all been explained.

Table 7.2. Data for local page data sets

Device no.	Activity rate A	Response time (ms) B	$A \times B$
576	0.583	24	13.992
C12	0.623	21	13.083
C17	0.662	21	13.902
577[1]	19.220	3	57.660
567	0.967	25	24.175
C11	2.750	19	52.250
Totals (excluding 577)	5.585		117.402

Note:
1 Device 577 has been excluded, as it would skew the response time to give an average which would not be correct to use in our calculations. It would mean that we derived a figure which would be too low.

Thus:

Average response time = 117.402/5.585 = 21 milliseconds (rounded)

Maximum I/O rate per second to a local page data set:

$(1/0.021) \times 0.30 \times 0.7 = 10$ I/Os per second

Figure 7.9 shows the column PAGE TRANS TIME highlighted. This is the time to transfer a block of pages to and/or from the page data sets. The average of the times for the local page data sets is 0.010 (10 milliseconds).

Taking the paging volumes as IBM 3380 DASD with a data transfer rate of 3 000 000 bytes per second (3000 bytes per millisecond), then 10 milliseconds to transfer the block means:

$10 \times 3K = 30K$ (8 pages, rounded) is transferred per paging I/O

10 paging I/Os per second at 8 pages per I/O
$= 80$ pages per second per local page data set

Our divisor of 80 pages per second is thus established.

A VIO page rate of 100 pages per second, and a hiperspace page rate also of 100 pages per second have been included to allow for future use of these features. This is sensible, as DIM techniques should be implemented as soon as possible in all installations.

7.11 The paging rate and the system multi-programming level

There is a relationship between the overall paging rate and the system multi-programming level (MPL) which is fundamental to the efficient working of your system. As a capacity planner you should be aware of it.

Intuitively we can accept that as the system MPL rises, the paging rate will also rise, but we can look at this from the other end. If we put a limit on the paging rate, then we are in effect putting a brake on the system MPL. Using this knowledge, and our previous calculations, we can be fairly sophisticated regarding our settings for the paging parameter which controls the system MPL.

The system MPL is controlled mainly (in MVS/ESA V4) by the RCCPTRT parameter in the IEAOPTxx member of SYS1.PARMLIB, and so our objective is to find the upper and lower values for this parameter. The default settings are (1000,1000), which in effect turns the parameter off!

So what should be our values? We have arrived at a page rate per second per local page data set, of 80, and we have calculated that we need 6 local page data sets. Therefore our total upper bound paging rate is $6 \times 80 = 480$ pages per second. We should subtract from this the VIO and swap paging, which in our case is 1 (see Fig. 7.14 to see how the VIO and paging rate of 1 is obtained).

Assuming (reasonably) that the page fault rate (page-ins) is 50 per cent of the total demand page rate, then this means that $480/2 = 240$ pages per second is our acceptable upper value for page fault rate. In other words, if our page fault rate goes above 240 pages per second, the system MPL will be lowered by the SRM. *Reasonable RCCPTRT values would be set at (200,240)*.

7.12 Where do the swapped address spaces go?

Figure 7.13 is the swap placement activity report of RMF Monitor I. It shows the destination of all swapped address spaces, logically swapped in central storage, swapped to expanded storage or to auxiliary storage. Analysis of this report is

MVS/ESA
SP/4.2.0
OPT = IEAOPT00

SYSTEM ID MAC1
RPT VERSION 4.2.1

PAGING ACTIVITY

DATE 28/06/93
TIME 09.00.00

PAGE 1
INTERVAL 15.00.00
CYCLE 1 SECOND

CENTRAL STORAGE PAGING RATES – IN PAGES PER SECOND

CATEGORY	PAGE RECLAIMS			PAGE IN				PAGE OUT			
	NON SWAP	% OF TOTL NON SWAP	SWAP	NON SWAP, BLOCK	NON SWAP, NON BLOCK	TOTAL RATE	% OF TOTL SUM	SWAP	NON SWAP	TOTAL RATE	% OF TOTL SUM
PAGEABLE SYSTEM AREAS (NON VIO)											
LPA	0.00	0			0.03	0.03	1		0.00	0.00	0
CSA	0.00	0			0.00	0.00	0		0.00	0.00	0
SUM	0.00	0			0.03	0.03	1		0.00	0.00	0
ADDRESS SPACES HIPERSPACE											
VIO	4.41	99		0.00		0.00	0		0.00	0.00	0
NON VIO	0.06	1	0.47	1.93	2.88	5.28	99	0.35	0.01	0.36	100
SUM	4.47	100	0.47	1.93	2.88	5.28	99	0.35	0.01	0.36	100
TOTAL SYSTEM HIPERSPACE											
VIO	4.41	99		0.00		0.00	0		0.00	0.00	0
NON VIO	0.06	1	**0.47**	1.93	2.91	5.31	100	**0.35**	0.01	0.36	100
SUM	4.47	100	0.47	1.93	2.91	5.31	100	0.35	0.01	0.36	100

PAGE MOVEMENT WITHIN CENTRAL STORAGE   55.40
AVERAGE NUMBER OF PAGES PER BLOCK   5.30
BLOCKS PER SECOND   0.37
PAGE-IN EVENTS (PAGE FAULT RATE)   3.28

Total swap and VIO paging = **0.82** (rounded = 1)

Figure 7.14. The VIO and swap paging rates per second.

required to see if the criterion that 99 per cent of all swaps are processor storage swaps (swaps to expanded storage or logical swaps) holds.

The report is split into three parts: starting from the left are those swaps that are real—they go to auxiliary storage; in the middle is the information on logical swaps; and on the right-hand side, expanded storage swaps information. You will see that the TOTAL rows at the bottom have been highlighted; this is the information to use. The three rows are the totals, the rate per second and the percentage of the total.

At the bottom of Fig. 7.13 you will see a field called OCCURRENCES OF TERMINAL OUTPUT WAIT. The value associated with this field is 1079 swaps. This is the number of TSO swaps that did not go into TERMINAL INPUT wait as they should have done, waiting for input from a user terminal. They are the TSO waits that were brought about by the lack of a virtual storage buffer, to write output to the terminal. Therefore the TSO user went into a terminal output wait, instead of a normal terminal input wait.

The value of 1079 represents 7 per cent of the total swaps ((1079/15 556) × 100). This is high, as it should be nearer 2–3 per cent of total TSO swaps, but it can be lowered by raising the value of the HIBFREXT parameter in the TSOKEYxx member of SYS1.PARMLIB. The default is 48 000 bytes of virtual storage, often not high enough for busy TSO installations. The TERMINAL OUTPUT WAIT occurs until the LOBFREXT value (default 24 000 bytes) is reached.

Check the HIBFREXT and LOBFREXT parameter values at your installations: this is a big factor in ensuring one swap per TSO transaction.

7.12.1 Analysis of swap placement activity report (Figure 7.13)

- *Logical swapping*
  Total logical swaps   = 16 460 swaps   99.9% of total (16 460/16 483)
  Logical swaps effective   = 12 262 swaps   74.5% of total (12 262/16 483)
                                 4 198 swaps

  To auxiliary from logical   =   3 swaps
  To expanded from logical   = 4 195 swaps
- *Expanded storage swapping*
  Expanded storage direct   =   23 swaps   1.0% of total (23/16 483)
  Migrated from logical swaps = 4 195 swaps
  Expanded storage effective = 4 218 swaps   25.6% of total (4218/16 483)
- *Logical + expanded swaps* = 16 480 swaps   c. 100% of total
                                                (16 460 + 23 − 3)

- *Auxiliary storage swapping*
  From logical swapping   =   3 swaps
  Auxiliary storage direct   =   0 swaps
  Auxiliary storage total   =   3 swaps

7.13 Primary (PLPA), common and duplex page data sets

The primary page data set should be about 5 per cent greater than the size of the Pageable Link Pack Area (PLPA), which can be ascertained from a virtual storage report obtained with RMF Monitor I or II. Alternatively, make the primary four megabytes to begin with, until you know the size of the PLPA. The overflow will go onto the common page data set. The rationale for allowing 5 per cent greater than the size of the PLPA is to allow for permanent I/O errors resulting in a loss of space.

The common page data set should start off the same size as the primary. Remember overflows from the primary will go to the common. Use RMF Monitor I reports to track the actual amount used, and reduce the size accordingly.

You can use the following information to help arrive at how much space will be required for your primary and common data sets. Four megabytes on an IBM 3390 DASD will require six cylinders, whereas on an IBM 3380 DASD you will need eight cylinders. So nine cylinders will be required on an IBM 3390 for a six megabytes primary.

If you are using a duplex page data set, then it must be equal to or greater than the combined size of the primary and common page data sets. So for example, if the primary and common require a combined total of 20 megabytes, then you will require 40 cylinders on an IBM 3380 DASD, or 30 cylinders on an IBM 3390 DASD for the duplex data set.

7.13.1 Initial sizing of local page data sets

For initial sizing of the local page data sets, use the following values:

- 8 megabytes per system address space (including non-swappables)
- 10 megabytes per batch address space
- 50 megabytes per TSO address space
- 40 megabytes for VIO data sets (allow for 200 data sets at 200 000 bytes each)

7.13.2 Data-in-virtual

If you are using data-in-virtual (DIV) data sets, then you must allow for this in your page data set calculations. Add whatever is the size of your DIV data sets to the page data sets, spread across all the local page data sets.

7.13.3 Performance recommendations

Spread local page data sets across different LCUs if possible. In the event of an LCU failure, you will still have at least one other local page data set to use, assuming that you are running with the minimum of two locals. *Do remember that two local page data sets are a bare minimum*, it is better for the performance of the I/O subsystem if you establish the 'best fit' number calculated previously. In our case this is six local page data sets, spread across all the LCUs.

Specify the primary page data set as the first 'dsname' in the PAGE parameter in IEASYSxx. This will ensure that the primary is used for the PLPA exclusively.

Put the primary page data set on a fast device (cached). There are no page-outs for the primary, and so if the RSM steals a PLPA module page, then a real page-in is required to replace it. Even better, use VLF to ensure that highly used PLPA modules remain in a data space, which will mean the best possible access times for your users.

7.14 Cache candidates—what data sets should you cache?

With the introduction of linklist lookaside (later upgraded to library lookaside (LLA), Virtual Lookaside Facility (VLF), Data Lookaside Facility (DLF) and batch local shared resource (LSR), we have the ability to give the read side of an I/O operation a boost in performance. Until the introduction of the IBM 3990 Model 3 cached controller, we did not have this same facility for the write part of the I/O operation. Now we have the ability to cache both reads and writes. Remember, caching *eliminates* disconnect time altogether, and reduces connect time to the amount of time to transfer the data to and from the cache to and from storage.

The following data sets are good candidates for read caching:

- Catalogs
- RACF and DFHSM control data sets
- VSAM indexes
- ISPF panels and CLISTs
- The IMS ACBLIB
- Program load libraries
- Any response time oriented data
- Data sets with a high I/O rate (greater than 15 I/Os per second)

Some simple rules should be noted for good cache candidates:

- Read/write ratio of at least 2:1
- Read hit percentage of greater than 70 per cent

Almost any data set is a good candidate for write caching, provided it has a write hit percentage of greater than 70 per cent. If the logical record is neither in the storage buffer, nor in the cache, then a write miss occurs. This means that the physical block is read from the DASD into the storage buffer, and at the same time a 'parallel transfer' I/O takes place into the cache. The next logical record will be found in the cache (assuming sequential reading), but the initial transfer takes a real I/O.

7.15 Data Facility—Systems Managed Storage

With the introduction of DFSMS in MVS/ESA, we can obtain, use and free up DASD space more easily. This means that we do not have to worry about the

Analysis of the I/O subsystem

placing of data sets when we allocate them; we let the system do it. It also has ramifications for the capacity of DASD required; we should be able to let DFSMS help us identify how many DASD and channels we need for *capacity* (space for data sets on DASD). We will still have to monitor for DASD *performance* though, as we have shown in this chapter.

The rationale of DFSMS is that we set up 'pools' of DASD, these pools having different characteristics. For example, there will be a pool of DASD under a cached controller for our fast response time applications to use. There will be another pool which has a high requirement for backup and/or migration criteria, in order that DFHSM (Data Facility Hierarchical Storage Manager) knows where to back-up/migrate the data.

DFSMS will enforce data set naming conventions through its interactions with RACF. Therefore, the whole function of maintaining data sets is much easier than it was. None the less, it is still essential to capacity plan. DFSMS will give you the information; but it will not consult the seller's systems engineer and order the DASD and channels for you in a timely manner!

DFSMS is not a panacea for all DASD ills: there are still some data sets that you will have to monitor outside DFSMS. These include:

- SYSRES
- Page and swap data set volumes
- Uncataloged data sets

On the other hand, the following are good DFSMS candidates:

- Temporary datasets (including VIO) for batch and TSO
- Permanent TSO and application data sets

7.16 ESCON channel support with MVS/ESA version 4.3.0

ESCON extended distance facility (XDF) laser channels and ESCON LED (light emitting diode channels) currently have 19 megabyte per second data transfer rate, *when attached to 520-based (Summit) machines*. They allow up to 1024 devices to be attached, thus increasing the number of devices that can be supported. This also means that fewer channels may possibly be required.

Capacity planning with ESCON channels up to 122 metres in length will give performance equal to or even slightly better than 4.5 megabytes per second channels. This means that there is no change in the methods for capacity planning.

ESCON channels will perform equal to or slightly worse than 4.5 megabyte channels, when the length of the channel is greater than 122 metres but less than 9 kilometres. So, again, there is little that needs to be done differently when considering capacity planning.

7.16.1 ESCON channels greater than 9 kilometres

When using the IBM ESCON XDF channels (laser channels as opposed to ESCON LED channels) allied to two ESCON directors, you can have ESCON channels up to 60 kilometres in length even in a PR/SM environment. Even though it is possible to have an ESCON channel of 20 kilometres between adaptor and director (or director to director), the critical distance still seems to be 9 kilometres for data transfer performance fall-off.

Therefore between 9 kilometres and 60 kilometres it is advisable to remember that it is not so much the path contention that matters, as much as the storage director and the channel busy. The methods of ascertaining the utilization do not change, but because of the enhanced data transfer rate, there will probably be a reduction in the number of channels and storage directors required.

7.17 RAID devices

There are five redundant array of independent disks (RAID) categories, each offering succeeding levels of function, starting with RAID 1, which is simply copying the data onto a second device, so that you in effect have a copy of the data. Performance of RAID 1 is not high, as you would expect. Even the performance of the dual copy feature of the IBM 3990 storage controller is not high, unless you ally it to DASD fast write feature.

RAID 2 and 3 are similar. They are effected by 'striping' the data onto multiple disks in parallel. The striping is at the byte level, and the performance improvement over RAID 1 is significant (no quantification available at the time of writing). RAID 1, 2 and 3 are better suited for sequential access of data.

RAID 4 and 5 use the striping method, but at the block level rather than the byte level. Performance over RAID 2 and 3 is better (again no figures are available). They are more suited to the random access of data.

7.17.1 IBM's RAID device—the IBM 9570 DASD array

The IBM 9570 DASD array is a RAID 3 device which is ideal for sequential access of data and will attach to ESCON channels. The data transfer rate is 50 megabytes per second, therefore use this value when calculating your capacity planning requirements. It would appear that it is possible to have almost double the I/O rate on a RAID channel, to that of an IBM 3390 (say) channel, again allowing you to reduce the number of channels required. No figures are available at the time of writing.

Whereas the IBM 3390 DASD and the IBM 9340 DASD are supported by the 'normal' access methods, the IBM 9570 DASD array is supported only by the RPQ High Performance Parallel Interface (HIPPI) on the IBM ES/3090 and IBM ES/9000 water-cooled processors, allied to the parallel I/O access method.

8
Storage analysis

8.1 Introduction

As with Chapter 7, the terms used will be defined before we begin the analysis for storage. Some of the newer features of MVS/ESA now available are described as well, in order that you are fully aware of the tools available to you. The chapter will then deal with analysis for both central and expanded storage. At the end of this chapter, you will be able to decide whether your installation needs either central or expanded storage, and how much.

The analysis is based on the amount of processor storage required to achieve 'zero paging', which is an ideal that will probably never be obtained; there will always be *some* paging, even if it is only on very few occasions. Any storage required for DIM will be in addition to the zero paging calculations, e.g. use of hiperspaces, VLF, CICS data tables, VIO, batch LSR.

There is a lot of new terminology and quite a few acronyms in this topic, so it would be advisable to define terms before we start to analyse the RMF Monitor I report. In particular, the paging terms can be confusing, therefore we will deal with them first.

Page fault

Page-ins from auxiliary storage, which result from a requirement for data or code by an application. The rate of page-ins is referred to as the 'page fault rate'.

Page steal

Changed pages written to auxiliary storage, as a result of a need for central storage. The rate of steals is referred to as the 'page steal' or 'page-out rate'.

Demand page rate

The sum of the page-in rate and the page steal or page-out rate.

Page reclaim

This was when the real storage manager (RSM) reclaimed a frame from the available queue, before it had been reallocated to another user. The frame still retained the 'old' user's data/code while it was on the available queue, until it was reallocated, only then was it reset to binary zeros. As of MVS version 3.1.3, this no longer happened. Increased storage sizes mean that the benefit is now outweighed by the code execution of reclaiming.

VIO page rate

The sum of the page-in rate and the page-out rate for VIO pages, to and from the page data sets. VIO pages are moved in a 'group' when movement has to take place. The group size is a function of the DASD type being emulated, and is referred to as the VIO 'window'. The window size is the track size of the emulated device, rounded up to a multiple of 4K.

Implicit block paging

This was introduced with MVS/ESA version 4.2. The normal page steal algorithms still apply but, in addition, there is now the function whereby a group of pages can be treated differently, if the SRM feels it would be beneficial to the overall working of the system and other users to do so. The group of pages must belong to the same address space or data space, and be contiguous in storage. If so, they can be moved *en masse* (up to a maximum of 256 pages) to either auxiliary or expanded storage.

The working set manager, which is a new component of the SRM, will enable implicit block paging as required for any individual address or data space. If the paging rate of a particular address or data space is high (and this is variable) relative to the total system paging rate, then it will be at first 'monitored' by the SRM. If necessary, after being monitored, implicit block paging will be invoked if the address or data space continues to maintain a high paging rate. Once this has happened, the address or data space is considered to be 'managed' by the SRM.

A page fault for any page within the block of pages sent to auxiliary or expanded storage results in the complete block of pages being brought into storage, and this is counted as one page fault. It is also recorded on the paging activity RMF Monitor I report under two separate headings, 'blocks per second' and 'average number of pages per block'.

Explicit block paging

The principle is the same as for implicit block paging. The difference is that this can be invoked by applications for their own data. The assembler REFPAT macro can be used to set the total size of the data, and the unit size to be block paged. COBOL, PL/1, C, Fortran and Pascal have a callable service—CSRIRP—to do the same thing.

This is a very useful function for users of large data arrays, and can be allied to data-in-virtual (DIV) VSAM linear data sets. By using explicit block paging, the application can avoid individual page steals which affect the response time.

8.2 Managing expanded storage

Expanded storage is managed in a similar manner to central storage, that is, if there is stress on the resource, then it is relieved by moving pages to auxiliary storage. Two criteria are used to manage expanded storage:

1 The rate of movement between expanded and auxiliary storage. This is referred to as the *migration rate*. All movement from expanded storage to auxiliary storage is via central storage, as there is no direct path from expanded storage to the I/O subsystem.
2 The average age (in seconds) of the pages migrated to auxiliary storage. This is referred to as the *migration age* (MA). The MA is analogous to the unreferenced interval count (UIC) for central storage.

8.3 Managing central storage

As with expanded storage, there are two major criteria to manage central storage:

1 The rate of movement between (to and from) central and expanded storage.
2 The UIC of each page frame. This is the time in seconds since the contents of the frame were last referenced. An overall system UIC is maintained by the SRM (expanded later), to use as a basis for swap decision-making.

8.4 Review of the swap process

Ever since the introduction of MVS/ESA version 3.1.3, the RSM always tries to avoid a physical swap if possible. It always tries to logically swap every type of address space (batch and TSO). If a physical swap cannot be avoided, then an expanded storage swap (a form of processor storage swap) is attempted before an auxiliary storage swap. The only exceptions to this fundamental rule are: an explicit requested swap; a transition to non-swappable swap; or a swap resulting from a shortage of central storage. All three result in a physical swap to auxiliary storage without preamble.

The attempt to logically swap all address spaces is even tried for wait state swaps such as terminal I/O waits (TSO), long waits and detected waits. As long as the user think time is less then the system think time, which is variable according to the system UIC, then these users will always be logically swapped. Even if the

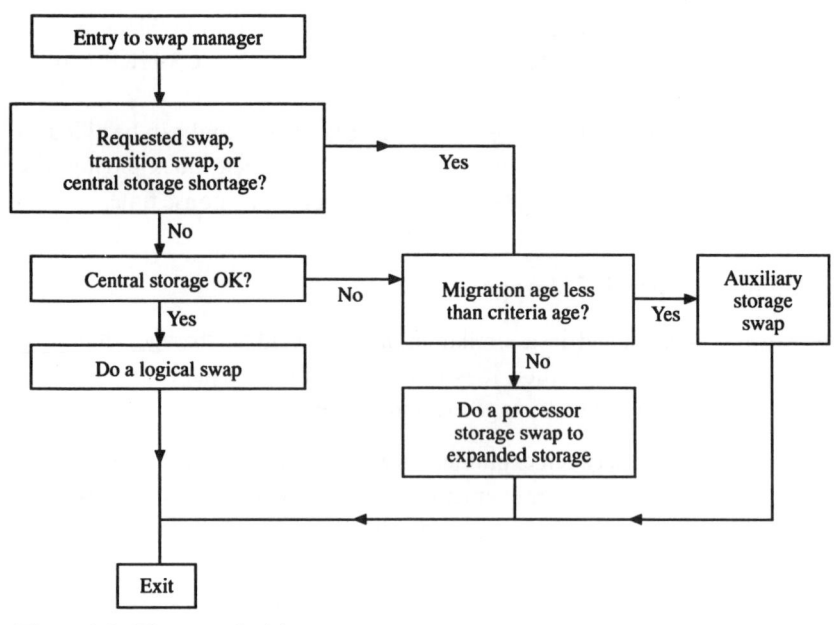

Figure 8.1. The swap decision process.

user think time is greater than the system think time, then logical swapping can still occur, if there is sufficient central storage (as defined by the RSM).

Non-wait-state swaps, such as unilateral swaps, exchange swaps and enqueue swaps, are only logically swapped if there is sufficient central storage, again defined by the RSM.

Swap working sets are 'trimmed' to a maximum of two megabytes in total, unless the primary working set is greater than this size, or storage isolation is in effect for the address space. Storage isolation is expanded at the end of this chapter.

Figure 8.1 summarizes the swapping process. Some of the expressions, e.g. migration age and criteria age, will be defined shortly.

8.5 Swap to expanded storage or auxiliary storage?

Figure 8.1 shows the decision-making process regarding whether an address space or data space is swapped to expanded storage or auxiliary storage. The decision is based upon the criteria age (CA) for a particular type of user. It is measured against the current system migration age (MA), which indicates the stress on expanded storage, modified by the system UIC, which indicates the stress on central storage. If the modified MA is less then the CA, then the swap will be to auxiliary storage. For TSO users there is an additional test. Swap criterion for a TSO user:

$$(MA + UIC - \text{User think time}) < CA?$$
Yes—Swap to auxiliary storage

Storage analysis

	Privileged users	Terminal wait users (TSO)	Other users
Criteria ages			
Working set and trimmed pages (changed and unchanged)	1200	800	1200

(Migration age ↕)

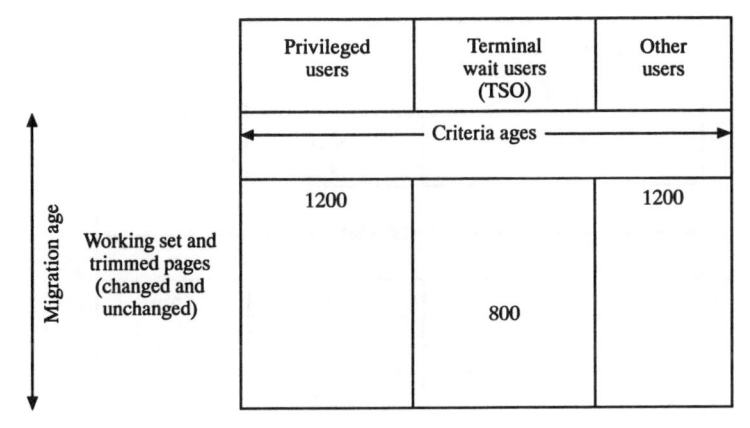

Figure 8.2. Default criteria age settings for swapping.

Swap criterion for other address spaces:

$(MA + UIC) < CA?$
Yes—Swap to auxiliary storage

So you can see that, for a batch user, the test of the CA is against the sum of the current system MA and the current system UIC. The higher the system UIC, the less the strain on central storage, resulting in a higher modified MA. The higher the system MA, the less the pressure on expanded storage, so the address space has a greater chance of being swapped to expanded storage. TSO users are penalized by their think time, as the modified MA is reduced by the length of the think time. The longer it is, the less the chance of the TSO user being swapped to expanded storage.

Figure 8.2 shows the default CA settings in the IEAOPTxx member of SYS1.PARMLIB for each type of user. Most defaults are in fact the same, therefore as the MA falls, so there is a greater likelihood that an address space of any type is swapped to auxiliary storage.

As the MA falls, so the various CAs are 'exposed' above the MA. When this happens, the address spaces and data spaces incorporated within the component whose CA is exposed are swapped to auxiliary storage rather than expanded storage.

8.6 Page steals, virtual fetch pages and VIO pages—page-outs

As stated in Sec. 8.5, the decision to swap to expanded storage instead of auxiliary storage is based upon the CA for that particular type of user, versus the current MA. The MA reflects the average age in seconds (almost) that pages have remained in expanded storage unreferenced. As this average age falls, this reflects the rising pressure on expanded storage. This will be complemented by a rise in the migration rate to auxiliary storage.

	Privileged user or Non-swappable user page	Batch user page	TSO user page
	Index 0	Index 1	Index 2
	←——————— Criteria ages ———————→		
VIO and hiperspace pages	1500	1500	1500
Specific request for page out	1200	1200	1200
Page steal pages		250	250
Virtual Fetch pages	100	100	100
Page steal pages	100		

(left axis: Migration age)

Figure 8.3. Default criteria age settings for various types of page-outs.

Figure 8.3 illustrates this decision-making process for a page to go to either expanded or auxiliary storage. The diagram shows the default CA settings in the IEAOPTxx parameter member, for various page-outs, to establish whether the page goes to either expanded storage or auxiliary storage. The users are described on a wide basis: privileged, non-swappable and common area pages, batch address space pages and TSO user address space pages. You will see that the lower the CA value, the less the likelihood of having to suffer an auxiliary storage page-out. For example, the virtual fetch pages of IMS are unlikely to go to auxiliary storage, as the default CA is set at 100, whereas VIO pages are less likely to go to expanded storage, as the default CA is set at 1500. Remember, as the MA drops, so it exposes users to auxiliary storage page-outs.

If a CA is set to 32 767 for a particular user, then all swaps and page outs will *always* go to auxiliary storage, as the MA will always be lower than 32 767. This is useful when allied to a new function in MVS version 4, whereby a domain can have its own value. Address spaces can be assigned to this domain, and therefore CA is now at the *individual* address space level instead of address space *type* level. This could be used, for example, to assign all swapping and page-outs for (say) test batch work to auxiliary storage, by setting the CA for the domain to which this work is assigned to 32 767 in the IEAOPTxx member.

8.7 Analysis for storage requirements

Now that we have defined our terms and explained exactly what is meant by different types of swaps and page movements, let us analyse our storage requirements proper. It should be noted that we will be analysing for zero paging in our system. You will be unlikely ever to achieve this, but if we aim for it, then we will be doing the best we can. Any DIM requirements will be in addition to the zero paging calculations.

It has been established over many capacity planning studies, by many capacity planning consultants both within and without IBM, that there is a distinct relationship between the utilized relative processor power (URPP) of an application, and the amount of storage used by that application. This has allowed 'standard' storage figures to be arrived at for a particular component of the workload, in order to attempt to achieve zero paging.

Recall that storage is purchased in 32, 64, 128 or even 256 megabyte units on today's mainframe central electronic complexes (CECs), and so the use of the standard amount of storage per component of the total workload is fully justified for our capacity planning purposes, and will in fact lead to good optimum values.

- *The standard amounts of storage per component*
    - —IMS full function   3.50 megabytes per URPP
    - —IMS fast path   4.00 megabytes per URPP
    - —CICS/DL1   3.75 megabytes per URPP
    - —CICS/DB2   5.50 megabytes per URPP
    - —Batch   3.25 megabytes per URPP
    - —TSO   10.00 megabytes per URPP
- *System-related storage*
    - —2.40 megabytes per production system
    - —1.25 megabytes per test system
- *Base storage*
    - —20 megabytes for MVS/ESA version 4
    - —16 megabytes for MVS/ESA version 3
    - —12 megabytes for MVS/XA version 2

8.7.1 Definition of a production system

Production systems include not only those which are clearly defined as such, but also those which incorporate system components that run in their own address space, for example, JES2 or JES3, Sysplex, TCAS, IMS Control Region, GRS, RACF, etc. So do not forget to allow for all of these when you calculate for zero paging.

Figure 8.4 shows a format that can be used to find the total amount of storage required. Once this figure is derived, it has to be broken into central and expanded storage, assuming you wish to use expanded storage.

Production systems:
TSO, JES2, TCAS, RMF, RACF, GRS, 8 MVS system address spaces, CICS/DL1. Total 15.

Test systems:
Batch and TSO
Total 2.

URPP-related storage:

Perf. grp.	Component	Standard	URPP	Req'd megabytes
–	CICS	3.75	40^1	150
2, 42, 999	TSO	10.00	15.23	153
1, 11, 111	Batch	3.25	8.85	29
			Subtotal	332 megabytes

System-related storage:

	Component	Standard	No. of systems	Req'd megabytes
	Production	2.40	15	36
	Test	1.25	2	3
			Subtotal	39

MVS base storage requirements:

	MVS/ESA Version 4		Subtotal	20
			Grand total	**391 megabytes**

Note:
1 Estimate based upon previous use of CICS/DL1 on another system.

Figure 8.4. Calculating the minimum storage requirements (all megabyte calculations are rounded up to the nearest megabyte).

The URPP figures for each application can be taken from the completed CPU analysis worksheet (Fig. 5.11).

CICS/DL1 has been included in the storage requirements, but not yet installed.

Note that the 391 megabytes was originally configured as 128 megabytes of central storage and 320 megabytes of expanded storage. DIM requirements have been added. These include hiperspaces, local shared resource buffers in expanded storage, DLF, etc. Therefore, the storage currently installed on this system is 128 megabytes of central storage, and 512 megabytes of expanded storage. This is why there is so little paging and swapping to auxiliary storage.

How to decide whether you need either additional central or expanded storage will be dealt with later in the chapter.

8.8 How is the storage being used?

Figure 8.5 shows the RMF Monitor I paging activity report (page 2). The lower half of the report indicates how central and expanded storage are currently being used for active and non-swappable address spaces. It does *not* show information

```
                                         PAGING ACTIVITY                                                    PAGE 2
MVS/ESA                    SYSTEM ID MAC1              DATE 28/06/93                               INTERVAL 15.00.00
SP/4.2.0                   RPT VERSION 4.2.1           TIME 09.00.00                               CYCLE 1 SECOND
OPT = IEAOPT00             EXPANDED STORAGE MOVEMENT RATES – IN PAGES PER SECOND

  ESF CONFIGURATION                                                                        HIGH UIC
INSTALLED    ONLINE                                                                          MIN    5                MIGR AGE
                                                                                             MAX   70                  2326
131072       131072                                                                          AVE   31.5                2326
                                                                                                                       2326
                           WRITTEN TO       READ FROM        MIGRATED         FREED              EXPANDED
                           EXP STOR         EXP STOR         FROM             WITHOUT        STORAGE FRAME COUNTS
                                                             EXP STOR         MIGRATION      MIN      MAX      AVE
  TOTAL        RT            1013.7           899.15            3.93            0.15         122791   130884   127162
  PAGES        %             100.0%           100.0%          100.0%
  HIPERSPACE   RT              68.12           10.62            0.00                          22989   28432    25175
  PAGES        %               6.7%             1.2%            0.0%
  VIO          RT               9.25            8.44            0.00                            387    1874     1127
  PAGES        %               0.9%             0.9%            0.0%

                        FRAME AND SLOT COUNTS

                    CENTRAL STORAGE              EXPANDED STORAGE             LOCAL PAGE DATA SET SLOT COUNTS
(181 SAMPLES)    MIN    MAX      AVE         MIN      MAX      AVE                              MIN      MAX      AVE
TOTAL FRAMES    32232  32232    32232       131072   131072   131072       AVAILABLE SLOTS    226846   232349   230297
  SQA            2350   2368     2361           51       53       51       VIO SLOTS               0        0        0
  LPA             899   1028      958           57      187      127
  CSA             435    630      600            0      192       26       NON-VIO SLOTS      37801    43304    39852
  LSQA           3175   4096     3625         1713     1803     1745
  REGIONS + SWA 20792  22893    22373       122788   130569   127009       BAD SLOTS              0        0        0
  AVAILABLE        74   1857      309          188     8281     3910
                                                                           TOTAL SLOTS        270150   270150   270150
FIXED FRAMES   10809  11831    11292
  NUCLEUS       1003   1003     1003
  SQA           2346   2364     2357
  LPA            104    107      104
  CSA            155    156      155
  LSQA          3014   3915     3453
  REGIONS + SWA 4140   4367     4218
  BELOW 16 MEG  1720   2024     1830
```

Figure 8.5. How are central and expanded storage being used?

for processor storage swapped users (logically swapped and expanded storage swapped).

If you wish to see information on *all* address spaces, then this can be done by using the RMF Monitor II address space data (ASD) report. The best way of using RMF Monitor II is as a TSO user. The current location of each address space is indicated by the CL field, after you have entered RMFMON and selected ASD and the following values can be seen:

- IN   Swapped in and active
- NS   Non-swappable
- WM   Processor storage swapped (logically or expanded)
- WT   Auxiliary storage swapped

Only the first three categories (IN, NS and WM) are of interest in this analysis.

Returning to the RMF Monitor I paging activity report (Fig. 8.5), Fig. 8.6 shows the information extracted from this report, indicating the current use of central and expanded storage. The lower half of Fig. 8.5 is highlighted, as this is the information we need at the moment. The AVE columns are used to extract the values. Do not use the MAX column, as this will mean that you overconfigure storage, because the maximum values are extreme in the sense that they are peak values.

Note that in Fig. 8.6:

- Available central storage relative to available expanded storage is low.
- Very little expanded storage used by the system, only 204 frames in total.
- There is no pressure on expanded storage, as reflected by the available frames (3910 frames).

	Central storage frames (average)	Expanded storage frames (average)
Total frames installed	32 768	131 072
SQA	2 361	51
LPA	958	127
CSA	600	26
Nucleus	1 003	0
High storage area (HSA)	536 (32 768 − 32 232)	0
System totals	**5 458**	**204**
LSQA	3 625	1 745
Regions + SWA	22 373	127 009
Private totals	**25 998**	**128 754**
Grand totals	**31 456**	**128 958**
Available	309	3 910

Figure 8.6. Current use of central and expanded storage.

8.9 How do we find out whether we need additional central or expanded storage?

To ascertain whether we need either central or expanded storage, we must monitor both of them via the RMF Monitor I paging activity report, page 2. Figure 8.7 shows this report, with the top half highlighted. Let us first of all look at how to monitor central storage, and then consider expanded storage.

8.9.1 Monitoring central storage

The pressure on central storage is indicated by the value of the average UIC, which ranges from 0 to 255. Each frame has its own UIC, and the RMF Monitor I paging activity report in Fig. 8.7 shows the minimum, maximum and the average. The UIC is the value in seconds that a frame has remained unreferenced, and you will see in the top right-hand corner of Fig. 8.7 the minimum, maximum and average values referred to. For capacity planning measurement purposes we always use the average. The average is calculated periodically using the current value and the previous average, therefore there is a smoothing effect, and the average becomes more representative the longer the system is up.

A UIC value approaching zero means that the pressure on central storage is very high, as the reference frequency is high and the paging rate is rising. In addition, the movement to and from central and expanded storage will be rising, but we will consider that in a moment. A value nearer to 255 shows that there is nothing to worry about regarding the amount of central storage installed. This will be reflected by low paging rates and lower movement between central and expanded storage.

What are the 'trigger for action' rates? An average UIC of 30 is normally accepted as the lower bound. When the average reaches this value, then central storage should be on order. *Never* let the average UIC remain consistently at or below 10, particularly if you do not have expanded storage installed. When this value is reached, the SRM gets involved and stops address spaces starting, and even stops some address spaces that are already active. In other words, the system is approaching the 'out of control' situation.

If you do not have expanded storage installed, then monitoring the average UIC and the overall paging rate to the page/swap data sets is all you can do. The page data set criteria and calculations were established in Chapter 7.

What are our UIC values and what do they tell us?

The minimum is 5, the maximum is 70 and the average is 31.5. What does this tell us? Disregarding the minimum and maximum, the average of 31.5 indicates that we are getting some pressure on central storage. It is very close to our accepted lower bound of 30, and so it would be prudent to get at least another 64 megabytes

PAGING ACTIVITY

MVS/ESA
SP/4.2.0
OPT = IEAOPT00

SYSTEM ID MAC1
RPT VERSION 4.2.1
EXPANDED STORAGE MOVEMENT RATES – IN PAGES PER SECOOND

DATE 28/06/93
TIME 09.00.00

PAGE 2
INTERVAL 15.00.00
CYCLE 1 SECOND

ESF CONFIGURATION								
INSTALLED	ONLINE					HIGH UIC		MIGR AGE
131 072	131 072					MIN 5		2326
						MAX 70		2326
						AVE 31.5		2326

		WRITTEN TO EXP STOR	READ FROM EXP STOR	MIGRATED FROM EXP STOR	FREED WITHOUT MIGRATION	EXPANDED STORAGE FRAME COUNTS		
						MIN	MAX	AVE
TOTAL PAGES	RT	1013.7	899.15	3.93	0.15	122 791	130 884	127 162
	%	100.0%	100.0%	100.0%				
HIPERSPACE PAGES	RT	68.12	10.62	0.00		22 989	28 432	25 175
	%	6.7%	1.2%	0.0%				
VIO PAGES	RT	9.25	8.44	0.00		387	1874	1127
	%	0.9%	0.9%	0.0%				

FRAME AND SLOT COUNTS

	CENTRAL STORAGE			EXPANDED STORAGE			LOCAL PAGE DATA SET SLOT COUNTS		
(181 SAMPLES)	MIN	MAX	AVE	MIN	MAX	AVE		MIN	MAX	AVE
TOTAL FRAMES	32 232	32 232	32 232	131 072	131 072	131 072	AVAILABLE SLOTS	226 846	232 349	230 297
SQA	2350	2368	2361	51	53	51	VIO SLOTS	0	0	0
LPA	899	1028	958	57	187	127				
CSA	435	630	600	0	192	26	NON-VIO SLOTS	37 801	43 304	39 852
LSQA	3175	4096	3625	1713	1803	1745				
REGIONS + SWA	20 792	22 893	22 373	122 788	130 569	127 009	BAD SLOTS	0	0	0
AVAILABLE	74		309	188	8281	3910				
		1857								
FIXED FRAMES	10 809	11 831	11 292				TOTAL SLOTS	270 150	270 150	270 150
NUCLEUS	1003	1003	1003							
SQA	2346	2364	2357							
LPA	104	107	104							
CSA	155	156	155							
LSQA	3014	3915	3453							
REGIONS + SWA	4140	4367	4218							
BELOW 16 MEG	1720	2024	1830							

Figure 8.7. The paging activity report.

on order. As CICS is to be installed at a later date, then 128 megabytes would be better, as this would ensure that DIM storage is not eroded.

This may seem to be unjustified, but recall that in Chapter 7 we found that our page/swap rate was 80 pages per second, requiring 6 page data sets (no swap data sets installed or required). This value was found by calculating that there are 8 pages per page/swap I/O, and that there are 10 page/swap I/Os per second. We also know from Chapter 7 that only three real swaps went to the page data sets throughout the whole period (see Fig. 7.13), therefore we can state that 80 pages per second is virtually all paging I/O as near as makes no difference.

If we allow for the VIO and hiperspace movement in the future of 100 pages per second each, then we need 6 page data sets. That is why we have 6 installed, based upon our upper bound paging rate of 480 pages per second, arrived at in Chapter 7. It would certainly give response times a boost if we could reduce the page stealing which clearly occurs, but is additional central storage *really* justified? Let us look a bit further in order to convince ourselves that central storage is indeed required.

If both central and expanded storage are installed

Continuing our analysis of central storage, if both central and expanded storage are installed, then in addition to monitoring the UIC to measure the intensity of central storage use, you will also monitor the rate at which pages move between central and expanded storage. This rate is another indication of the pressure on central storage.

There are two fields on Fig. 8.7 which show the information we require on page movements between central and expanded storage: WRITTEN TO EXP STOR and READ FROM EXP STOR. Each field consists of three pairs of entries: TOTAL PAGES, HIPERSPACE PAGES and VIO PAGES. Each pair of entries consists of two rows of information: the 'rate per second' and the 'percentage of the total' for each subset. The 'total pages' rows include VIO, hiperspace and application data/code, but the application data/code is not shown separately; it is obtained by subtracting the VIO and hiperspace values from the total, if required.

The sum total of the pages read from and written to expanded storage is collectively defined as the pages that are *moved*. As you will see, we can set an upper bound to this total which we are prepared to tolerate.

What are our rates of movement between central and expanded storage?

The simple way of extracting the required information is to show the subset of the fields from Fig. 8.7. The third column 'total pages moved' is not included in Fig. 8.7, but is added here in Table 8.1 to show the information we require for completeness. The figures are rounded to the nearest integer.

Table 8.1. Page movements between central and expanded storage

		Written to exp. storage	Read from exp. storage	Total pages moved
Total pages	Rate	1013	899	1912
	%	100%	100%	100%
Hiperspace pages	Rate	68	11	79
	%	6.7%	1.2%	7.9%
VIO pages	Rate	9	8	17
	%	0.9%	0.9%	1.8%
Totals		1090	918	2008

As you can see from Table 8.1, there was some VIO and hiperspace movement in addition to the normal application data and code, the total movement being 2008 pages per second. How much is this total rate a reflection of pressure on central storage?

Note also that all expanded storage (512 megabytes) is online, as can be seen from Fig. 8.7.

What is an acceptable rate of movement between central and expanded storage?

The amount of movement between central and expanded storage is dictated by a criterion stated by you, the system designer. The question you must ask yourself is, 'How much processor power am I prepared to use on this function of moving pages between central and expanded storage?' All movement of pages uses processor power, and we therefore need to know how much is being used to execute the movement.

So, let us suppose we say that we are prepared to allow 5 per cent of our processor engine(s) power to be used for this function. Five per cent is a reasonable initial upper bound for this, but more on this later. As you do this more often, so will you get a feel for your configuration's limits, but none the less, 5 per cent is a good starting figure.

It takes between 70 and 75 microseconds (0.000 070–0.000 075 seconds) to *synchronously* transfer a page between central and expanded storage (and vice versa). Knowing this, it is possible to work out how many pages a second this represents. Using the slower speed to ensure we do not overstate our case:

$1/0.000\,075 = 13\,333$ pages per second

or

133 pages per 1/100th of a second (1 percent of the processor engine(s) power).

If we allow 5 per cent of the processor to be used, then:

$5 \times 133 = 665$ pages per second as the upper bound *on a uni-processor*.

As each engine in a multi-processor can execute this function in parallel, then on a processor with (say) three engines, the upper bound will be:

$3 \times 5 \times 133 = 1995$ pages per second on a three-engine processor

Thus on our system, we are prepared to tolerate a page movement of 665 pages per second between central and expanded storage.

Summary—more central storage required

Now we can confirm that we will be justified in installing another 64/128 megabytes of central storage. Our acceptable upper bound is 665 pages per second, representing 5 per cent of the processor's engine(s). We are using $(2008/665) \times 5 = 15.1$ per cent of the processor for the function—three times what we are prepared to accept. Adding more expanded storage will make no difference, as the movement is initiated by the pressure on central storage, not expanded storage.

Monitoring the amount of processor power used for *movement* between central and expanded storage has another ramification. We stated that 30 was the lower bound beyond which we should not allow the average UIC to fall, but if expanded storage is installed, then we can allow this value to fall a little. An average UIC of 25 will be acceptable in this case, as excessive paging will go to expanded storage, not result in real paging I/O to the page data sets—but *never* let it reach 10!

Why can we let the UIC fall? The reason for being a bit more benevolent towards central or expanded movement is because the page faults to and from expanded storage are managed *synchronously*. This means that the application is not suspended while the page fault is resolved; the page is fetched from expanded storage by code which is invoked on behalf of the application, by a branch to the code that effects the function, thereby removing entries to the MVS dispatcher.

The alternative is the normal method of effecting a paging I/O, which is *asynchronous*. This means that the application is suspended while the page fault is resolved. The I/O supervisor is dispatched to start the page fetch function, and there will probably be at least three entries into the MVS dispatcher, as another application or user will be dispatched while the page is fetched. All this adds time to the overall transaction response time. This is not the case with the synchronous page fault to and from expanded storage, which takes about 70 to 75 microseconds per page, and so results in shorter transaction response times; less time in MVS's code, more time in user's code, hence increased productivity of MVS/ESA.

8.9.2 Monitoring expanded storage

As with central storage, there are two values to monitor in order to monitor expanded storage correctly. These are the *average migration age* and the *page migration rate*. We will deal with the migration age first, and again, we will need Fig. 8.7.

The migration age

The migration age (MA) is shown at the top right-hand corner of Fig. 8.7 and, as with the UIC, it has three values: minimum, maximum and average. Again, as with the UIC, we always use the average in our capacity planning computations. Finally, as with the UIC, there is an MA for each frame. The MA values are incremented internally about every $\frac{2}{3}$ second. Therefore multiplying the average MA values by 0.67 will give the values in seconds, since a page in expanded storage was referenced on average.

When the number of frames on the expanded storage available queue drops below the lower bound of the MCCAECTH parameter in IEAOPTxx (default 150, 300), frames are stolen from address spaces. The selection is based upon the average MA, and the contents of the page frame are migrated to auxiliary storage. There is a direct relationship between the *falling* average MA, and the *rising* migration rate of pages from expanded storage to auxiliary storage.

This is similar to the way the average UIC is used as the criterion to select page frames in central storage. When the number of frames on the central storage available queue drops below the lower bound of the MCCAFCTH parameter in IEAOPTxx (default values are 50, 100), central storage frames are stolen from address spaces.

Recall also, that as the average MA falls, so the criteria age (CA) of different components of the workload is exposed, thus stopping those components from using expanded storage; they are forced to use auxiliary storage for their paging.

You can see VIO and hiperspace movements to and from central and expanded storage on Fig. 8.7, and you can see that there is little pressure on expanded storage. Even hiperspaces are going to expanded storage (68.12 pages per second, representing 6.7 per cent of the total).

What are our migration age values?
The MA values extracted from Figs. 8.7 and 8.8 are:

- Minimum migration age = 2326
- Maximum migration age = 2326
- Average migration age = 2326

What does this tell—and what is a reasonable value? An average MA of 150 is about as low as you should let this value go. This would in fact represent $150 \times 0.67 = 100$ seconds on average between references. As you can see, our value is way above this, about 26 minutes between references ($(2326 \times 0.67)/60$). Therefore it would appear that there is no pressure on expanded storage, but, the migration age should always be evaluated in conjunction with the migration rate, and so we will cover this point now.

PAGING ACTIVITY

MVS/ESA
SP/4.2.0
OPT = IEAOPT00

SYSTEM ID MAC1
RPT VERSION 4.2.1

DATE 28/06/93
TIME 09.00.00

PAGE 2
INTERVAL 15.00.00
CYCLE 1 SECOND

EXPANDED STORAGE MOVEMENT RATES – IN PAGES PER SECOOND

ESF CONFIGURATION					HIGH UIC		
INSTALLED	ONLINE				MIN	5	
131 072	131 072				MAX	70	
					AVE	31.5	

		WRITTEN TO EXP STOR	READ FROM EXP STOR	MIGRATED FROM EXP STOR	FREED WITHOUT MIGRATION	STORAGE FRAME COUNTS		
						MIN	MAX	AVE
TOTAL PAGES	RT	1013.7	899.15	3.93	0.15	122 791	130 884	127 162
	%	100.0%	100.0%	100.0%				
HIPERSPACE PAGES	RT	68.12	10.62	0.00		22 989	28 432	25 175
	%	6.7%	1.2%	0.0%				
VIO PAGES	RT	9.25	8.44	0.00		387	1874	1127
	%	0.9%	0.9%	0.0%				

							MIGR AGE
							2326
							2326
							2326.0

FRAME AND SLOT COUNTS

	CENTRAL STORAGE			EXPANDED STORAGE			LOCAL PAGE DATA SET SLOT COUNTS		
(181 SAMPLES)	MIN	MAX	AVE	MIN	MAX	AVE		MIN	MAX	AVE
TOTAL FRAMES	32 232	32 232	32 232	131 072	131 072	131 072	AVAILABLE SLOTS	226 846	232 349	230 297
SQA	2350	2368	2361	51	53	51	VIO SLOTS	0	0	0
LPA	899 1028	958	57	187	127					
CSA	435	630	600	0	192	26	NON-VIO SLOTS	37 801	43 304	39 852
LSQA	3175	4096	3625	1713	1803	1745				
REGIONS + SWA	20 792	22 893	22 373	122 788	130 569	127 009	BAD SLOTS	0	0	0
AVAILABLE	74	1857	309	188	8281	3910				
FIXED FRAMES	10 809	11 831	11 292				TOTAL SLOTS	270 150	270 150	270 150
NUCLEUS	1003	1003	1003							
SQA	2346	2364	2357							
LPA	104	107	104							
CSA	155	156	155							
LSQA	3014	3915	3453							
REGIONS + SWA	4140	4367	4218							
BELOW 16 MEG	1720	2024	1830							

Figure 8.8. Monitoring central and expanded storage.

The migration rate

Use Fig. 8.8 for this analysis. Figure 8.8 has a column named MIGRATED FROM EXP STOR. This represents the migration of pages from expanded storage to auxiliary storage, as a result of pressure on expanded storage (we will see what reflects this pressure in a moment). All migration from expanded storage is to auxiliary storage, via central storage; there is no direct path from expanded storage to the DASD subsystem.

There are three pairs of entries associated with the 'migrated from expanded storage' field: VIO PAGES, HIPERSPACE PAGES and TOTAL PAGES. Like the movement to and from central and expanded storage, each of these pairs shows the 'rate per second' and the 'percentage of the total' that this component makes up.

The rate per second and percentage of the application data/code are not shown separately, but included in the total. That is why the value in the TOTAL PAGES field is 3.93 and 100 per cent. As there is no VIO or hiperspace movement from expanded storage to auxiliary storage, then all of this value (3.93 pages per second) is made up of application data/code, and no VIO or hiperspace data.

A rate of 3.93 (say 4) pages per second is very low; even the VIO and hiperspace are being left alone! This suggests that there is more than sufficient expanded storage installed. Remember though, CICS is coming, and so a new analysis will be required when it is installed.

What is an upper bound for migration rate?
As with pages moved to and from central and expanded storage, there is an upper *rate* of migration from expanded to auxiliary storage above which we cannot tolerate, and which should be taken as an indication of the requirement for additional expanded storage. The manner in which this is arrived at is a little more complex than for page movement between central and expanded storage; it has to be forced out.

8.10   Page migration and page management

Migrating pages from expanded storage to auxiliary storage is page *migration*, a form of movement, and as such there is a cost in processor cycles to *migrate* pages. In addition, however, there is a cost in processor cycles to *manage* the pages in central and expanded storage. Managing pages includes the functions of scanning the frames in central and expanded storage, in order to find out the UIC and migration age of the individual frames and to calculate the average.

We can find out what the time is to manage pages and convert it to processor seconds. Once we know this value, we can subtract it from the upper limit of time that we are prepared for our engine(s) to use on combined page management and migration, thereby forcing out the amount of time that we are prepared to allow on page migration, and in turn, changing this into a page rate. It sounds complex,

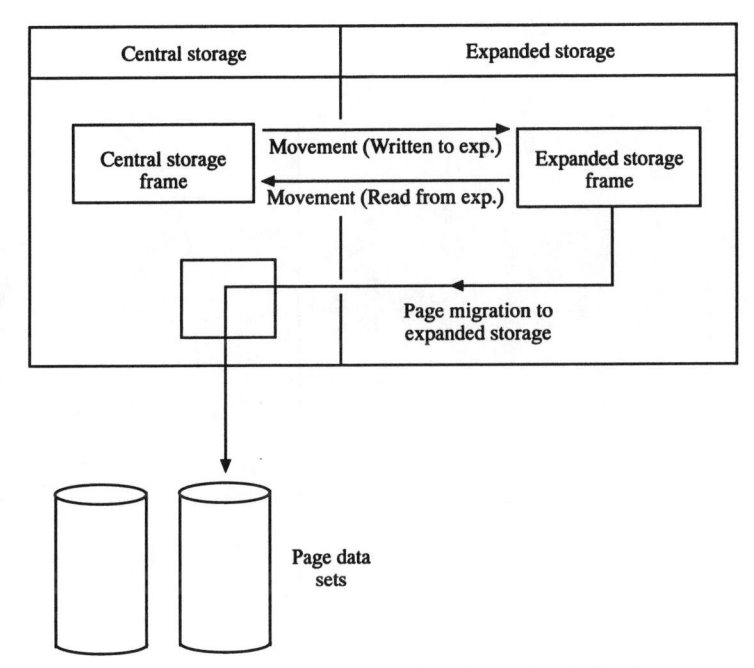

Figure 8.9. Page movement and page migration—the distinction.

but let us see how this is done; it is not so bad really. Figure 8.9 illustrates the difference between page movement and page migration.

8.10.1 Calculating the processor time used on page management

The SUs absorbed on the function of page management in central and expanded storage are recorded as SRB time in performance group 0. MVS version 4.2 shows this as processor seconds as well, therefore we do not have to go through the conversion exercise, although you know how to do this if you have to, for example, if you have an earlier version of MVS installed.

Using Fig. 8.10 (the WAR for PG 0) we can extract the value in seconds directly from the RMF Monitor I report. Do not divide this by the capture ratio, as this would distort our criterion. Our value is 18.4 seconds. This could have been calculated by dividing the SRB SUs of 214 659 by the service definition coefficient of 10 and the number of SUs per second (1162.3):

$$214\,659/(10 \times 1162.3) = 18.47 \text{ seconds}$$

18.4 seconds as a percentage of the processor use is:

$$(18.4/900) \times 100 = 2.04 \text{ per cent}$$

Therefore 2.04 per cent of the processor engine(s) (of the single and only engine in our case) is being used for page management. We can do nothing about this, and

WORKLOAD ACTIVITY

```
MVS/ESA                    SYSTEM ID MAC1                        DATE 28/06/93              INTERVAL 15.00.000
SP4.2.0                    RPT VERSION 4.2.1                     TIME 09.00.000             IPS = IEAIPS00

OPT = IEAPT00              REPORT BY PERFORMANCE GROUP           SERVICE DEFINITION COEFFICIENTS   SU/SEC = 1162.3
ICS = IEAICS00                     PERIOD                        IOC = 5.0   CPU = 10.0   SRB = 10.0   MSO = 0.100
```

PGN	PGP	DMN	TIME SLICE GROUP	INTERVAL SERVICE		AVERAGE AVE TRX TCB + SRB	ABSORPTION SERV RATE SECONDS, %	PAGE-IN RATES	RATES		STORAGE		TRANSACTIONS		AVE TRANS TIME, STD DEVIATION HHH.MM.SS.TTT	
0000	1	000	**	IOC =	1435	ABSRPTN	109	SINGLE	0.00		AVERAGE	309.92	AVE	5.14	TRX	000.00.00.000
				CPU =	260 715	TRX SERV	109	BLOCK	0.00		TOTAL	1595.7	MPL	5.14	SD	000.00.00.000
				MSO =	28 413	TCB	22.4	HSP	0.00		CENTRAL	1214.7	ENDED	0		
				SRB =	**214 659**	SRB	18.4	HSP MISS	0.00		EXPAND	381.08	ENDED/SEC	0.00	QUE	000.00.00.000
				TOT =	505 222	TCB + SRB%	4.5	EXP SINGL	0.33				#SWAPS	43		
				PER SEC =	561			EXP BLK	0.00						TOT	000.00.00.000

Figure 8.10. The WAR for performance group 0—SRB information.

so we must accept this amount of our single engine being used for this function. We can, however, state what our upper bound of engine percentage is for both page management and migration, and subtract the management time from this value leaving the amount of time for page migration.

Assuming that we let our upper bound for managing and migrating be 5 per cent (again this is a reasonable initial value), then this leaves $5 - 2.04 = 2.96$ per cent available for page migration. We must now find out what page rate 2.96 per cent represents.

To move 133 pages per second between central and expanded storage uses 1 per cent of each engine (only one in our case), therefore $2.96 \times 133 \times 1 = 394$ pages per second as the upper bound that we are prepared to tolerate. The current rate is 4 pages per second and so we are well within our calculated criterion; we do not need expanded storage, only central storage.

8.10.2 Summary

Central storage page movement to and from expanded storage

We have stated that 5 per cent is the upper bound of processor time that we are prepared to tolerate for moving pages between central and expanded storage. We have found that, in fact, we are using more than three times that amount of the processor engine for this function—15.1 per cent. This fact, allied to our low UIC of 31.5, which is very close to our lower acceptable bound of 30 (possibly 25), indicates that it is time to order another 64/128 megabytes of central storage.

Expanded storage page migration to auxiliary storage

We have also calculated that we are prepared to allow 2.96 per cent of the processor engine to be used for migrating pages from expanded storage to auxiliary storage (via central storage). We have found that we are using a lot less than that $((4/133) \times 100) = 0.03$ per cent, in fact. This indicates that there is no need for more expanded storage, as we would expect if we look at the amount installed; 512 megabytes, as opposed to only 128 megabytes of central storage. Even the VIO and hiperspace pages are not only going to expanded storage, but they are also staying there and not being migrated to auxiliary storage. This is exceptionally benevolent to VIO and hiperspace pages. Remember though, CICS is coming!

Managing central and expanded storage

We have calculated that we are using 2.04 per cent of the processor to manage central and expanded storage. This allowed us to arrive at the expanded storage migration value of 2.96 per cent, by subtracting it from our upper bound for managing and migrating pages of 5 per cent. There is nothing we can do about the 2.04 per cent used for this function; we calculate it merely to derive the migration rate value.

8.10.3 Additional storage—to buy or not to buy

The decision whether to buy additional storage, either central or expanded, can be simplified by comparing the price of the additional storage against the amortized value of the CEC. For example, if the current value of the CEC is 2 000 000 units of currency, and the current cost of the additional storage is (say) 100 000, then the cost of storage as a percentage of the written value of the processor is 5 per cent.

Therefore, the break-even point is when 5 per cent of the CEC's engine(s) is (are) being used for managing and migrating pages when considering expanded storage, or 5 per cent for moving pages when looking at central storage.

8.11 Storage isolation

We have looked at a number of features to help us control the use of storage, for example:

- System MPL adjustment via page fault rate (Chapter 7)
- Page data set configuration (Chapter 7)
- Swap data set configuration (if necessary) (Chapter 7)
- The use of the criteria age versus the migration age (this chapter)

Now let us look at another method of controlling the use of storage, *storage isolation* (SI). SI is very useful for applications that need fast response times, for example CICS, IMS or favoured TSO users. If there is a lull in the transaction rate, it is possible that CICS pages can be stolen. When a transaction arrives, there will be a delay while there is momentary heavy paging for the necessary pages, before the transaction can be processed. To avoid the pages being stolen, CICS can be protected by SI.

SI is invoked by parameters in the IEAIPSxx member of SYS1.PARMLIB, and allows you to state that a working set will be protected. This working set is made up of pages in both central and expanded storage, and is protected by ensuring that it does not drop below a certain size, except in very exceptional circumstances. The rationale is that as the paging rate for the application rises, you allow the target working set size to increase. As the paging rate falls, indicating less activity for the application, the target working set size can be allowed to fall. The target moves up and down within the minimum and maximum working set sizes, as stated with the PWSS parameter. In other words, you are stopping your application's pages from being stolen or trimmed, beyond the point that protects your application's response time.

Use RMF Monitor II to monitor the paging rate and working set sizes of the applications you wish to protect, then set up the necessary values in the IEAIPSxx member. See Fig. 8.11 for an illustration of SI.

Figure 8.11. Storage isolation—the parameters.

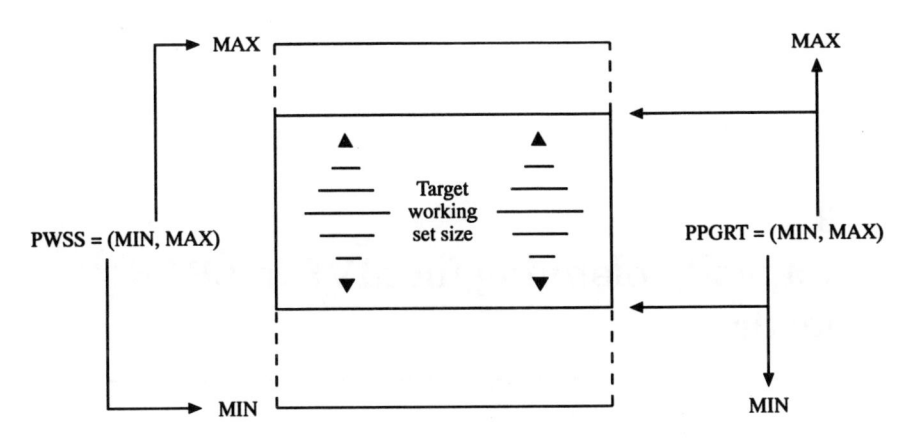

Target working set consists of pages in central and expanded storage

8.11.1 How SI works

As PPGRT (the private page rate) falls, so does the target working set size fall, down to a lower bound stated by the 'min' value of PWSS. Conversely, as it rises then so does the target working set rise up to the maximum stated by the 'max' value. It is possible to have an 'open ended' maximum target working set size, by replacing the 'max' value in the PWSS parameter by '*', for example PWSS = (60,*).

The value of 60 in this parameter is a reasonable value for TSO first period, until you ascertain what a more finely tuned value should be. This can be obtained from the workload activity report for the performance group 'storage' field. This field shows the average number of frames per address space, and the breakdown into central and expanded storage frames. Notice that 60 is a multiple of 30, which is the burst size that the ASM uses for IBM 3380 devices that are being used for page data sets (there are no swap data sets!). Make the value 64 for IBM 3390 devices (or a multiple of 32).

If it is necessary, page stealing will take place first of all, for pages beyond the maximum working set size stated in the 'max' value of PWSS, and so it is essential to ensure that the maximum value is reasonable, otherwise all the good work of SI is negated. Use '*' to ensure that the target rises to the 'correct' value; this can be ascertained by RMF Monitor I or II. As a last resort only will stealing be invoked for a working set down to the target working set level.

The common area can also be protected in the same manner by the CWSS and CPGRT parameters. These work in exactly the same manner as PWSS and PPGRT.

9
Capacity planning for MVS in LPAR mode

9.1 Introduction

There are now three ways of dividing a CEC. First, physical partitioning (as reflected in Figs. 9.1, 9.2, 9.3), which involves splitting a CEC along power boundaries into two separate processors, each capable of running a different operating system, and each side having its own dedicated DASD (which can be SHARED), channels and storage. Secondly, we have software partitioning, which is made possible by combining the LPAR PR/SM feature with the multiple high-performance guests (MHPG) feature of VM/XA and VM/ESA. This allows the V=R machine to be supplemented by up to five V=F machines, to give six production partitions per physical image, in addition to any number of V=V partitions for test purposes. If a CEC is physically divided, then each side can have 6 production partitions, giving 12 partitions in total. This will be expanded in Chapter 10. Finally, we now have partitioning via the LPAR PR/SM feature.

Logical partitioning (LPAR) is the ability to run multiple operating system images in one CEC. IBM introduced the PR/SM feature (Processor Resource/Systems Manager), which allows IBM ES/3090 models (primarily S and J models), and IBM ES/9000 (all models), to be divided into up to 7 separate logical partitions (10 with MVS/ESA V4.3 on 520-based processors). Each partition supports a standalone MVS or VM (V=V) operating system and its environment of DASD, channels and storage. Channels and storage are dedicated to the partition, but engines, along with their associated vector facility (VF), can be either dedicated or shared with other partitions. There is the capability of moving storage between partitions, but it cannot be shared. If an engine is dedicated to a partition, then it cannot be used by any other partition, and it reduces the pool of available engines that can be used by other shared partitions.

This chapter will cover the fundamentals of PR/SM mode, and the points that are important for capacity planners and performance analysts. It will explain the RMF Monitor I partition data report, which is required for LPAR analysis.

9.2 RMF Monitor I and LPAR mode

Before we start, it is essential that you ensure that the correct PTFs are installed on your RMF Monitor I, otherwise the results from RMF Monitor I are 'unpredictable', as IBM would say!

RMF uses the Systems Management Facility (SMF) records 70–79 for the source of its data. SMF type 70 records produced by RMF Monitor I running in an LPAR logical partition, with the LPAR PTFs installed, can be processed only by an RMF Monitor I post-processor which also has the LPAR PTFs installed. The second RMF Monitor I can be on a different processor, and the other processor need not have the PR/SM feature installed. If you do not ensure that this is the case, the following will happen:

- The CPU report will show 100 per cent busy, no matter what it really is, and
- If you request a CPU duration report, you will get an 0C4 ABEND.

9.2.1 Other manufacturers' logical partitioning

- *Multiple Domain Facility (MDF)* This is offered by Amdahl, and is a hardware feature, which offers multiple MVS support within one CEC, without the need for VM.
- *Multiple Logical Processor Facility (MLPF)* This is a similar software offering from Hitachi Data Systems (HDS). This feature requires IBM's LPAR management time support feature when using IBM's RMF.
- *Capacity planning tools for LPAR mode* IBM's LPAR/CE and Amdahl's MDFCAL assist in the defining of required configurations within a logical partition, but do not rely solely on these, as they are fairly insensitive.

9.3 The capture ratio—general point

One of the most important pieces of information that we require in order to capacity plan is the capture ratio. This is what we have to calculate in any environment, and it is no different in LPAR mode. Therefore, everything we do is designed to help us arrive at an accurate capture ratio.

9.4 CPU utilization and LPAR mode

You will find that LPAR mode is very accurate as far as CPU utilization is concerned, particularly at the higher utilization end. LPAR overhead is recorded separately from system and application CPU use, providing you have the management time APAR OY36668 installed, so ensure that you have this on your system.

The LPAR overhead mainly consists of setup and waiting for work. The busier the system, the lower is the LPAR overhead, and so RMF Monitor I CPU utilization is almost 1:1 for busy systems, particularly in those partitions running with a dedicated engine or engines.

Partitions running in shared mode (sharing engines with other partitions) will show a higher proportion of CPU being used for LPAR management, but again, the LPAR use reduces the busier the partition is.

The number of engines available to shared partitions comprises those left after the dedicated engines have been 'removed'. For example, on a CEC with six engines and four partitions, if two of the engines are dedicated to one partition, then only four engines are available to be shared among the other three partitions. In addition, these three sharing partitions can only be set up with a maximum of four engines—they cannot have five or six.

The sharing of the engines is carried out on either a time-slice basis, or is event driven, whichever occurs first, unlike Amdahl's MDF which is just time-sliced.

9.5 The RMF Monitor I partition data report for LPAR mode

RMF Monitor I uses the partition data report for two purposes: to report on the overall use of the physical processor; and to report on the use of the logical processors in each logical partition that is active.

RMF Monitor I reports on the total utilization of the physical CPUs for each partition. This data is found in the PHYSICAL PROCESSORS, EFFECTIVE and TOTAL columns in Fig. 9.1. It also reports on the logical use of the CPUs by each partition in the LOGICAL PROCESSORS, EFFECTIVE and TOTAL columns. Each engine in a shared partition is referred to as a 'logical processor'.

RMF Monitor I shows the physical use of the engines in a partition as a percentage of the number of engines in the partition. For example, if there are two engines (shared) in a partition on a CEC with six engines, and the busy percentage is shown as 40 per cent, then this represents 40 per cent of two engines. Thus in reality, this is 40 per cent of $\frac{1}{3}$ of the available total capacity; $0.4 \times 0.33 = 0.132$. The partition is in fact using 13.2 per cent of the total available physical capacity. This will be expanded in more detail later.

To turn the logical partition CPU busy into physical CPU busy (real use of the engines), divide the busy percentage for the logical partition by the real number of engines (six in the above case), and multiply by the number of logical processors in the partition (two in the above case).

9.6 Performance aspects of LPAR

There are a number of reasons for reduced effectiveness under LPAR mode. As previously stated, if engines are dedicated to a partition, then there is very little LPAR overhead. On the other hand, the more the engines are shared, the greater is the LPAR overhead. In other words, the greater the ratio of the total of all logical processors in all partitions (which is variable depending on the number of

PARTITION DATA REPORT

MVS/ESA SP 4.2.0	SYSTEM ID MAC1 RPT VERSION 4.2.1	DATE 28/06/93 TIME 11.15.35	INTERVAL 4.59.999 CYCLE 1.000 SECONDS

MVS PARTITION NAME   BAM3
NUMBER OF CONFIGURED PARTITIONS   4
NUMBER OF PHYSICAL PROCESSORS   3 (IBM ES/9021 MODEL 580)
WAIT COMPLETION   NO
DISPATCH INTERVAL   DYNAMIC

PARTITION DATA				LOGICAL PARTITION PROCESSOR DATA			AVERAGE PROCESSOR UTILIZATION PERCENTAGES				
					Logical Processor information				Physical Proc'r Info.		
					DISPATCH TIME DATA		LOGICAL PROCESSORS			PHYSICAL PROCESSORS	
NAME	STATUS	WEIGHTS	CAPPING	NUMBER OF LOG PRCRS	EFFECTIVE	TOTAL	EFFECTIVE	TOTAL	LPAR MGMT	EFFECTIVE	TOTAL
BAM1	A	DED	NO	1	00.04.59.534	00.04.59.907	99.84	99.97	0.04	33.28	33.32
BAM2	A	1	YES	2	00.00.24.224	00.00.27.294	4.03	4.54	0.34	2.69	3.03
BAM3	**A**	**10**	**NO**	**2**	**00.05.24.812**	**00.05.25.594**	**54.13**	**54.26**	**0.08**	**36.09**	**36.17**
BAM4	A	10	NO	1	00.04.02.396	00.04.02.788	80.80	80.93	0.04	26.93	26.97
PHYSICAL						00.00.03.935			0.43		0.43
TOTAL					00.14.50.966	00.14.59.518			0.93	98.99	99.92

Figure 9.1. Partition data report: BAM3 is highlighted.

partitions that are active and the number of available engines) to physical processors (which is fixed), the greater will be the impact of LPAR overhead.

This factor has been found to have the highest effect on the efficiency of LPAR via PR/SM. Figure 9.4 analyses the efficiency of the logical and physical processors, but this will be expanded later in the chapter.

9.6.1 Running VM/XA or VM/ESA as V=R or V=F in an LPAR partition

VM/XA and VM/ESA can be run in an LPAR partition in V=V mode only. Running VM V=R in LPAR gains no benefit, as it is running 'third level' (after LPAR and VM CP), and so will suffer bad response time. Running V=F just cannot be done, as the PR/SM feature is already being used when you IML (initial microcode load) the CEC in LPAR mode, and so it is just not available as the basis for VM MHPG.

9.6.2 Low utilization effect

There is a low utilization effect which manifests itself in higher LPAR overhead, and is brought about by the LPAR dispatcher continually looking for work in a low-use partition. As the partitions get busier this effect will fall, but it is compounded by the number of logical processors within the partition; the greater the number of logical processors, the greater is the low utilization effect, even if the partitions are busy.

Low utilization can have an effect on your capacity planning, because the wait time becomes less accurate. One way around this is to have CPU 'soaker' jobs running in their own partition. There should be as many of these jobs as there are engines available (less the dedicated ones). This will allow you to remove the CPU time for this partition, and ensure that the wait time is accurate; in fact, it will be removed all together. The soaker partition should be the lowest rank.

The shared partitions will probably show a lower ITR than dedicated partitions; the difference being due to the LPAR overhead. This can be partially offset by *capping* the partition. This means that there is a limit on the amount of the shared processors that this partition can use. Care should be taken with capping, as it can impact the peak time response times. So do not use it on a true production partition unless you are prepared to accept the consequences.

9.7 Capacity planning under LPAR

We can see the differences in the RMF Monitor I reports in LPAR mode by examining the reports in Figs. 9.1 and 9.2. These are respectively the RMF Monitor I CPU activity report for partition BAM3, and the overall partition data report

```
                              CPU ACTIVITY

MVS/ESA              SYSTEM ID BAM3              DATE 28/06/93              INTERVAL 4.59.999
SP 4.2.0             RPT VERSION 4.2.1           TIME 11.15.35              CYCLE 1.000 SECONDS

CPU MODEL 9021 VERSION 38 (ES/9021 MODEL 580)

CPU      VF       VF AFFINITY   BUSY TIME     WAIT TIME     CPU SERIAL    I/O TOTAL          % I/O INTERRUPTS
NUMBER   ONLINE   PERCENTAGE    PERCENTAGE    PERCENTAGE    NUMBER        INTERRUPT STATE    HANDLED VIA TPI
0        —        ****          55.10         —             ******        *****              ****
1        —        ****          53.16         —             ******        *****              ****

                                              SAMPLES = 300

TOTAL/AVERAGE     ****          54.13
```

Figure 9.2. RMF Monitor I CPU activity report for partition BAM3.

with partition BAM3 highlighted. We will use BAM3 to expand the necessary points.

We will be analysing the data supplied for an IBM ES/9021 Model 580. This is a triadic machine with a stated RPP of 75 RPP. Four partitions have been defined, BAM1, BAM2, BAM3 and BAM4, all of which are active. One partition, BAM1, has a dedicated processor, therefore there are only two engines available for the other three partitions. This also means that partitions BAM2, BAM3 and BAM4 can, at best, be defined to run diadic processors. The BAM3 partition shares the two available engines, and is in fact emulating an IBM ES/9021 Model 500, a diadic machine.

Notice that the CPU utilization shown on the CPU activity report, of 54.13 per cent (Fig. 9.2), is the same as shown for the LOGICAL PROCESSORS EFFECTIVE value in the partition data report (Fig. 9.1).

9.7.1 The high storage area in LPAR mode

One aspect of LPAR mode that you must be aware of is that your high storage area (HSA) will be much larger under LPAR than it will be in native mode. The different configurations in each of the partitions that LPAR must be aware of are held there, and so finding your HSA growing to 1.5 megabytes (yes, megabytes) is not unusual. Be aware of this in your capacity planning for storage.

9.7.2 Understanding the analysis of the BAM3 partition data report

The partition data report has two main sections: the logical processor information and the physical processor information. The two fields of data have been identified on Fig. 9.1, but this is not the case on the normal RMF Monitor I partition data report. Let us look at how each piece of data is arrived at, reading from left to right for the line of data associated with LPAR partition BAM3 in Fig. 9.1.

We need information that allows us to capacity plan both *within* the logical partition and for *all* partitions. We need to know the application and system RPP use within each and every partition, and the RPP use by all partitions. Finally, we need to find the amount of RPP used by LPAR within each partition, and by all partitions, but the first thing we need to know is the capture ratio.

9.8 The capture ratio—calculation

To begin with we need the captured seconds; this can be worked out from the information in the workload activity—system summary report for partition BAM3. A subset of this report is illustrated in Fig. 9.3. Only the CPU and SRB numbers are shown, and we can work out the captured seconds from the SUs as described in Chapter 5:

PARTITION DATA REPORT

MVS/ESA
SP4.2.0

SYSTEM ID MAC1
RPT VERSION 4.2.1

DATE 28/06/93
TIME 11.15.35

INTERVAL 4.59.000
CYCLE 1.000 SECONDS

OPT = IEAOPT00
ICS = IEAICS00

SYSTEM SUMMARY

SERVICE DEFINITION COEFFICIENTS
IOC = 3.0   CPU = 10.0   MSO = 5.0   SU/SEC = 1104.2   SRB = 10.0

PERFORMANCE GROUP NUM.	GROUP PER'D	OBJ. NUM.	DOMAIN NUMBER	TIME SLICE GROUP	INTERVAL SERVICE (TOTAL, BY TYPE AND PER SECOND)	AVERAGE ABSORPTION, AVG TRX SERV RATE, WORKLOAD LEVEL	PAGE IN RT, HSP PIN RT, HSP MISS RT	STORAGE AVERAGE, TOTAL	AVERAGE TRANS, MPL	ENDED TRANS, # SWAPS	AVE TRANS. TIME, STD DEV HHH.MM.SS.TTT.
ALL	ALL	ALL	ALL	ALL	IOC = CPU = 2 624 264 MSO = SRB = 600 000						

Figure 9.3. WAR system summary report for partition BAM3.

- Total TCB SUs = 2 624 264
- Total SRB SUs = 600 000
- SUs per second for an IBM ES/9021 Model 500 = 1104.2
- Service definition coefficient (SDC) for CPU and SRB = 10
- Number of engines = 2
- Interval duration = 5 minutes (300 seconds)

Therefore:

$$\text{Captured seconds} = \frac{\text{TCB SUs} + \text{SRB SUs}}{\text{SDC} \times \text{No. of engines} \times \text{SUs per second}}$$

$$= \frac{2\,624\,264 + 600\,000}{10 \times 2 \times 1104.2} = 146 \text{ seconds}$$

We know that the percentage of processor use for BAM3 is 54.13 per cent, and that the interval duration is 5 minutes (300 seconds). This represents:

$$0.5413 \times 300 = 162.39 \text{ seconds}$$

Our captured seconds are 146 seconds, therefore the capture ratio for BAM3 is:

$$\text{Capture ratio} = 146/162.39 = 0.8991$$

Warning: do not use the *total* processor percentage (54.25 per cent) to calculate the capture ratio, otherwise you will end up with a capture ratio lower than you need. This will result in inflated RPP values for your applications, because they will *all* include an inflation for LPAR. This in turn will overstate your requirement for processor power.

If you win your case, and a more powerful processor than you really require is installed, you may have to explain why the applications appear to be like a fistful of marbles in an oil drum!

9.9 Capacity planning for a partition

9.9.1 The logical processor data

Under the field DISPATCH TIME DATA on the partition data report (Fig. 9.1), you will see the effective and total minutes of execution time. They are, respectively:

Effective time 00.05.24.812 = 5 minutes and 24.812 seconds
Total time 00.05.25.594 = 5 minutes and 25.594 seconds

How do we get more execution time than there is in the interval duration (5 minutes)? Well, the effective and total times are the total times summed across *both* the logical processors defined in this partition. Therefore, if we divide either of these times by the number of engines in the partition (two), the quotient represents the real elapsed time. It will be easier if we turn all the times into seconds:

Capacity planning for MVS in LPAR mode

Effective time   324.812 seconds/2 = 162.406 seconds elapsed time
Total time   325.594 seconds/2 = 162.797 seconds elapsed time

As a percentage of the total duration (300 seconds):

Effective time   (162.406/300) × 100 = 54.13 per cent
Total time   (162.797/300) × 100 = 54.26 per cent

These are, respectively, the two times shown under the fields LOGICAL PROCESSORS, EFFECTIVE and TOTAL. The difference between them represents the LPAR use of the processors *within* the BAM3 partition; 0.13 per cent (intra-partition LPAR time). This is the sort of LPAR intrapartition engine use you can expect with a two-engine shared partition. It will fall a little as the partition gets busier, but not by much.

9.9.2 The physical processor data

Moving across the line of data on the partition data report, you will come to the physical processor data. It is under the field PHYSICAL PROCESSORS, and there are three pieces of information supplied:

- The LPAR management percentage use
- Effective processor percentage use
- Total processor percentage use

LPAR management percentage use

This is the percentage of engine use, apportioned to partition BAM3, which LPAR used while managing *all* the partitions, for example, scanning for an active partition with ready work. The amount used for partition BAM3 is 0.08 per cent. The total of this type of LPAR use for all partitions is 0.93 per cent, which is highlighted on Fig. 9.1.

Effective physical processor percentage

The effective physical processor percentage is calculated by multiplying the effective logical processor percentage, by the ratio of the number of processors in the partition to the total number of physical processors (as explained earlier):

Effective logical percentage = 54.13 per cent
Number of logical processors in the partition = 2
Total number of physical processors = 3

Therefore:

54.13 × (2/3) = 36.09 per cent

Total physical processor percentage

The totals are arrived at in the same manner as described above, but using the total physical processor percentage, and the total logical processor percentage:

$$54.26 \times (2/3) = 36.17 \text{ per cent}$$

The difference, 0.08 per cent, is LPAR interpartition time.

9.9.3 RPP calculations for capacity planning

Now that we have discovered how the data is derived, we can use this to calculate both the amount of power (RPP) used within partition BAM3, and the total amount of power used by all partitions.

RPP used within partition BAM3

Partition BAM3 is running a diadic processor, an IBM ES/9021 Model 500, with an overall RPP of 52. In addition, 54.13 per cent of the power available to partition BAM3 has been used. Therefore the RPP used in BAM3 is:

$$0.5413 \times 52 = 28.15 \text{ RPP (rounded) for the applications and system}$$

The total (including LPAR overhead) logical processor RPP is:

$$0.5426 \times 52 = 28.22 \text{ RPP (rounded) including the LPAR overhead}$$

This is the value you use for capacity planning within BAM3, i.e. for logical partition calculations. This is the total RPP used by real work within the partition, plus the LPAR intrapartition overhead, which you cannot ignore. This is the RPP that must be recovered across all applications, even though we know that, in reality, only 28.15 RPP was used by the applications and system components within partition BAM3.

Figure 9.4, which shows a summary of this and other information, has slightly different numbers, but the differences above are due to rounding. In Fig. 9.4, the value of 28.218 for BAM3 including LPAR intrapartition overhead, is calculated by multiplying the LPAR percentage use (0.13 per cent) by the RPP of the processor in the partition (52), $0.0013 \times 52 = 0.068$ RPP, and then adding it to 28.15.

9.9.4 Capacity planning for all partitions

Total physical processor RPP used

In order to capacity plan for the total physical processor requirements, we need to know the amount of RPP that is used by applications in BAM3, in terms of the physical processor.

Capacity planning for MVS in LPAR mode

Physical processor RPP for partition BAM3

We know that the physical processor is an IBM ES/9021 Model 580, with an RPP of 75. We also know that the effective physical processor percentage is 36.09 per cent. This represents:

$$0.3609 \times 75 = 27.07 \text{ RPP}$$

The total physical processor RPP is:

$$0.3617 \times 75 = 27.13 \text{ RPP including LPAR overhead}$$

The difference is 0.06 RPP, which is used by LPAR for intrapartition work. This represents $(0.06/75) \times 100 = 0.08$ per cent, as shown by the LPAR MGMT column on the partition data.

This exercise must be done for each of the partitions, in order to ascertain the true RPP use within each partition. Only in this way can you be sure that you are correct in your individual partition RPP use. The final step is to find the total RPP use for all partitions.

Total physical processor load

The total physical processor load is 99.92 per cent. See Fig. 9.1, where this is highlighted. This includes the LPAR interpartition overhead, and this is the value you must use to establish the overall processor requirements. In terms of RPP:

$$0.9992 \times 75 = 74.94 \text{ RPP}$$

In effect, the physical processor is full, and it is not possible to run any more work on our ES/9021 Model 580, unless we stop one of the other partitions.

9.10 How efficient is LPAR?

Figure 9.4 is a summary of the information extracted from the partition data report in Fig. 9.1 for all partitions. Part (a) shows the efficiency of the logical partitions, and part (b) the efficiency of the physical processor within each partition. On the right-hand side you will find the efficiencies in percentage terms (highlighted).

BAM1 is a dedicated partition, and this is reflected by the highest efficiency of 99.87 per cent. BAM2 on the other hand is a capped partition with a low utilization, probably because of the capping. The low utilization effect is well illustrated in this partition—88.79 per cent. The other two partitions, BAM3 and BAM4, show that the efficiency of LPAR logical partitioning is normally quite good. The respective efficiency percentages are 99.76 and 99.84 per cent.

On the physical processor side (Fig. 9.4(b)), you can see the same thing reflected in the efficiency percentages. BAM2 is particularly low, 86.6 per cent, but remember, it is a low utilized partition.

Partition name	Logical processor in partition	RPP of logical processor A	Effective workload (%) B	Utilized RPP A × B	LPAR URPP	Total partition URPP C	Partition efficiency (%) (A × B)/C
BAM1	9021/340	27	99.84	26.96	0.035	26.995	**99.87**
BAM2	9021/500	52	4.03	2.10	0.265	2.365	**88.79**
BAM3	9021/500	52	54.13	28.15	0.068	28.218	**99.76**
BAM4	9021/340	27	80.80	21.82	0.035	21.855	**99.84**

(a)

Partition name	Physical processor in partition	RRP of physical processor A	Effective workload (%) B	Utilized RPP A × B	LPAR URPP	Total partition URPP C	Partition efficiency (%) (A × B)/C
BAM1	9021/580	75	33.28	24.96	0.03	24.99	**99.88**
BAM2	9021/580	75	2.69	2.02	0.26	2.28	**88.60**
BAM3	9021/580	75	36.09	27.07	0.06	27.13	**99.78**
BAM4	9021/580	75	26.93	20.20	0.03	20.23	**99.85**
Physical	9021/580	75	–	–	0.32	0.32	
			Totals	74.25	0.70	74.95	**99.07**

(b)

Figure 9.4. Partition efficiency: (a) logical and (b) physical.

The analysis in Fig. 9.4 is not one you will do often, but it is worth while on a few occasions when your workload has settled down. It will help your capacity planning, as it will identify the real use of the processor, warts and all!

10
Capacity planning for MVS in a VM guest partition

10.1 Introduction

Both physical and logical partitioning have now been dealt with; this chapter introduces software partitioning under VM, VM/XA or VM/ESA. As usual, the terms will be explained before discussing what you have to be aware of when analysing for capacity planning or performance under VM.

The term 'VM' will be used in this chapter, but generically, in the sense that we are referring to VM, VM/XA and VM/ESA systems. If a particular point relates only to one or two of these systems, then this will be mentioned.

RMF Monitor I reports are very accurate when running under VM in every area, except in one, arriving at the capture ratio. As with logical partitioning, if you are not careful, you will overstate your case by ending up with a capture ratio which is too low.

The reason that the capture ratio will be too low is because the CPU wait time will be less than for the same MVS system in native mode, for the same interval duration, running the same workload. The captured time will not change, and so the effect is that the CPU busy percentage is inflated, thus giving a larger denominator for the capture ratio calculation, thereby resulting in a smaller capture ratio. This will be expanded upon.

As with logical partitioning, the background information will be covered, and then the capture ratio for an MVS system under VM will be calculated.

10.2 Multiple high-performance guests

VM multiple high-performance guests (MHPG) is another way of using the PR/SM microcode/hardware feature of IBM 3090 S and J models and ES/9000 systems. Instead of initial microcode loading (IML) the system in LPAR mode, and running native MVS/ESA systems in up to seven partitions, it is possible to IML in BASIC mode under VM/XA or VM/ESA, and use the MHPG feature of

Figure 10.1 (a): Basic mode layout

| V=R | V=F | V=F | V=F | V=F | V=F |

VM/XA or VM/ESA + MHPG

BASIC mode

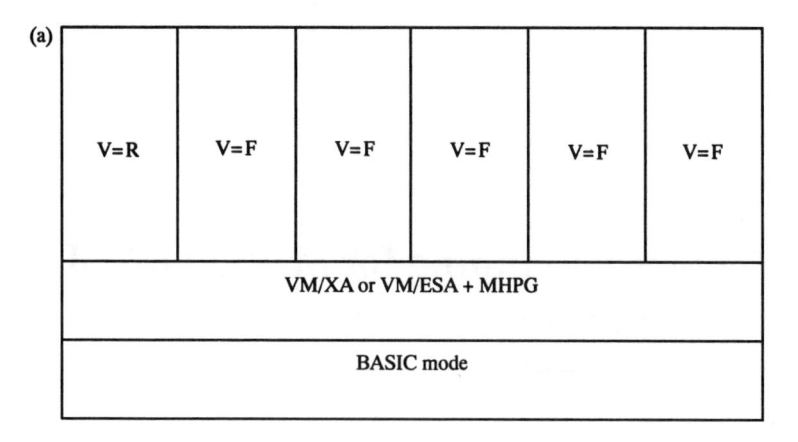

Figure 10.1 (b): LPAR mode layout

| Partition 1 | Partition 2 | Partition 3 | Partition 4 | Partition 5 | Partition 6 | Partition 7 |

LPAR mode

Figure 10.1. LPAR or BASIC mode? (a) Basic: VM/XA or VM/ESA + MHPG; (b) LPAR: PR/SM + Logical partitioning.

PR/SM to run five additional production partitions, in addition to the normal one V=R partition. The extra partitions are V=F and are run in an identical manner to the V=R partition. The only difference is that they are offset in storage from location 0. Other than that, they are identical in function, and almost identical in performance.

If PR/SM is used for the MHPG feature, then it cannot at the same time be used to initialize the CEC in LPAR mode. Figure 10.1 indicates the difference between the two modes of IML.

10.3   Start Interpretive Execution mode

Start Interpretive Execution (SIE) mode is really a long running instruction. When VM passes control to a guest, it does so by executing the SIE instruction. The effect of this is to pass control to the guest by entering SIE mode. SIE mode will be maintained until the guest gives up control. The guest is now running within the SIE instruction.

Now, when engines are dedicated to a VM guest (and in LPAR mode), there is little entry and exit to and from SIE mode. The effect of this is that the guest may appear to be 100 per cent busy all the time. The way around this, is to use the system activity display (SAD) frame on the system console. The CPU busy will be accurate and can be used as the VTIME (see Sec. 10.7) calculation for the capture ratio.

The signal processor (SIGP) instruction is no longer used (as from VM/HPO 3.4), to 'shoulder tap' another engine in a multi-engined processor (a small group of instructions is now 'spun' on until work is available). This feature is also now incorporated in the PR/SM feature, so that it can be used by MHPG. To remove the effect of this from the SAD frame information, EXCLUDE Key 3 from the display, as this is the supervisor key in which this loop of instructions runs.

10.4 CP mode and involuntary wait time

Control can be surrendered to VM from the guest, because either a function has to be executed by VM on behalf of the guest, for example, an I/O operation, or another guest of higher priority has to be given control from VM. If another guest is given control, then this is referred to as *involuntary wait* (IW) *time*. This is involuntary from the perception of the monitored guest.

The time that VM uses to execute a function on behalf of a guest operating system, or is in involuntary wait time, is called *control program time*, or more usually, CP time. CP time = VM execution time for the guest + IW time.

10.5 MVS clocks

There are three clocks used in MVS, MVS/XA and MVS/ESA (generically referred to as 'MVS clocks'). These are: the time-of-day (TOD) clock, the CPU timer and the clock comparator (CC). A short review on how they work will be advantageous to your understanding of RMF reports under VM. A fourth clock, the interval timer, is still incorporated within MVS, but it is not used now.

10.5.1 Time-of-day clock

This is the normal 'wall clock'. It is constantly running, and is very accurate. Like any other clock, it has to be set (normally at COLD start IPL time), but once set it need not be touched again, unless the system has to be reset. RMF uses this clock to set the start time for measuring an interval duration.

10.5.2 Clock comparator

This is the 'alarm clock'. It is set to a time ahead of the current TOD, and when the TOD reaches the CC, an interrupt is presented to MVS. RMF uses this clock in conjunction with the TOD clock, to set the RMF interval duration time. In the case of the native system analysed in the earlier chapters, the interval was 15 minutes (900 seconds).

10.5.3 CPU timer

The CPU timer is the 'egg timer'. When a task is dispatched, the MVS dispatcher sets the maximum value into the CPU timer. As the task executes, the CPU timer decrements (like an egg timer), and when the task gives up control, the MVS dispatcher calculates the amount of CPU time absorbed by the executing task, by subtracting the current value of the CPU timer from the maximum value that can be placed into it. The difference is the amount of CPU time for the task (again, like an egg timer!). This time is calculated for each dispatch of the task, and so the total task execution time is accumulated.

SRB time is handled in exactly the same manner. Even under VM, the CPU time is accurate, and so TCB and SRB SUs and seconds are accurate on RMF Workload Activity reports.

10.6 The RMF weakness

Now that you have an overview of how the clocks work, we can look at how the weakness of RMF occurs, and how to get over it to calculate the correct capture ratio.

The CPU timer is no problem, as it stops when the task is no longer dispatched. The problem lies with the CPU busy time, which is calculated by subtracting the CPU wait time from the difference between the CC and the TOD. This at first seems perfectly acceptable; the only problem is that it includes the CP time, and that should *not* be included if it incorporates involuntary wait time. It *is* acceptable if it is entirely made up of time in VM executing a function on behalf of the guest, as it would be for a V=V MVS guest.

It is unlikely that you will want to analyse an MVS guest running V=V, therefore we are really talking about V=R or V=F guests, which will execute their own I/O without exiting from SIE mode back to VM. Indeed, V=F and V=R guests very seldom exit from SIE mode back to VM, therefore there is little or no time in CP mode for executing functions on behalf of the guest. If there is any CP time, it will be for VM to run a higher priority guest; in other words, the CP time will consist of involuntary wait time. The trick is, therefore, to extract the CP time from the total busy time, otherwise you will end up with a busy time that is too long, with a resulting capture ratio that is too low.

Capacity planning for MVS in a VM guest partition

```
|◄─────────── Interval duration ───────────►|
|◄── TOD value ──|           Clock comparator value ──►|
```

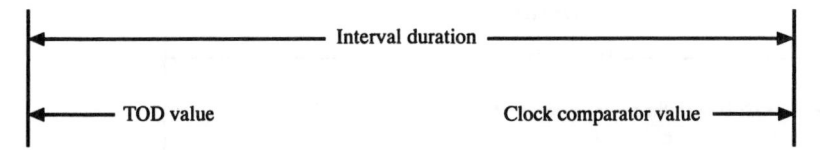

Figure 10.2. Setting the duraton value with TOD and CC.

Figure 10.2 shows how the interval duration is calculated under VM, using the TOD and CC.

10.6.1 *How do we extract CP time from the CPU busy time?*

We now know that all of the guest's interval time which is non-MVS wait time is recorded as busy time, and that this includes the CP time (if any). The CP time is probably only made up of time running another higher priority guest—involuntary wait time. We cannot tell from RMF Monitor I reports what part of the total CPU busy time is used for running the monitored guest, and what part is used by VM in CP mode running the involuntary wait time within CP time.

As we cannot tell the breakdown of CPU busy time from the RMF Monitor I report, we have to turn to VM for the information. VM accumulates the time running a guest in SIE mode, and calls it VTIME. *This does not include the CP mode time.* The total CPU busy time recorded by RMF will be made up of the VTIME and the CP mode time. CP mode has already been defined. Finally, VM refers to the total of VTIME and CP time as TTIME. TTIME is analogous to CPU busy time for a V=R or V=F guest.

How do we find VTIME?

What we need, therefore, is to be able to extract the CP time to leave the VTIME. Once we have the VTIME, we can calculate the correct capture ratio. VM will help us here by giving us the VTIME. We can obtain the VTIME in a number of ways:

1. The ACNT command places an accounting record, which also contains the TTIME, into a nominated virtual machine. This virtual machine can collect accounting records for all guests.
2. An alternative method is to enter the QUERY TIME command. This displays the VTIME and TTIME on the monitor screen, and is accurate to one-hundredth of a second.
3. The IND USER command also displays the information on the monitor screen, but in addition shows the reads and writes for the guest.
4. At a lower level, you can incorporate the DIAGNOSE x'0C' instruction in some code. This instruction retrieves VTIME and TTIME in microseconds

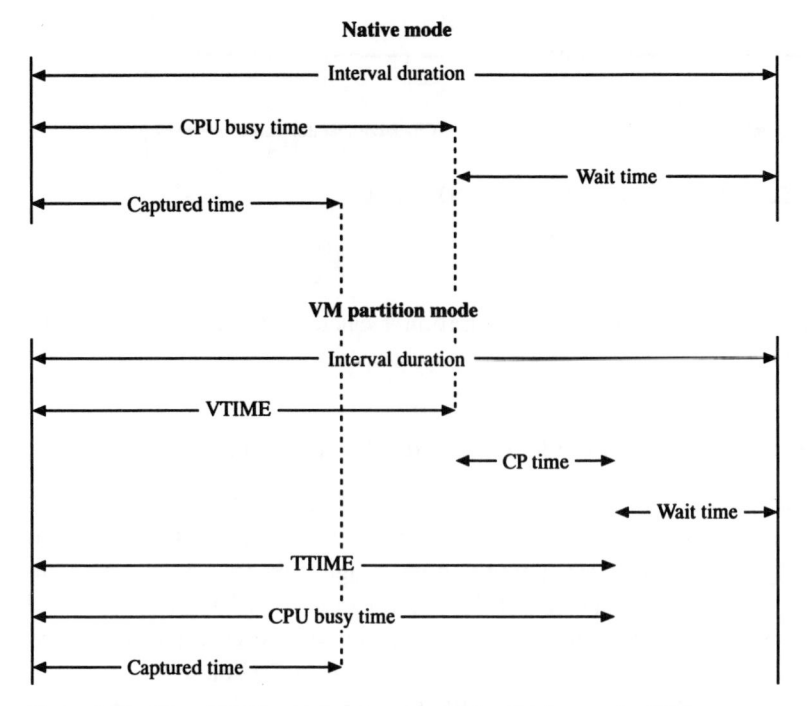

Figure 10.3. How CPU busy time is extended by CP time under VM.

from its low storage location, and places it into a specified address in your code.
5   There is also the DIAGNOSE x'70' instruction. This can be issued from any operating system screen, and lifts the VTIME value from its low storage location, and displays it in CPU timer units.

Figure 10.3 shows CPU busy time in native mode, and in VM software partition mode. It shows how CPU busy time in VM mode is extended by the CP time for the guest. It also illustrates the terms just defined.

10.7 The capture ratio for an MVS guest under VM

10.7.1 Capture ratio in native mode

The capture ratio in native mode is obtained by dividing the total of the TCB and SRB seconds (the captured time) by the product of the CPU busy percentage and interval duration:

$$\text{Native capture ratio} = \frac{\text{TCB} + \text{SRB seconds}}{\text{CPU busy percentage} \times \text{Interval time}}$$

10.7.2 Capture ratio under VM

The capture ratio for a guest under VM is obtained by dividing the captured seconds (which will be the same as in native mode) by the VTIME:

$$\text{VM partition mode capture ratio} = \frac{\text{TCB} + \text{SRB seconds}}{\text{VTIME}}$$

10.8 Summary

Analysing for capacity planning or performance under VM is no different than for a native MVS system. The CPU timer is accurate, therefore we can use the TCB and SRB seconds without modification.

The only problem lies with the CPU busy time, which incorporates the CP time. You now know how to ensure that you remove the CP time from the CPU busy time, by finding the VTIME. The VTIME is analogous to the CPU percentage × Interval duration that you would extract for a native MVS system.

Other than that, all other RMF Monitor I data is correct, and the analysis for the I/O subsystem and storage is exactly the same.

Appendix 1
Relevant SYS1.PARMLIB members for the system analysed in this book

A1.1 IEAIPS00 member of SYS1.PARMLIB

```
DATASET:   SYS1.PARMLIB                                           DATE: 28/06/93
MEMBER  :  IEAIPS00                  LEVEL : 01.06                TIME: 09.00
                                     USERID: MAC1                PAGE: 01 OF 01

START                                                                        MOD
COL    ----+----1----+----2----+----3----+----5----+----6----+----7----+----8
  2    /*                 IEAIPS00 FOR THE MAC1 SYSTEM             */ 00010001
  2    /*                                                          */ 00020001
  1    CPU=10.0,IOC=5.0,MSO=0.1,SRB=10   /* MSO REDUCED            */ 00030001
  1    APGRNG=(0,15)                     /* ALL APGs INCLUDED      */ 00040001
  1    PVLDP=F7                          /* PRIV. USER DISP PRTY.  */ 00050001
  1    IOQ=PRTY                          /* I/O QUEUED BY DISP PTY */ 00060001
  2    /*                                                          */ 00070001
  2    /*                                                          */ 00080001
  1    DMN=1,DSRV=(0,2800)       /* TEST BATCH FIRST PERIOD        */ 00090001
  1    DMN=2,DSRV=(0,1600)       /* TEST BATCH SECOND PERIOD       */ 00100001
  2    /*                                                          */ 00110001
  1    DMN=11,DSRV=(1150,2200),  /* PROD BATCH FIRST PERIOD        */ 00120001
  8         ESCRTABX=4                                              */ 00130001
  1    DMN=12,DSRV=(400,800),    /* PROD BATCH SECOND PERIOD       */ 00140001
  8         ESCRTABX=4                                              */ 00150001
  2    /*                                                          */ 00160001
  1    DMN=21,ASRV=(460,600)     /* DEV TSO SHORT                  */ 00170001
  1    DMN=22,ASRV=(460,600)     /* DEV TSO MEDIUM                 */ 00180001
  1    DMN=23,ASRV=(375,500)     /* DEV TSO LONG                   */ 00190001
  2    /*                                                          */ 00200001
  1    DMN=31,ASRV=(700,1000),   /* PROD TSO SHORT                 */ 00210001
  8         ESCRTABX=3                                              */ 00220001
  1    DMN=32,ASRV=(675,900),    /* PROD TSO MEDIUM                */ 00230001
  8         ESCRTABX=3                                              */ 00240001
  1    DMN=33,ASRV=(675,900),    /* PROD TSO LONG                  */ 00250001
  8         ESCRTABX=3                                              */ 00260001
  2    /*                                                          */ 00270001
  1    DMN=80,ASRV=(460,2000)    /* HOT BATCH                      */ 00280001
  1    DMN=99,CNSTR=(0,0)        /* DELAY DOMAIN                   */ 00290001
  1    DMN=100,CNSTR=(0,30)      /* SYSTEM ADDRESS SPACES          */ 00300001
  1    DMN=128,CNSTR=(5,15),     /* SYSPROGS DOMAIN                */ 00310001
  8         ASRV=(4000,4000)     /*                                */ 00320001
  2    /*                                                          */ 00330001
  2    /*                                                          */ 00340001
  1    PGN=1,(DMN=1,DP=M3,DUR=30K)      /* PERIOD 1 TEST BATCH     */ 00350001
  7          (DMN=2,DP=M2)              /* PERIOD 2 TEST BATCH     */ 00360001
  1    PGN=11,(DMN=11,DP=M6,DUR=30K)    /* PERIOD 1 PROD BATCH     */ 00370001
  8          (DMN=12,DP=M5)             /* PERIOD 2 PROD BATCH     */ 00380001
```

```
1      PGN=2,(DMN=21,DP=F43,DUR=200)      /* DEV TSO SHORT           */ 00390001
7             (DMN=22,DP=F42,DUR=1800)    /* DEV TSO MEDIUM          */ 00400001
7             (DMN=23,DP=M4)              /* DEV TSO LONG            */ 00410001
1      PGN=42,(DMN=31,DP=F73,DUR=200)     /* PROD TSO SHORT          */ 00420001
8             (DMN=32,DP=F72,DUR=850)     /* PROD TSO MEDIUM         */ 00430001
8             (DMN=33,DP=M7,PWSS=(500,*)) /* PROD TSO LONG           */ 00440001
1      PGN=3,(DMN=80,DP=F30)              /* HOT BATCH               */ 00450001
1      PGN=13,(DMN=1,DP=M0)               /* LOW PRTY BATCH          */ 00460001
1      PGN=99,(DMN=99,DP=M1)              /* DELAY JOBS              */ 00470001
1      PGN=100,(DMN=100,DP=M8)            /* STARTED TASKS           */ 00480001
1      PGN=101,(DMN=100,DP=M8)            /* CATALOG                 */ 00490001
1      PGN=102,(DMN=100,DP=M8)            /* LLA                     */ 00500001
1      PGN=103,(DMN=100,DP=M8)            /* VLF                     */ 00510001
1      PGN=104,(DMN=100,DP=M8)            /* VTAM                    */ 00520001
1      PGN=105,(DMN=100,DP=M8)            /* JES2                    */ 00530001
1      PGN=106,(DMN=100,DP=M8)            /* RMF                     */ 00540001
1      PGN=107,(DMN=100,DP=M8)            /* MOUNT                   */ 00550001
1      PGN=111,(DMN=1,DP=M0)              /* CPU USER                */ 00560001
1      PGN=999,(DMN=128,DP=F9)            /* HIGH PRIORITY TSO       */ 00570001
```

A1.2   IEAICS00 member of SYS1.PARMLIB

```
DATASET:  SYS1.PARMLIB                                      DATE: 28/06/93
MEMBER :  IEAICS00              LEVEL : 01.06               TIME: 09.00
                                USERID: MAC1                PAGE: 01 OF 01

START                                                                    MOD
COL      ----+----1----+----2----+----3----+----5----+----6----+----7----+----8
 2      /*                IEAICS00 FOR THE MAC1 SYSTEM            */ 00010001
 2      /*                                                        */ 00020001
 1      SUBSYS=JES2,PGN=1             /* DEFAULT BATCH - PGN 1    */ 00030001
 3        TRXNAME=ROCK(1),RPGN=201    /* REPORT PG FOR BATCH      */ 00040001
 3        TRXNAME=BAM(1),PGN=11       /* SPECIFIC PROD BATCH      */ 00050001
 3        TRXNAME=NED(1),PGN=11       /* SPECIFIC PROD BATCH      */ 00060001
 3        TRXNAME=SID(1),PGN=11       /* SPECIFIC PROD BATCH      */ 00070001
 3        TRXNAME=ROB(1),PGN=11       /* SPECIFIC PROD BATCH      */ 00080001
 3        TRXNAME=NIK(1),PGN=11       /* SPECIFIC PROD BATCH      */ 00090001
 3        TRXNAME=CPU(1),PGN=111      /* SPECIFIC CPU INTENSIVE   */ 00100001
 3        TRXNAME=BOR(1),PGN=11       /* SPECIFIC PROD BATCH      */ 00110001
 3        TRXNAME=ALB(1),PGN=11       /* SPECIFIC PROD BATCH      */ 00120001
 3        TRXNAME=CB8(1),PGN=11       /* SPECIFIC PROD BATCH      */ 00130001
 3        TRXNAME=VEC(1),PGN=3        /* HOT BATCH                */ 00140001
 1      SUBSYS=TSO,PGN=2              /* TSO                      */ 00150001
 3        USERID=7(6),PGN=42          /* USERIDS XXXXXX70 - 79    */ 00160001
 3        USERID=8(6),PGN=42          /* USERIDS XXXXXX80 - 89    */ 00170001
 3        USERID=9(6),PGN=42          /* USERIDS XXXXXX90 - 99    */ 00180001
 3        USERID=MARY,PGN=999         /* SYSPROGS PGN             */ 00190001
 3        USERID=BRIAN,PGN=999        /* SYSPROGS PGN             */ 00200001
 3        USERID=JOHN,PGN=999         /* SYSPROGS PGN             */ 00210001
 3        USERID=GEORGE,PGN=999       /* SYSPROGS PGN             */ 00220001
 3        USERID=SID,PGN=999          /* SYSPROGS PGN             */ 00230001
 1      SUBSYS=STC,PGN=100            /* STARTED TASKS            */ 00240001
 3        TRXNAME=CATALOG,PGN=101     /* CATALOG                  */ 00250001
 3        TRXNAME=LLA,PGN=102         /* LLA                      */ 00260001
 3        TRXNAME=VLF,PGN=103         /* VLF                      */ 00270001
 3        TRXNAME=VTAM,PGN=104        /* VTAM                     */ 00280001
 3        TRXNAME=JES2,PGN=105        /* JES2                     */ 00290001
 3        TRXNAME=RMF,PGN=106         /* RMF                      */ 00300001
 3        TRXNAME=IEEVMPCR,PGN=107    /* MOUNT                    */ 00310001
```

A1.3 IEAOPT00 member of SYS1.PARMLIB

```
DATASET:  SYS1.PARMLIB                                            DATE: 28/06/93
MEMBER :  IEAOPT00              LEVEL : 01.06                     TIME: 09.00
                                USERID: MAC1                      PAGE: 01 OF 01

START                                                                        MOD
  COL   ----+----1----+----2----+----3----+----5----+----6----+----7----+----8
  2     /*                  IEAOPT00 FOR THE MAC1 SYSTEM          */ 00010001
  2     /*                                                        */ 00020001
  1     CCCSIGUR=45,        /* MIN MEAN-TIME-TO-WAIT THRESHOLD    */ 00030001
  1     CNTCLIST=NO,        /* SEPARATE CLIST COMMANDS            */ 00040001
  1     CPENABLE=(10,30),   /* I/O INT. % FOR TPI                 */ 00050001
  1     DVIO=YES,           /* DIRECTED VIO IS ACTIVE             */ 00060001
  1     ERV=500,            /* ENQUEUE RESIDENCY VALUE            */ 00070001
  1     ESCTBDS=1500,       /* HIPERSPACE PAGE CRITERIA AGE       */ 00080001
  1     ESCTPOC(0)=1200,    /* PAGED OUT PAGE CRITERIA AGE        */ 00090001
  1     ESCTPOC(1)=1200,    /* PAGED OUT PAGE CRITERIA AGE        */ 00100001
  1     ESCTPOC(2)=1200,    /* PAGED OUT PAGE CRITERIA AGE        */ 00110001
  1     ESCTPOC(3)=500,     /* PAGED OUT PAGE CRITERIA AGE        */ 00120001
  1     ESCTPOC(4)=700,     /* PAGED OUT PAGE CRITERIA AGE        */ 00130001
  1     ESCTSTC(0)=100,     /* STOLEN PAGE CRITERIA AGE           */ 00140001
  1     ESCTSTC(1)=250,     /* STOLEN PAGE CRITERIA AGE           */ 00150001
  1     ESCTSTC(2)=250,     /* STOLEN PAGE CRITERIA AGE           */ 00160001
  1     ESCTSTC(3)=100,     /* STOLEN PAGE CRITERIA AGE           */ 00170001
  1     ESCTSTC(4)=150,     /* STOLEN PAGE CRITERIA AGE           */ 00180001
  1     ESCTSWTC(0),1200,   /* TRIMMED PAGE CRITERIA AGE          */ 00190001
  1     ESCTSWTC(1),1200,   /* TRIMMED PAGE CRITERIA AGE          */ 00200001
  1     ESCTSWTC(2),800,    /* TRIMMED PAGE CRITERIA AGE          */ 00210001
  1     ESCTSWTC(3),500,    /* TRIMMED PAGE CRITERIA AGE          */ 00220001
  1     ESCTSWTC(4),700,    /* TRIMMED PAGE CRITERIA AGE          */ 00230001
  1     ESCTSWWS(0),1200,   /* SWAPPED OUT PAGE CRITERIA AGE      */ 00240001
  1     ESCTSWWS(1),1200,   /* SWAPPED OUT PAGE CRITERIA AGE      */ 00250001
  1     ESCTSWWS(2),800,    /* SWAPPED OUT PAGE CRITERIA AGE      */ 00260001
  1     ESCTSWWS(3),800,    /* SWAPPED OUT PAGE CRITERIA AGE      */ 00270001
  1     ESCTSWWS(4),800,    /* SWAPPED OUT PAGE CRITERIA AGE      */ 00280001
  1     ESCTVF=100,         /* VIRTUAL FETCH PAGE CRITERIA AGE    */ 00290001
  1     ESCTVIO=1500,       /* VIO PAGE CRITERIA AGE              */ 00300001
  1     LSCTFET=(76,82),    /* FIXED BELOW 16MB % FOR LOG. THINK  */ 00310001
  1     LSCTFTT=(58,66),    /* FIXED ONLINE % FOR LOG. THINK      */ 00320001
  1     LSCTMTE=(5,30),     /* LOW/HIGH LOG. THINK TIME VALUES    */ 00330001
  1     LSCTUCT=(20,30),    /* LOW/HIGH UIC FOR LOG. THINK TIME   */ 00340001
  1     MCCAECTH=(150,300), /* LOW/OK EXP. STOR. AV. FRAME QUEUE  */ 00350001
  1     MCCAFCTH=(50,100),  /* LOW/OK CENT. STOR. AV. FRAME QUEUE */ 00360001
  1     MCCFXEPR=92,        /* FIXED % BELOW 16MB                 */ 00370001
  1     MCCFXTPR=80,        /* TOTAL FIXED %                      */ 00380001
  1     MCCMAXSW=512,       /* MAX. SWAPSET SIZE FOR IN FRAMES    */ 00390001
  1     RCCCPUT=(101.0,106.0), /* LOW/HIGH CPU UTIL. FOR MPL ADJ. */ 00400001
  1     RCCFXET=(82,88),    /* LOW/HI FIXED STOR. < 16MB FOR MPL ADJ */ 00410001
  1     RCCFXTT=(66,72),    /* LOW/HI ONLINE STOR. FOR MPL ADJ.   */ 00420001
  1     RCCPTRT=(50,70),    /* LOW/HI PAGE FAULT FOR MPL ADJ.     */ 00430001
  1     RCCUICT=(2,4),      /* LOW/HI UIC FOR MPL ADJ.            */ 00440001
  1     RMPTTOM=1000,       /* SRM INVOCATION INTERVAL            */ 00450001
  1     SELTAPE=NEXT,       /* TAPE DRIVE ALLOCATION METHOD       */ 00460001
  1     SWAPRSF=10.0        /* WEIGHT FOR COST OF EXCHANGE SWAP   */ 00470001
```

A1.4 IEASYS00 member of SYS1.PARMLIB

```
DATASET:   SYS1.PARMLIB                                          DATE: 28/06/93
MEMBER :   IEASYS00              LEVEL : 01.06                   TIME: 09.00
                                 USERID: MAC1                    PAGE: 01 OF 01

START                                                                        MOD
COL    ----+----1----+----2----+----3----+----5----+----6----+----7----+----8
  2    /*                   IEASYS00 FOR THE MAC1 SYSTEM          */ 00010001
  2    /*                                                         */ 00020001
  1    APF=46,                    /* AUTHORISED LIB'Y LIST        */ 00030001
  1    APG=07,                    /* AUTOMATIC PRIORITY GROUP = 7 */ 00040001
  1    CLOCK=00,                  /* CLOCK00 IS TIME BASE         */ 00050001
  1    CMB=(UNITR,COMM,GRAPH,CHRDR), /* MORE CMB ENTRIES          */ 00060001
  1    CMD=(00,01),               /* TOD PROMPT,SDUMO,TRACE/RMF ON */ 00070001
  1    CON=00,                    /* SELECT CONSOL00              */ 00080001
  1    CSA=(2000,4000),           /* CSA RANGE                    */ 00090001
  1    DUMP=(DASD,04-07),         /* SVC DUMPS TO DASD            */ 00100001
  1    FIX=00,                    /* MODULES TO BE FIXED          */ 00110001
  1    GRS=NONE,                  /* NO GRS CONTROL               */ 00120001
  1    ICS=00,                    /* USE IEAICS00                 */ 00130001
  1    IPS=00,                    /* USE IEAIPS00                 */ 00140001
  1    LNK=00,                    /* USE LNKLST00                 */ 00150001
  1    LNKAUTH=LNKLST,            /* LNKLST00 IS AUTHORISED LIBS  */ 00160001
  1    LOGCLS=L,                  /* SYSOUT FOR SYSTEM LOG        */ 00170001
  1    LOGLMT=999999,             /* MAX NO. WTL MESSAGES         */ 00180001
  1    LPA=00,                    /* USE IEALPA00                 */ 00190001
  1    MAXUSER=200,               /* MAX. NO. TSO USERS           */ 00200001
  1    MLPA=00,                   /* TEST MODULES                 */ 00210001
  1    MSTRJCL=00,                /* USE MSTJCL00                 */ 00220001
  1    PAGTOTL=(9,9),             /* 9 MORE PAGE & SWAP DATA SETS */ 00230001
  1    PAK=00,                    /* USE IEAPAK00                 */ 00240001
  1    OPI=YES,                   /* OPERATOR CAN OVERRIDE IEASYS */ 00250001
  1    OPT=00,                    /* USE IEAOPT00 FOR SRM         */ 00260001
  1    PAGE=(PAGE.VMVSCAT.PLPA.CYL20, /* PLPA PAGE DATA SET       */ 00270001
  7         PAGE.VMVSCAT.COMMON,  /* COMMON PAGE DATA SET         */ 00280001
  7         PAGE.VAKESM1.LOCAL,   /* LOCAL ON AKESM1              */ 00290001
  7         PAGE.VESCCAT.LOCAL,   /* LOCAL ON ESCCAT              */ 00300001
  7         PAGE.VCB84LB.LOCAL,   /* LOCAL ON CB84LB              */ 00310001
  7         PAGE.VMVS576.LOCAL),  /* LOCAL ON MVS576              */ 00320001
  1    REAL=64,                   /* 1*64 K JOB CAN RUN V=R       */ 00330001
  1    RSU=0,                     /* NO RECONFIG. STORAGE UNITS   */ 00340001
  1    RSVSTRT=5,                 /* RESERVED ASVT ENTRIES        */ 00350001
  1    RSVNONR=5,                 /* RESERVED ASVT ENTRIES        */ 00360001
  1    SCH=00,                    /* USE SCHED00                  */ 00370001
  1    SMF=00,                    /* USE IEASMF00                 */ 00380001
  1    SQA=(10,4),                /* SQA C. 640K                  */ 00390001
  1    SSN=00,                    /* SUBSYSTEMS TO BE STARTED     */ 00400001
  1    SVC=00,                    /* USE IEASVC00                 */ 00410001
  1    SYSNAME=MAC1,              /* SYSTEM NAME AS IN SMFPRM00   */ 00420001
  1    VAL=00,                    /* USE VATLST00                 */ 00430001
  1    VRREGN=64                  /* V=R REGION                   */ 00440001
```

A1.5   COFVLF00 member of SYS1.PARMLIB

```
DATASET:  SYS1.PARMLIB                                     DATE: 28/06/93
MEMBER :  COFVLF00                   LEVEL : 01.06         TIME: 09.00
                                     USERID: MAC1          PAGE: 01 OF 01

START                                                                 MOD
COL       ----+----1----+----2----+----3----+----5----+----6----+----7----+----8
  2    /*                   COFVLF00 FOR THE MAC1 SYSTEM           */ 00000001
  2    /*                                                          */ 00010001
  2    /*  NAME: COFVLF00                                           */ 00020001
  2    /*                                                          */ 00030001
  2    /*  VIRTUAL LOOKASIDE FACILITY MEMBER                        */ 00040001
  2    /*                                                          */ 00050001
  2    /*  COPYRIGHT =                                              */ 00060001
  2    /*     5685-001                                              */ 00070001
  2    /*       This macro is "RESTRICTED MATERIALS OF IBM"         */ 00080001
  2    /*       (C) Copyright of IBM Corporation 1988               */ 00090001
  2    /*       Licensed materials - Property of IBM                */ 00100001
  2    /*                                                          */ 00110001
  2    /*  Status: JBB3311                                          */ 00120001
  2    /*                                                          */ 00130001
  2    /*  Function:                                                */ 00140001
  2    /*    COFVLF00 specifies the VLF CLASS and Major Name        */ 00150001
  2    /*    used for objects stored by Library Lookaside (LLA)     */ 00160001
  2    /*    The class of objects is named "CSVLLA" with a          */ 00170001
  2    /*    major name of "LLA".                                   */ 00180001
  2    /*                                                          */ 00190001
  2    /*  Change activity:                                         */ 00200001
  2    /*    $L0=VLF    HBB3310 871023 PDAM: Virt. Lookaside        */ 00210001
  2    /*    $P1=VLF    HBB3310 880209 PDAM: Change class name      */ 00220001
  2    /*    $P2=PCG0085 JBB3311 880419 PDAM: Lib'y Loo'de  name    */ 00230001
  2    /*                                                          */ 00240001
  2    /* Start of specifications ********************************/ 00250001
  1    CLASS NAME(CSVLLA)           /* CLASS NAME FOR LLA           */ 00260001
  7          EMAJ9LLA),             /* MAJOR NAME FOR LLA           */ 00270001
  1    CLASS NAME(IKJEXEC)          /* CLASS NAME FOR CLISTS & REXX */ 00280001
  7          EDSN(IPO1.CMDPROC)     /* MAJOR NAME                   */ 00290001
  7          EDSN(ICQ.ICQCCLIB)     /* MAJOR NAME                   */ 00300001
  7          EDSN(TSOISPF.ISPCLIB)* MAJOR NAME                      */ 00310001
  1    CLASS NAME(IGGCAS)           /* CLASS NAME FOR CATALOG       */ 00320001
  7          EMAJ(CATALOG.MVSICF1.VMVSRES)  /* CATALOG              */ 00330001
  7          EMAJ(CATALOG.MAC1TEAM)         /* USER CAT             */ 00340001
  7          EMAJ(UCAT001)          /* TSO USERCAT                  */ 00350001
  7          EMAJ(UCAT002)          /* TSO USERCAT                  */ 00360001
  7          EMAJ(UCAT003)          /* TSO USERCAT                  */ 00370001
  7          EMAJ(UCAT004)          /* TSO USERCAT                  */ 00380001
  7          EMAJ(UCAT005)          /* TSO USERCAT                  */ 00390001
  7          EMAJ(UCAT006)          /* TSO USERCAT                  */ 00400001
  7          EMAJ(UCAT007)          /* TSO USERCAT                  */ 00410001
  7          EMAJ(UCAT008)          /* TSO USERCAT                  */ 00420001
  7          EMAJ(UCAT009)          /* TSO USERCAT                  */ 00430001
  7          EMAJ(UCAT00A)          /* TSO USERCAT                  */ 00440001
  7          EMAJ(UCAT00B)          /* TSO USERCAT                  */ 00450001
  1    CLASS NAME(IRRGTS)           /* CLASS NAME FOR RACF 1.9 GTS  */ 00460001
  7          EMAJ(GTS)              /* MAJOR NAME OF IRRGTS CLASS   */ 00470001
  2    /* End of specifications ********************************/ 00480001
```

A1.6 COFDLF00 member of SYS1.PARMLIB

```
DATASET: SYS1.PARMLIB                                    DATE: 28/06/93
MEMBER :  COFDLF00              LEVEL : 01.06            TIME: 09.00
                                USERID: MAC1             PAGE: 01 OF 01

START                                                                 MOD
COL     ----+----1----+----2----+----3----+----5----+----6----+----7----+----8
  2     /*                  COFDLF00 FOR THE MAC1 SYSTEM        */ 00010001
  2     /*                                                      */ 00020001
  2     /*  NAME: COFDLF00                                      */ 00030001
  2     /*                                                      */ 00040001
  2     /*  DATA LOOKASIDE FACILITY MEMBER                      */ 00050001
  2     /*                                                      */ 00060001
  2     /*  COPYRIGHT =                                         */ 00070001
  2     /*     5685-001                                         */ 00080001
  2     /*     This macro is "RESTRICTED MATERIALS OF IBM"      */ 00020001
  2     /*     (C) Copyright of IBM Corporation 1988            */ 00090001
  2     /*     Licensed materials - Property of IBM             */ 00100001
  2     /*                                                      */ 00110001
  2     /*  Status: JBB3313                                     */ 00120001
  2     /*                                                      */ 00130001
  2     /*  Function:                                           */ 00140001
  2     /*    COFDLF00 specifies the initialisation parameters  */ 00150001
  2     /*    used for DLF.                                     */ 00160001
  2     /*                                                      */ 00170001
  2     /*                                                      */ 00180001
  2     /*                                                      */ 00190001
  2     /*  Change activity:                                    */ 00200001
  2     /*    $L0=VLF     JBB3313 890718 PDAM: Data Look'de Fac.*/ 00210001
  2     /*                                                      */ 00220001
  2     /*                                                      */ 00230001
  2     /*                                                      */ 00240001
  2     /* Start of specifications ******************************/ 00250001
  1     CLASS                                                      00260001
  7         MAXEXPB(150)        /* USE 150Mb. OF EXP. STORAGE   */ 00270001
  7         PCTRETB(50)         /* % OF MAX. TO RETAIN          */ 00280001
  7         CONEXIT(COFXDLF1)   /* INSTALLATION EXIT NOT USED   */ 00290001
  2     /* End of specifications ********************************/ 00300001
```

A1.7 VATLST00 member of SYS1.PARMLIB

```
DATASET:  SYS1.PARMLIB                                          DATE: 28/06/93
MEMBER :  VATLST00                   LEVEL : 01.06              TIME: 09.00
                                     USERID: MAC1               PAGE: 01 OF 01

START                                                                       MOD
COL       ----+----1----+----2----+----3----+----5----+----6----+----7----+----8
  2       /*                    VATLST00 FOR THE MAC1 SYSTEM       */ 00010001
  2       /*                                                       */ 00020001
  1       VATDEF IPLUSE(PRIVATE),SYSUSE(PRIVATE)                   */ 00030001
  1       BAT*,1,2,3380                                            */ 00040001
  1       TSOA9%,1,2,3380                                          */ 00050001
  1       TSO1C%,1,2,3380                                          */ 00060001
  1       CACHE1,1,2,3380                                          */ 00070001
  1       CACHE3,1,2,3380                                          */ 00080001
  1       CACHE2,1,0,3380                                          */ 00090001
  1       CACHE4,1,0,3380                                          */ 00100001
  1       MVS576,1,2,3380                                          */ 00110001
  1       MVS577,1,2,3380                                          */ 00120001
  1       CB84LB,1,2,3380       ,Y                                 */ 00130001
  1       CIC570,1,2,3380       ,Y                                 */ 00140001
  1       AKESM1,1,2,3380       ,Y                                 */ 00150001
  1       IDAVOL,1,2,3380       ,Y                                 */ 00160001
  1       MVSRES,1,2,3380       ,Y                                 */ 00170001
  1       MVSDLB,1,2,3380       ,Y                                 */ 00180001
  1       MVSCAT,1,2,3380       ,Y                                 */ 00190001
  1       CICIPO,1,2,3380       ,Y                                 */ 00200001
  1       ESCDLB,1,2,3380                                          */ 00210001
  1       ESCRES,1,2,3380                                          */ 00220001
  1       ESCCAT,1,2,3380                                          */ 00230001
  1       WRK571,1,0,3380                                          */ 00240001
  1       SPL89A,1,0,3380                                          */ 00250001
  1       SC189A,1,0,3380                                          */ 00260001
  1       DLB89A,1,0,3380                                          */ 00270001
  1       RS189A,1,1,3380                                          */ 00280001
  1       RS289A,1,1,3380                                          */ 00290001
  1       CAT89A,1,0,3380                                          */ 00300001
  1       DL289A,1,1,3380                                          */ 00310001
  1       MVSTS3,1,2,3380                                          */ 00320001
  1       SMP89A,1,0,3380                                          */ 00330001
```

Appendix 2
Formatted worksheet for CPU analysis of RMF Monitor I report

See Fig. A2.1 on page 174.

RMF MONITOR I REPORT—ANALYSIS WORKSHEET																
DATE 28/06/93 PROC'R ES9021-340			TIME 09.00 DUR'N 900 secs		SYSID MAC1 CPU % 89.19			CYCLE 1 second PROC'R RPP 27			SAMPLES 900 URPP		AVE. CAPTURE RATIO MVS VER. 4.2.0 RMF VER. 4.2.1			
APPL. PERF. GROUP	CPU SECS	PG %	PG URPP	←——SYSTEM PGs——→						TOTAL PG URPP	TOTAL CPU %	TOTAL CPU SECS	No. TRANS	No. USERS	ETR	ITR
TOTAL URPP——→																

Figure A2.1. CPU analysis worksheet.

Appendix 3
IBM internal throughput rates

Table A3.1. IBM ITRs using ES/3090 Model 180 J as base of 100[1] (*Continues*)

Model	Batch CB84	MVS/ESA SP 3.1 Interactive CICS	MVS/ESA SP 3.1 Interactive IMS	MVS/ESA SP 3.1 Interactive TSO	VM/XA SP 2.1 Interactive PD3	VM/XA SP 2.1 Interactive HT4
IBM ES/4381						
4381-90E	15	16	15	17	14	15
4381-91E	20	19	20	21	16	18
4381-92E	38	35	35	38	34	36
IBM ES/3090E						
3090-120E	39	28	30	35	38	36
3090-150E	49	40	44	45	46	45
3090-180E	76	65	66	73	77	75
3090-200E	149	125	124	139	156	149
3090-280E	147	122	120	136	152	145
3090-300E	220	177	172	197	226	211
3090-400E	282	219	212	252	298	272
3090-500E	343	260	251	300	366	332
3090-600E	397	295	283	342	431	389
IBM ES/3090S						
3090-100S	31	20	21	27	31	28
3090-120S	39	28	30	35	38	36
3090-150S	61	45	47	55	65	60
3090-170S	72	58	60	67	72	68
3090-180S	94	87	89	92	95	92
3090-200S	185	169	168	173	191	183
3090-250S	121	91	88	104	131	118
3090-280S	182	165	161	171	189	180
3090-300S	272	243	238	246	282	265
3090-380S	270	244	240	254	279	260
3090-400S	353	308	297	322	370	347
3090-500S	429	371	354	390	457	427
3090-600S	504	435	418	444	541	506
IBM ES/3090J						
3090-110J	39	28	30	35	38	36
3090-120J	47	37	39	43	45	43
3090-150J	67	52	53	62	69	65
3090-170J	76	65	66	73	77	75
3090-180J	100	100	100	100	100	100
3090-200J	197	191	190	185	201	199
3090-250J	129	98	96	109	139	127

Table A3.1. IBM ITRs using ES/3090 Model 180 J as base of 100[1] (Concluded)

Model	MVS/ESA SP 3.1				VM/XA SP 2.1	
	Batch	Interactive			Interactive	
	CB84	CICS	IMS	TSO	PD3	HT4
IBM ES/3090J (cont.)						
3090-280J	195	189	183	183	200	196
3090-300J	290	275	271	265	302	288
3090-380J	290	280	275	274	299	284
3090-400J	377	350	339	346	401	379
3090-500J	458	422	405	421	491	463
3090-600J	538	492	477	480	588	552
IBM ES/3090T						
3090-15T	74	56	58	69	79	75
3090-17T	85	69	72	81	88	85
3090-18T	100	100	100	100	100	100
3090-25T	145	109	107	123	157	143
3090-28T	195	189	183	183	200	196
IBM ES/9000						
9121-190	43	27	27	37	56	48
9121-210	59	43	42	54	70	65
9121-260	75	62	61	71	82	79
9121-320	89	85	83	88	91	95
9021-330	94	87	89	92	96	93
9021-340	100	100	100	100	100	100
9021-440	146	118	112	133	164	154
9021-480	172	160	146	162	180	181
9021-500	197	191	190	185	201	199
9021-580	290	275	271	265	302	288
9021-620	377	350	339	346	401	379
9121-720	538	492	477	480	588	552
9021-820[2]	754	700	678	692	802	758
9021-900[2]	1076	984	954	960	1176	1104

Notes:
1 Source: announcement material issued by IBM in 5/91.
2 The ITRs for the IBM ES/9021 Models 820 and 900 are, respectively, twice the IBM ES/9021 Model 620 (IBM 3090 Model 400J) and the IBM ES/9021 Model 720 (IBM 3090 Model 600J). The value of 2 was chosen, as it is the average of all the information announced by IBM in their announcement guide (May 1991). Originally IBM claimed the multiplier to be in the range 1.7 to 1.9, but as usual with IBM, it is conservative in its choice of stating power improvements, rather than overstating its case.

Appendix 4
Complete quarter-hour RMF Monitor 1 report for the system analysed in this book

See Figs. A4.1 to A4.9 starting on page 178.

CPU REPORT

| MVS/ESA SP 4.2.0 | | | SYSTEM ID MAC1 RPT VERSION 4.2.1 | | | | DATE 28/06/93 TIME 09.00.00 | | | | | INTERVAL 15.00.000 CYCLE 1.000 SECOND | | SP4.2.0 |

CPU MODEL 9021 VERSION 49 — The Version Code for the IBM ES/9021 Model 340

CPU NUMBER	VF ONLINE	VF AFFINITY PERCENTAGE	BUSY TIME PERCENTAGE	WAIT TIME PERCENTAGE	CPU SERIAL NUMBER	% I/O TOTAL INTERRUPT RATE	% I/O INTERRUPT HANDLED VIA TPI
1	—	****	89.19	10.80	******	744.9	3.39
TOTAL/AVERAGE		****	89.19	10.80		744.9	3.39

SYSTEM ADDRESS SPACE ANALYSIS

SAMPLES = 900

TYPE	NUMBER OF ASIDS			DISTRIBUTION OF QUEUE LENGTHS (%)											
	MIN	MAX	AVE	0	1	2	3	4	5	6	7-8	9-10	11-12	13-14	14+
IN READY	0	34	9.0	11.2	6.2	6.3	4.7	5.5	4.5	5.0	8.7	9.8	8.0	6.4	23.1
				0	1-2	3-4	5-6	7-8	9-10	11-15	16-20	21-25	26-30	31-35	35+
IN	34	69	48.9	0.0	0.0	0.0	0.0	0.0	0.0	0.0	0.0	0.0	0.0	0.0	99.8
OUT READY	0	17	4.1	17.8	25.6	19.7	11.8	10.0	6.3	8.0	0.4	0.0	0.0	0.0	0.0
OUT WAIT	149	195	175.1	0.0	0.0	0.0	0.0	0.0	0.0	0.0	0.0	0.0	0.0	0.0	100.0
LOGICAL OUT RDY	0	7	0.3	79.6	17.8	2.4	0.0	0.0	0.0	0.0	0.0	0.0	0.0	0.0	0.0
LOGICAL OUT WAIT	35	79	56.5	0.0	0.0	0.0	0.0	0.0	0.0	0.0	0.0	0.0	0.0	0.0	99.9
BATCH	14	20	19.8	0.0	0.0	0.0	0.0	0.0	0.0	0.0	99.9	0.0	0.0	0.0	0.0
STC	21	27	21.3	0.0	0.0	0.0	0.0	0.0	0.0	0.0	0.0	0.0	0.0	0.0	0.0
TSO	240	249	243.9	0.0	0.0	0.0	0.0	0.0	0.0	0.0	0.0	99.9	0.0	0.0	100.0
ASCH	0	0	0.0	100.0	0.0	0.0	0.0	0.0	0.0	0.0	0.0	0.0	0.0	0.0	0.0

Figure A4.1. CPU report.

MVS/ESA SP/4.2.0			SYSTEM ID MAC1 RPT VERSION 4.2.1		I/O QUEUING ACTIVITY DATE 28/06/93 TIME 09.00.00				INTERVAL 15.00.00 CYCLE 1 SECOND
TOTAL SAMPLES = 900		IOP 02	ACTIVITY RATE 668.081	AVE Q LNGTH 0.03	IODF = 99 NO CREATION DATE AVAILABLE				ACT: ACTIVATE

LCU	CONTENTION RATE	DELAY Q LNGTH	% ALL CH PATH BUSY	CONTROL UNITS	CHAN PATHS	CHPID TAKEN	%DP BUSY	%CU BUSY	
097	0.005	0.00	1.18	1C0	01	43.842		0.39	OFFLINE
					81				OFFLINE
				1C1	25	43.858		0.48	OFFLINE
					A5				OFFLINE
0CD	0.094	0.55	3.57	560	05	58.598		1.51	OFFLINE
				561	85				OFFLINE
				562	21	58.530		1.46	OFFLINE
				563	A1				OFFLINE
0D5	0.000	0.00	12.54	620	06	92.761		0.04	OFFLINE
				621	86				OFFLINE
				622	22	92.747		0.03	OFFLINE
				623	A2				OFFLINE
0F0	0.710	0.27	5.53	780	07	44.458		5.06	OFFLINE
					87				OFFLINE
				781	23	44.254		5.12	OFFLINE
					A3				OFFLINE
15C	0.025	0.13	2.65	A90	0A	53.623		0.64	OFFLINE
					8A				OFFLINE
				A91	2E	53.421		0.63	OFFLINE
					AE				OFFLINE
173	0.000	0.00	1.30	C10	19	41.051		0.01	OFFLINE
					99				
				C11	1D	40.938		0.00	OFFLINE
					9D				

Figure A4.2. I/O queueing activity report.

CHANNEL PATH ACTIVITY

MVS/ESA SYSTEM ID MAC1 DATE 28/06/93 INTERVAL 15.00.00
SP/4.2.0 RPT VERSION 4.2.1 TIME 09.00.00 CYCLE 1 SECOND

IODF = 99   NO CREATION DATE AVAILABLE   ACT: ACTIVATE

CHANNEL PATH ID	TYPE	PERCENT CH PATH BUSY	CHANNEL PATH ID	TYPE	PERCENT CH PATH BUSY	CHANNEL PATH ID	TYPE	PERCENT CH PATH BUSY	CHANNEL PATH ID	TYPE	PERCENT CH PATH BUSY
60		OFFLINE	68		OFFLINE	80	BY	0.00	88	BL	0.05
61		OFFLINE	69		OFFLINE	81	BL	11.55	89	BL	0.00
62		OFFLINE	6A		OFFLINE	82	BL	0.00	8A	BL	16.31
63		OFFLINE	6B		OFFLINE	83	BL	0.00	8B	BL	0.00
64		OFFLINE	6C		OFFLINE	84	BL	0.00	8C	BL	0.00
65		OFFLINE	6D		OFFLINE	85	BL	18.61	8D	BL	0.00
66		OFFLINE	6E		OFFLINE	86	BL	34.65	8E	BL	0.00
67		OFFLINE	6F		OFFLINE	87	BL	23.49	8F	BL	0.00
90	BL	0.00	98	BL	0.00	A0	BL	0.00	A8	BL	0.00
91	BL	0.00	99	BL	11.13	A1	BL	19.20	A9	BL	0.00
92	BL	0.00	9A	BL	0.00	A2	BL	36.20	AA	BL	0.00
93	BL	0.00	9B	BL	0.00	A3	BL	23.52	AB	BL	0.00
94	BL	0.00	9C	BL	0.00	A4	BL	0.00	AC	BL	1.28
95	BL	0.00	9D	BL	11.65	A5	BL	10.19	AD	BL	0.00
96	BL	0.00	9E	BL	0.00	A6	BL	0.00	AE	BL	16.24
97	BL	0.00	9F	BL	0.00	A7	BL	0.00	AF	BL	0.00

All channel paths 00–5F are OFFLINE.
All channel paths B0–FF are OFFLINE.

Figure A4.3. Channel path activity report.

DIRECT ACCESS DEVICE ACTIVITY

MVS/ESA
SP/4.2.0
TOTAL SAMPLES = 900

SYSTEM ID MAC1
RPT VERSION 4.2.1

DATE 28/06/93
TIME 09.00.00
IODF = 99

INTERVAL 15.00.00
CYCLE 1 SECOND
ACT: ACTIVATE

STORAGE GROUP	DEV NUM	DEVICE TYPE	IOP	VOLUME SERIAL	LCU	DEVICE ACTIVITY RATE	AVE RESP TIME	AVE Q LNGTH IOSQ TIME	AVE DPB DLY	AVE CUB DLY	AVE DB DLY	AVE PEND TIME	AVE DISC TIME	AVE CONN TIME	% DEV CONN	DEV UTIL	% DEV RESV	AVE NUMBER ALLOC	% ANY ALLOC	% MT PEND
	1C0	3380D		CACHE1	097	18.794	3	0	0.0	0.0	0.1	0.2	0.7	2.2	4.05	5.51	2.6	7.7	100.0	0.0
	1C1	3380D		CACHE2	097	3.127	11	1	0.0	0.0	1.2	1.4	5.8	2.9	0.90	3.37	1.2	61.5	100.0	0.0
	1C2	3380D		CACHE3	097	26.931	3	0	0.0	0.0	0.1	0.2	0.0	2.8	7.52	7.60	0.0	1282	100.0	0.0
	1C3	3380D		CACHE4	097	25.537	2	0	0.0	0.0	0.1	0.2	0.0	2.2	5.55	5.68	0.0	241	100.0	0.0
	1C4	3380D		TSO1C4	097	6.758	9	1	0.0	0.0	1.3	1.5	3.5	3.6	2.43	7.06	3.5	127	100.0	0.0
	1C5	3380D		TSO1C5	097	6.554	8	1	0.0	0.0	1.5	1.6	2.7	3.2	2.09	4.60	2.7	173	100.0	0.0
				LCU	097	87.701	4	0			0.3	0.4	0.8	2.6	3.76	5.64	1.6	1892	100.0	0.0
	564	3380J		BAT564	0CD	20.039	4	1	0.0	0.0	0.0	0.3	0.4	3.0	6.08	19.37	13.9	5.6	100.0	0.0
	565	3380J		BAT565	0CD	10.908	5	0	0.0	0.0	0.0	0.3	0.5	3.5	3.85	10.69	6.7	2.7	100.0	0.0
	566	3380J		IDAVOL	0CD	15.489	2	0	0.0	0.0	0.0	0.1	0.0	1.7	2.66	2.71	0.0	7.2	100.0	0.0
	567	3380J		CB84LB	0CD	0.967	25	1	0.0	0.0	0.0	0.2	18.0	5.6	0.54	2.29	0.0	1.9	100.0	0.0
	570	3380J		CIC570	0CD	0.043	24	0	0.0	0.0	0.0	0.5	12.2	11.2	0.05	0.32	0.3	1.1	100.0	0.0
	571	3380J		WRK571	0CD	0.284	4	0	0.0	0.0	0.0	0.8	0.5	2.8	0.08	0.09	0.0	3.3	100.0	0.0
	572	3380J		BAT572	0CD	16.357	5	1	0.0	0.0	0.0	0.2	0.4	3.5	5.65	10.44	4.7	3.5	100.0	0.0
	573	3380J		BAT573	0CD	13.686	6	0	0.0	0.0	0.0	0.2	0.7	4.2	5.80	57.97	52.9	3.7	100.0	0.0
	574	3380J		BAT574	0CD	6.857	7	1	0.0	0.0	0.0	0.2	1.3	4.9	3.33	5.03	1.3	3.8	100.0	0.0
	575	3380J		BAT575	0CD	12.697	5	0	0.0	0.0	0.0	0.3	0.6	3.5	4.41	5.16	0.0	3.3	100.0	0.0
	576	3380J		MVS576	0CD	0.583	24	0	0.0	0.0	0.0	0.1	18.6	5.3	0.31	1.39	0.0	1.0	100.0	0.0
	577	3380J		MVS577	0CD	19.220	3	0	0.0	0.0	0.0	0.2	0.5	1.8	3.54	4.50	0.0	2674	100.0	0.0
				LCU	0CD	117.129	4	0			0.0	0.2	0.7	3.1	3.03	10.00	6.6	2711	100.0	0.0
	630	3380J		BAT630	0D5	27.962	69	44	0.0	0.0	0.1	0.2	21.2	3.6	10.08	69.47	9.6	9.1	100.0	0.0
	631	3380J		BAT631	0D5	21.071	58	35	0.0	0.0	0.1	0.2	20.2	3.4	7.27	64.11	29.3	7.3	100.0	0.0
	632	3380J		BAT632	0D5	25.570	59	34	0.0	0.0	0.1	0.2	21.4	3.5	8.95	63.96	2.6	7.4	100.0	0.0
	633	3380J		BAT633	0D5	23.764	69	44	0.0	0.0	0.1	0.2	21.0	3.4	8.13	58.75	5.3	7.5	100.0	0.0
	634	3380J		BAT634	0D5	26.511	58	34	0.0	0.0	0.1	0.2	20.3	3.2	8.50	64.35	10.9	8.6	100.0	0.0
	635	3380J		BAT635	0D5	18.199	46	21	0.0	0.0	0.1	0.2	19.9	4.0	7.30	48.37	12.9	6.2	100.0	0.0
	636	3380J		BAT636	0D5	20.493	45	22	0.0	0.0	0.1	0.2	19.5	3.4	6.87	66.43	33.2	6.6	100.0	0.0
	637	3380J		BAT637	0D5	21.946	74	46	0.0	0.0	0.1	0.2	23.3	4.3	9.54	76.82	51.5	7.9	100.0	0.0
				LCU	0D5	185.517	60	36			0.1	0.2	20.9	3.6	8.33	64.03	19.4	60.6	100.0	0.0
	780	3380E		RS189A	0F0	21.638	33	14	0.0	0.0	2.0	2.3	10.8	6.0	12.93	40.85	31.3	16.2	100.0	0.0
	781	3380E		RS289A	0F0	21.848	28	10	0.0	0.0	1.2	1.4	10.9	5.3	11.57	41.21	30.5	36.6	100.0	0.0
	782	3380E		CAT89A	0F0	4.999	18	2	0.0	0.0	2.7	3.1	10.1	3.5	1.76	7.66	2.5	115	100.0	0.0

Figure A4.4. Direct access device activity report (*Continues*).

DIRECT ACCESS DEVICE ACTIVITY

MVS/ESA SP/4.2.0
TOTAL SAMPLES = 900
SYSTEM ID MAC1
RPT VERSION 4.2.1
DATE 28/06/93
TIME 09.00.00
IODF = 99
INTERVAL 15.00.00
CYCLE 1 SECOND
ACT: ACTIVATE

STORAGE GROUP	DEV NUM	DEVICE TYPE	VOLUME SERIAL	LCU	DEVICE ACTIVITY RATE	AVE RESP TIME	AVE IOSQ TIME	AVE Q LNGTH DPB DLY	AVE CUB DLY	AVE DB DLY	AVE PEND TIME	AVE DISC TIME	AVE CONN TIME	% DEV CONN	DEV UTIL	% DEV RESV	AVE NUMBER ALLOC	% ANY ALLOC	% MT PEND
	783	3380E	SPL89A	0F0	4.822	19	2		0.0	2.6	3.0	11.1	3.5	1.67	7.62	2.4	125	100.0	0.0
	784	3380E	SC189A	0F0	5.332	20	3		0.0	2.8	3.2	11.1	3.4	1.81	8.34	2.7	123	100.0	0.0
	785	3380E	DL189A	0F0	4.547	19	1		0.0	2.5	2.9	11.6	3.3	1.49	7.61	2.6	123	100.0	0.0
	786	3380E	DL289A	0F0	19.243	30	11		0.0	1.3	1.6	11.8	5.6	10.79	37.45	29.3	27.1	100.0	0.0
	787	3380E	MVSTS3	0F0	0.000	0	0		0.0	0.0	0.0	0.0	0.0	0.00	0.00	0.0	0.0	100.0	0.0
	788	3380E	SMP89A	0F0	6.284	22	4		0.0	3.1	3.5	10.7	3.3	2.05	9.35	3.1	121	100.0	0.0
			LCU	0F0	88.713	27	9		0.0	1.9	2.2	11.1	5.0	4.90	17.79	11.6	686	100.0	0.0
	A90	3380D	TSOA90	15C	8.906	28	7		0.0	0.1	0.2	17.6	3.0	2.65	19.93	5.8	137	100.0	0.0
	A91	3380D	TSOA91	15C	20.838	28	11		0.0	0.2	0.2	13.7	2.7	5.66	34.93	7.6	153	100.0	0.0
	A92	3380D	TSOA92	15C	12.107	25	8		0.0	0.2	0.2	13.8	3.0	3.64	21.97	5.8	139	100.0	0.0
	A93	3380D	TSOA93	15C	6.753	23	3		0.0	0.1	0.2	16.9	2.9	1.97	15.56	5.1	151	100.0	0.0
	A94	3380D	TSOA94	15C	6.622	28	7		0.0	0.1	0.2	17.9	3.0	2.01	15.34	4.2	122	100.0	0.0
	A95	3380D	TSOA95	15C	4.586	25	4		0.0	0.2	0.2	17.7	2.8	1.28	9.92	2.9	121	100.0	0.0
	A96	3380D	TSOA96	15C	9.090	32	10		0.0	0.1	0.2	19.8	2.4	2.15	22.46	8.4	163	100.0	0.0
	A97	3380D	TSOA97	15C	7.821	24	4		0.0	0.1	0.2	17.0	2.8	2.22	17.66	6.8	125	100.0	0.0
	A98	3380D	TSOA98	15C	8.099	24	4		0.0	0.1	0.2	16.9	3.0	2.47	17.57	5.4	177	100.0	0.0
	A99	3380D	TSOA99	15C	6.767	25	4		0.0	0.1	0.2	17.2	3.6	2.42	15.48	4.8	145	100.0	0.0
	A9A	3380D	TSOA9A	15C	7.977	27	6		0.0	0.1	0.2	17.8	2.9	2.30	18.87	7.1	163	100.0	0.0
	A9B	3380D	TSOA9B	15C	7.476	23	3		0.0	0.1	0.2	17.2	2.7	2.04	16.48	3.7	134	100.0	0.0
			LCU	15C	107.040	26	7		0.0	0.1	0.2	16.4	2.9	2.57	18.85	5.6	1729	100.0	0.0
	C10	3380E	MVSDLB	173	17.546	19	2		0.0	0.0	0.1	14.7	1.8	3.10	29.01	0.3	115	100.0	0.0
	C11	3380E	CICIPO	173	2.750	19	1		0.0	0.1	0.2	14.9	2.9	0.80	4.89	0.0	3.0	100.0	0.0
	C12	3380E	AKESM1	173	0.623	21	0		0.0	0.3	0.3	15.3	5.2	0.32	1.28	0.0	5.4	100.0	0.0
	C13	3380E	MVSRES	173	28.394	115	90		0.0	0.4	0.5	20.3	4.3	12.24	69.99	3.6	7903	100.0	0.0
	C14	3380E	ESCDLB	173	0.000	0	0		0.0	0.0	0.0	0.0	0.0	0.00	0.00	0.0	0.0	100.0	0.0
	C15	3380E	MVSCAT	173	32.017	10	1		0.0	0.0	0.1	6.6	1.9	6.06	28.42	7.2	734	100.0	0.0
	C16	3380E	ESCRES	173	0.000	0	0		0.0	0.0	0.0	0.0	0.0	0.00	0.00	0.0	4.0	100.0	0.0
	C17	3380E	ESCCAT	173	0.662	21	0		0.0	0.2	0.2	14.9	5.6	0.37	1.36	0.0	1.0	100.0	0.0
			LCU	173	81.992	49	32		0.0	0.2	0.2	13.5	2.8	2.86	16.87	1.4	8765	100.0	0.0

Figure A4.4. Direct access device activity report (*Concluded*).

```
                    CENTRAL STORAGE PAGING RATES—IN PAGES PER SECOND                      PAGE 1

MVS/ESA              SYSTEM ID MAC1                    DATE 28/06/93               INTERVAL 15.00.00
SP/4.2.0             RPT VERSION 4.2.1                 TIME 09.00.00                CYCLE 1 SECOND

OPT = IEAOPT00
```

	PAGE RECLAIMS			PAGE IN				PAGE OUT			
CATEGORY	NON SWAP	% OF TOTL NON SWAP	SWAP	NON SWAP, BLOCK	NON SWAP, NON BLOCK	TOTAL RATE	% OF TOTL SUM	SWAP	NON SWAP	% OF TOTAL RATE	TOTL SUM
PAGEABLE SYSTEM AREAS (NON VIO)											
LPA	0.00	0			0.03	0.03	1		0.00	0.00	0
CSA	0.00	0			0.00	0.00	0		0.00	0.00	0
SUM	0.00	0			0.03	0.03	1		0.00	0.00	0
ADDRESS SPACES											
HIPERSPACE				0.00		0.00	0		0.00	0.00	0
VIO	4.41	99		0.00		0.00	0		0.00	0.00	0
NON VIO	0.06	1	0.47	1.93	2.88	5.28	99	0.35	0.01	0.36	100
SUM	4.47	100	0.47	1.93	2.88	5.28	99	0.35	0.01	0.36	100
TOTAL SYSTEM											
HIPERSPACE				0.00		0.00	0		0.00	0.00	0
VIO	4.41	99		0.00		0.00	0		0.00	0.00	0
NON VIO	0.06	1	0.47	1.93	2.91	5.31	100	0.35	0.01	0.36	100
SUM	4.47	100	0.47	1.93	2.91	5.31	100	0.35	0.01	0.36	100

```
PAGE MOVEMENT WITHIN CENTRAL STORAGE        55.40
AVERAGE NUMBER OF PAGES PER BLOCK            5.30
BLOCKS PER SECOND                            0.37
PAGE-IN EVENTS (PAGE FAULT RATE)             3.28
```

Figure A4.5(a). Central storage paging rates—in pages per second.

```
MVS/ESA                                      PAGING ACTIVITY                                    PAGE 2
SP/4.2.0                    SYSTEM ID MAC1              DATE 28/06/93                INTERVAL 15.00.00
                            RPT VERSION 4.2.1           TIME 09.00.00                 CYCLE 1 SECOND
OPT = IEAOPT00              EXPANDED STORAGE MOVEMENT RATES – IN PAGES PER SECOND

  ESF CONFIGURATION                                                               HIGH UIC
INSTALLED     ONLINE                                                              MIN    5
                                                                                  MAX   70
131072        131072                                                              AVE   31.5

                        WRITTEN TO        READ FROM        MIGRATED         FREED              EXPANDED
                        EXP STOR          EXP STOR         FROM             WITHOUT            STORAGE FRAME COUNTS          MIGR AGE
                                                           EXP STOR         MIGRATION          MIN      MAX       AVE
TOTAL         RT        1013.7            899.15           3.93             0.15               122791   130884    127162     2326
PAGES         %         100.0%            100.0%           100.0%                                                            2326
HIPERSPACE    RT        68.12             10.62            0.00                                22989    28432     25175      2326
PAGES         %         6.7%              1.2%             0.0%
VIO           RT        9.25              8.44             0.00                                387      1874      1127
PAGES         %         0.9%              0.9%             0.0%
```

FRAME AND SLOT COUNTS

```
                  CENTRAL STORAGE            EXPANDED STORAGE            LOCAL PAGE DATA SET SLOT COUNTS
(181 SAMPLES)     MIN    MAX     AVE         MIN      MAX      AVE                           MIN       MAX       AVE
TOTAL FRAMES      31232  31232   31232       131072   131072   131072     AVAILABLE SLOTS    226846    232349    230297
SQA               2350   2368    2361        51       53       51         VIO SLOTS          0         0         0
LPA               899    1028    958         57       187      127
CSA               435    630     600         0        192      26         NON-VIO SLOTS      37801     43304     39852
LSQA              3175   4096    3625        1713     1803     1745
REGIONS + SWA     20792  22893   22373       122788   130569   127009     BAD SLOTS          0         0         0
AVAILABLE         74     1857    309         188      8281     3910
                                                                          TOTAL SLOTS        270150    270150    270150
FIXED FRAMES      10809  11831   11292
NUCLEUS           1003   1003    1003
SQA               2346   2364    2357
LPA               104    107     104
CSA               155    156     155
LSQA              3014   3915    3453
REGIONS + SWA     4140   4367    4218
BELOW 16 MEG      1720   2024    1830
```

Figure A4.5(b). Expanded storage movement rates—in pages per second.

		TOTAL	AUX STOR TOTAL	AUX STORAGE — AUX STOR DIRECT	AUX STOR VIA TRANSITION	LOGICAL SWAP — LOG SWAP	LOG SWAP EFFECTIVE	EXP STOR DIRECT	EXPANDED STORAGE — EXP STOR TOTAL	MIGRATED FROM EXP STOR	EXP STOR EFFECTIVE	LOG SWAP /EXP STOR EFFECTIVE
TERMINAL INPUT/OUTPUT WAIT	CT RT %	15 556 17.28 94.4%	3 0.00 0.0%	0 0.00 0.0%	3 0.00 100.0%	15 556 17.28 100.0%	12 013 13.35 77.2%	0 0.00 0.0%	3 540 3.93 22.8%	0 0.00 0.0%	3 540 3.93 100.0%	15 553 17.28 100.0%
LONG WAIT	CT RT %	7 0.01 0.0%	0 0.00 0.0%	0 0.00 0.0%	0 0.00 0.0%	7 0.01 100.0%	5 0.01 71.4%	0 0.00 0.0%	2 0.00 28.6%	0 0.00 0.0%	2 0.00 100.0%	7 0.01 100.0%
DETECTED WAIT	CT RT %	99 0.11 0.6%	0 0.00 0.0%	0 0.00 0.0%	0 0.00 0.0%	99 0.11 100.0%	54 0.06 54.5%	0 0.00 0.0%	45 0.05 45.5%	0 0.00 0.0%	45 0.05 100.0%	99 0.11 100.0%
UNILATERAL	CT RT %	776 0.86 4.7%	0 0.00 0.0%	0 0.00 0.0%	0 0.00 0.0%	755 0.84 97.3%	189 0.21 25.0%	21 0.02 2.7%	587 0.65 75.6%	0 0.00 0.0%	587 0.65 100.0%	776 0.86 100.0%
EXCHANGE ON RECOMMENDATION VALUE	CT RT %	14 0.02 0.1%	0 0.00 0.0%	0 0.00 0.0%	0 0.00 0.0%	13 0.01 92.9%	0 0.00 0.0%	1 0.00 7.1%	14 0.02 100.0%	0 0.00 0.0%	14 0.02 100.0%	14 0.02 100.0%
TRANSITION TO NON-SWAPPABLE	CT RT %	1 0.00 0.0%	0 0.00 0.0%	0 0.00 0.0%	0 0.00 0.0%	0 0.00 0.0%	0 0.00 0.0%	0 0.00 100.0%	0 0.00 100.0%	0 0.00 0.0%	0 0.00 100.0%	1 0.00 100.0%
IMPROVE CENTRAL STORAGE	CT RT %	30 0.03 0.2%	0 0.00 0.0%	0 0.00 0.0%	0 0.00 0.0%	30 0.03 100.0%	1 0.00 3.3%	0 0.00 0.0%	29 0.03 96.7%	0 0.00 0.0%	29 0.03 100.0%	30 0.03 100.0%
TOTAL	CT RT %	16483 18.31 100.0%	3 0.00 0.0%	0 0.00 0.0%	3 0.00 100.0%	16460 18.29 99.9%	12 262 13.62 74.5%	23 0.03 0.1%	4218 4.69 25.6%	0 0.00 0.0%	4218 4.69 100.0%	16480 18.31 100.0%

AUXILIARY STORAGE – AVERAGE PAGES PER SWAP OUT – 105   AVERAGE PAGES PER SWAP IN – 140
OCCURRENCES OF TERMINAL OUTPUT WAIT – 1079

Figure A4.5(c). Swap placement activity report.

PAGE/SWAP DATA SET ACTIVITY

MVS/ESA SP/4.2.0		SYSTEM ID MAC1 RPT VERSION 4.2.1									INTERVAL 15.00.00 CYCLE 1 SECOND	

NUMBER OF SAMPLES = 900

DATE 28/06/93
TIME 09.00.00

PAGE DATA SET USAGE

PAGE SPACE TYPE	VOLUME SERIAL	DEV NUM	DEVICE TYPE	SLOTS ALLOC	SLOTS USED MIN	SLOTS USED MAX	SLOTS USED AVE	BAD SLOTS	% IN USE	PAGE TRANS TIME	NUMBER IO REQ	PAGES XFER'D	V I O	DATA SET NAME
PLPA	MVSCAT	C15	3380E	3000	2986	2986	2986	0	0.06	0.018	38	28		PAGE.VMSCAT.PLPA.CYL20
COMMON	MVSCAT	C15	3380E	1950	520	525	521	0	0.06	0.062	8	8		PAGE.VMSCAT.COMMON
LOCAL	MVS576	576	3380J	60000	5998	6985	6333	0	1.50	0.010	525	1402	Y	PAGE.VMVS576.LOCAL
LOCAL	AKESM1	C12	3380E	42000	6723	7747	7097	0	0.83	0.005	515	1417	Y	PAGE.VAKESM1.LOCAL
LOCAL	ESCCAT	C17	3380E	32100	6827	7899	7276	0	2.06	0.011	596	1678	Y	PAGE.VESCCAT.LOCAL
LOCAL	MVS577	577	3380J	16050	5469	6060	5693	0	1.33	0.011	687	1064	Y	PAGE.VMVS577.LOCAL
LOCAL	CB84LB	567	3380J	60000	6189	7138	6568	0	1.83	0.012	518	1362	Y	PAGE.VCB84LB.LOCAL
LOCAL	CICIPO	C11	3380E	60000	6460	7476	6876	0	1.89	0.011	850	1528	Y	PAGE.VCICIPO.LOCAL

Figure A4.6. Page/swap data set activity report.

WORKLOAD ACTIVITY

```
MVS/ESA                SYSTEM ID MAC1              DATE 28/06/93           INTERVAL 15.00.000
SP4.2.0                RPT VERSION 4.2.1           TIME 09.00.000          IPS = IEAIPS00

OPT = IEAOPT00         REPORT BY PERFORMANCE GROUP    SERVICE DEFINITION COEFFICIENTS   SU/SEC = 1162.3
ICS = IEAICS00                    PERIOD               IOC = 5.0   CPU = 10.0           MSO = 0.1000
                                                       SRB = 10.0
```

PGN	PGP	DMN	TIME SLICE GROUP	INTERVAL SERVICE	AVERAGE AVE TRX TCB+SRB	ABSORPTION SERV RATE SECONDS, %	PAGE-IN RATES	RATES	STORAGE		TRANSACTIONS		AVE TRANS TIME, STD DEVIATION HHH.MM.SS.TTT	
SUBSYS = JES2 USERID =				TRXCLASS = TRXNAME =		ACCTINFO = NO								
0001	1	001	**	IOC = 602955	ABSRPTN	216	SINGLE	0.00	AVERAGE	224.42	AVE	9.58	TRX	000.00.35.345
				CPU = 795915	TRX SERV	172	BLOCK	0.00			MPL	8.63	SD	000.00.51.890
				MSO = 31690	TCB	68.4	HSP	0.00	TOTAL	1713.5	ENDED	202		
				SRB = 56777	SRB	4.8	HSP MISS	0.00	CENTRAL	1277.4	END/SEC	0.22	QUE	003.40.53.885
				TOT = 1487337	TCB+SRB%	8.1	EXP SNGL	1.05	EXPAND	436.09	#SWAPS	169		
				PER SEC = 1652			EXP BLK	0.51					TOT	003.41.29.230
0001	2	002	**	IOC = 262405	ABSRPTN	148	SINGLE	0.00	AVERAGE	440.75	AVE	4.75	TRX	000.04.26.383
				CPU = 275065	TRX SERV	132	BLOCK	0.00			MPL	4.21	SD	000.02.38.300
				MSO = 7792	TCB	23.6	HSP	0.00	TOTAL	1859.8	ENDED	12		
				SRB = 20364	SRB	1.7	HSP MISS	0.00	CENTRAL	495.88	END/SEC	0.01	QUE	038.53.38.679
				TOT = 565626	TCB+SRB%	2.8	EXP SNGL	0.49	EXPAND	1363.9	#SWAPS	36		
				PER SEC = 628			EXP BLK	0.27					TOT	038.58.05.062
0001	ALL	ALL	ALL	IOC = 865360	ABSRPTN	192	SINGLE	0.00	AVERAGE	301.42	AVE	14.33	TRX	000.00.48.300
				CPU = 1070980	TRX SERV	159	BLOCK	0.00			MPL	11.85	SD	000.01.21.700
				MSO = 39482	TCB	92.1	HSP	0.00	TOTAL	3573.3	ENDED	214		
				SRB = 77141	SRB	6.6	HSP MISS	0.00	CENTRAL	1773.3	END/SEC	0.23	QUE	005.39.22.191
				TOT = 2052963	TCB+SRB%	10.9	EXP SNGL	0.85	EXPAND	1800.0	#SWAPS	205		
				PER SEC = 2281			EXP BLK	0.42					TOT	005.40.10.492

Figure A4.7(a). RMF Monitor I workload activity report—the application performance groups.

WORKLOAD ACTIVITY

MVS/ESA SP4.2.0
OPT = IEAOPT00
ICS = IEAICS00

SYSTEM ID MAC1
RPT VERSION 4.2.1
REPORT BY PERFORMANCE GROUP PERIOD

DATE 28/06/93
TIME 09.00.000

INTERVAL 15.00.000
IPS = IEAIPS00

SERVICE DEFINITION COEFFICIENTS
IOC = 5.0   CPU = 10.0   SRB = 10.0
SU/SEC = 1162.3   MSO = 0.1000

SUBSYS = TSO   TRXCLASS =   ACCTINFO = NO
USERID =   TRXNAME =

PGN	PGP	DMN	TIME SLICE GROUP	INTERVAL SERVICE	AVERAGE AVE TRX TCB + SRB	ABSORPTION SERV RATE SECONDS. %	PAGE-IN RATES	RATES	STORAGE		TRANSACTIONS		AVE TRANS TIME, STD DEVIATION HHH.MM.SS.TTT	
0002	1	021	**	IOC = 189230	ABSRPTN	792	SINGLE	0.77	AVERAGE	450.51	AVE	1.75	TRX	000.00.00.064
				CPU = 883683	TRX SERV	740	BLOCK	0.41			MPL	1.63	SD	000.00.00.148
				MSO = 35159	TCB	76.0	HSP	0.00	TOTAL	738.07	ENDED	9515		
				SRB = 60968	SRB	5.2	HSP MISS	0.00	CENTRAL	368.82	END/SEC	10.57	QUE	000.00.00.000
				TOT = 1169040	TCB + SRB%	9.0	EXP SNGL	244.00	EXPAND	369.25	#SWAPS	9482		
				PER SEC = 1298			EXP BLK	0.00					TOT	000.00.00.064
0002	2	022	**	IOC = 405240	ABSRPTN	447	SINGLE	0.14	AVERAGE	456.53	AVE	4.86	TRX	000.00.01.834
				CPU = 1306511	TRX SERV	415	BLOCK	0.08			MPL	4.51	SD	000.00.02.063
				MSO = 64266	TCB	112.4	HSP	0.00	TOTAL	2062.2	ENDED	1891		
				SRB = 43403	SRB	3.7	HSP MISS	0.00	CENTRAL	1165.9	END/SEC	2.10	QUE	000.17.43.702
				TOT = 1819420	TCB + SRB%	12.9	EXP SNGL	15.72	EXPAND	896.26	#SWAPS	2216		
				PER SEC = 2021			EXP BLK	0.12					TOT	000.17.45.536
0002	3	023	**	IOC = 278040	ABSRPTN	368	SINGLE	0.70	AVERAGE	514.53	AVE	3.85	TRX	000.00.12.762
				CPU = 706309	TRX SERV	301	BLOCK	0.00			MPL	3.15	SD	000.00.10.670
				MSO = 37464	TCB	60.7	HSP	0.00	TOTAL	1624.2	ENDED	408		
				SRB = 25485	SRB	2.1	HSP MISS	0.00	CENTRAL	847.50	END/SEC	0.45	QUE	000.00.00.000
				TOT = 1047298	TCB + SRB%	6.9	EXP SNGL	8.75	EXPAND	776.70	#SWAPS	555		
				PER SEC = 1163			EXP BLK	3.36					TOT	000.00.12.762
0002	ALL	ALL	ALL	IOC = 872510	ABSRPTN	481	SINGLE	0.20	AVERAGE	475.10	AVE	10.47	TRX	000.00.00.786
				CPU = 2896503	TRX SERV	428	BLOCK	0.11			MPL	9.31	SD	000.00.03.189
				MSO = 136889	TCB	249.2	HSP	0.00	TOTAL	4424.5	ENDED	11814		
				SRB = 129856	SRB	11.1	HSP MISS	0.00	CENTRAL	2382.2	END/SEC	13.12	QUE	000.02.50.260
				TOT = 4035758	TCB + SRB%	28.9	EXP SNGL	53.52	EXPAND	2042.2	#SWAPS	12253		
				PER SEC = 4484			EXP BLK	1.19					TOT	000.02.51.047

Figure A4.7(b). RMF Monitor I workload activity report—the application performance groups.

WORKLOAD ACTIVITY

```
MVS/ESA                    SYSTEM ID MAC1                              DATE 28/06/93         INTERVAL 15.00.000
SP4.2.0                    RPT VERSION 4.2.1                           TIME 09.00.000        IPS = IEAIPS00

OPT = IEAOPT00             REPORT BY PERFORMANCE GROUP                 SERVICE DEFINITION COEFFICIENTS    SU/SEC = 1162.3
ICS = IEAICS00                        PERIOD                           IOC = 5.0    CPU = 10.0            MSO = 0.1000
                                                                       SRB = 10.0
```

SUBSYS = JES2   TRXCLASS =   ACCTINFO = NO
USERID =   TRXNAME =

PGN	PGP	DMN	TIME SLICE GROUP	INTERVAL SERVICE	AVERAGE AVE TRX TCB + SRB	ABSORPTION SERV RATE SECONDS, %	PAGE-IN RATES		STORAGE		TRANSACTIONS		AVE TRANS TIME, STD DEVIATION HHH.MM.SS.TTT	
0011	1	011	**	IOC = 430170	ABSRPTN	619	SINGLE	0.00	AVERAGE	162.60	AVE	2.67	TRX	000.00.25.472
				CPU = 771356	TRX SERV	524	BLOCK	0.00			MPL	2.26	SD	000.00.20.030
				MSO = 21216	TCB	66.3	HSP	0.00	TOTAL	368.34	ENDED	117		
				SRB = 39799	SRB	3.4	HSP MISS	0.00	CENTRAL	291.54	END/SEC	0.13	QUE	005.02.04.127
				TOT = 1262541	TCB + SRB%	7.7	EXP SNGL	1.38	EXPAND	76.80	#SWAPS	67		
				PER SEC = 1402			EXP BLK	0.22					TOT	005.02.29.600
0011	2	012	**	IOC = 173705	ABSRPTN	1746	SINGLE	0.00	AVERAGE	206.29	AVE	0.63	TRX	000.01.47.140
				CPU = 372921	TRX SERV	1003	BLOCK	0.00			MPL	0.36	SD	000.00.42.980
				MSO = 14003	TCB	32.0	HSP	0.00	TOTAL	74.96	ENDED	13		
				SRB = 10406	SRB	0.8	HSP MISS	0.00	CENTRAL	57.19	END/SEC	0.01	QUE	078.04.23.336
				TOT = 571035	TCB + SRB%	3.6	EXP SNGL	4.24	EXPAND	17.77	#SWAPS	23		
				PER SEC = 634			EXP BLK	2.63					TOT	078.06.10.477
0011	ALL	ALL	ALL	IOC = 603875	ABSRPTN	775	SINGLE	0.00	AVERAGE	168.64	AVE	3.30	TRX	000.00.33.639
				CPU = 1144277	TRX SERV	615	BLOCK	0.00			MPL	2.62	SD	000.00.33.730
				MSO = 35219	TCB	98.4	HSP	0.00	TOTAL	443.41	ENDED	130		
				SRB = 50205	SRB	4.3	HSP MISS	0.00	CENTRAL	348.74	END/SEC	0.14	QUE	012.20.18.048
				TOT = 1833576	TCB + SRB%	11.4	EXP SNGL	1.78	EXPAND	94.57	#SWAPS	90		
				PER SEC = 2037			EXP BLK	0.56					TOT	012.20.51.688

Figure A4.7(c). RMF Monitor I workload activity report—the application performance groups.

WORKLOAD ACTIVITY

MVS/ESA SP4.2.0
OPT = IEAOPT00
ICS = IEAICS00

SYSTEM ID MAC1
RPT VERSION 4.2.1
REPORT BY PERFORMANCE GROUP PERIOD

DATE 28/06/93
TIME 09.00.000

INTERVAL 15.00.000
IPS = IEAIPS00

SERVICE DEFINITION COEFFICIENTS
IOC = 5.0 CPU = 10.0 SRB = 10.0
SU/SEC = 1162.3 MSO = 0.1000

SUBSYS = TSO
USERID =
TRXCLASS =
TRXNAME =
ACCTINFO = NO

PGN	PGP	DMN	TIME SLICE GROUP	INTERVAL SERVICE		AVERAGE AVE TRX TCB + SRB	ABSORPTION SERV RATE SECONDS, %	PAGE-IN RATES		RATES	STORAGE			TRANSACTIONS			AVE TRANS TIME, STD DEVIATION HHH.MM.SS.TTT	
0042	1	031	**	IOC =	58 875	ABSRPTN	1059	SINGLE		0.74	AVERAGE		470.88	AVE		0.39	TRX	000.00.00.049
				CPU =	276 936	TRX SERV	1024	BLOCK		0.77				MPL		0.38	SD	000.00.00.225
				MSO =	12 696	TCB	23.8	HSP		0.00	TOTAL		180.69	ENDED		2564		
				SRB =	17 391	SRB	1.4	HSP MISS		0.00	CENTRAL		91.06	END/SEC		2.84	QUE	000.00.00.000
				TOT =	365 898	TCB + SRB%	2.8	EXP SNGL		304.67	EXPAND		89.63	#SWAPS		2554		
				PER SEC =	406			EXP BLK		0.00							TOT	000.00.00.049
0042	2	032	**	IOC =	134 290	ABSRPTN	724	SINGLE		0.20	AVERAGE		479.25	AVE		0.91	TRX	000.00.01.217
				CPU =	407 099	TRX SERV	699	BLOCK		0.11				MPL		0.88	SD	000.00.01.087
				MSO =	21 769	TCB	35.0	HSP		0.00	TOTAL		424.72	ENDED		573		
				SRB =	14 934	SRB	1.2	HSP MISS		0.00	CENTRAL		252.38	END/SEC		0.63	QUE	001.15.14.522
				TOT =	578 092	TCB + SRB%	4.0	EXP SNGL		19.33	EXPAND		172.34	#SWAPS		609		
				PER SEC =	642			EXP BLK		0.01							TOT	001.15.15.739
0042	3	033	**	IOC =	96 205	ABSRPTN	605	SINGLE		0.01	AVERAGE		513.31	AVE		0.60	TRX	000.00.06.913
				CPU =	204 427	TRX SERV	589	BLOCK		0.00				MPL		0.59	SD	000.00.05.150
				MSO =	12 502	TCB	17.5	HSP		0.00	TOTAL		304.19	ENDED		131		
				SRB =	9643	SRB	0.8	HSP MISS		0.00	CENTRAL		198.22	END/SEC		0.14	QUE	000.00.00.000
				TOT =	322 777	TCB + SRB%	2.0	EXP SNGL		6.24	EXPAND		105.97	#SWAPS		137		
				PER SEC =	358			EXP BLK		0.00							TOT	000.00.06.913
0042	ALL	ALL	ALL	IOC =	289 370	ABSRPTN	755	SINGLE		0.25	AVERAGE		488.36	AVE		1.92	TRX	000.00.00.529
				CPU =	888 462	TRX SERV	731	BLOCK		0.21				MPL		1.86	SD	000.00.01.789
				MSO =	46 967	TCB	76.4	HSP		0.00	TOTAL		909.61	ENDED		3268		
				SRB =	41 968	SRB	3.6	HSP MISS		0.00	CENTRAL		541.66	END/SEC		3.63	QUE	000.13.11.560
				TOT =	1 266 767	TCB + SRB%	8.9	EXP SNGL		73.95	EXPAND		367.95	#SWAPS		3300		
				PER SEC =	1407			EXP BLK		0.00							TOT	000.13.12.090

Figure A4.7(d). RMF Monitor I workload activity report—the application performance groups.

WORKLOAD ACTIVITY

MVS/ESA SP4.2.0				SYSTEM ID MAC1 RPT VERSION 4.2.1		DATE 28/06/93 TIME 09.00.000				INTERVAL 15.00.000 IPS = IEAIPS00	
OPT = IEAOPT00 ICS = IEAICS00				REPORT BY PERFORMANCE GROUP PERIOD		SERVICE DEFINITION COEFFICIENTS IOC = 5.0 CPU = 10.0 SRB = 10.0				SU/SEC = 1162.3 MSO = 0.1000	

PGN	PGP	DMN	TIME SLICE GROUP	INTERVAL SERVICE	AVERAGE AVE TRX TCB + SRB	ABSORPTION SERV RATE SECONDS, %	PAGE-IN RATES	RATES	STORAGE		TRANSACTIONS		AVE TRANS TIME, STD DEVIATION HHH.MM.SS.TTT
SUBSYS = JES2 USERID =				TRXCLASS = TRXNAME = CPU(1)		ACCTINFO = NO							
0111	1	**		IOC = 3015	ABSRPTN 166		SINGLE	0.00	AVERAGE	91.67	AVE	0.05	TRX 000.00.06.437
				CPU = 2669	TRX SERV 121		BLOCK	0.00			MPL	0.03	SD 000.00.06.450
				MSO = 4	TCB 0.2		HSP	0.00	TOTAL	3.60	ENDED	9	
				SRB = 188	SRB 0.0		HSP MISS	0.00	CENTRAL	2.85	END/SEC	0.01	QUE 000.00.00.000
				TOT = 5876	TCB + SRB% 0.0		EXP SNGL	1.01	EXPAND	0.75	#SWAPS	2	
				PER SEC = 6			EXP BLK	0.00					TOT 000.00.06.437
SUBSYS = TSO USERID =				TRXCLASS = TRXNAME =		ACCTINFO = NO							
0999	1	128	**	IOC = 14675	ABSRPTN 377		SINGLE	0.30	AVERAGE	536.79	AVE	0.26	TRX 000.00.01.917
				CPU = 69251	TRX SERV 376		BLOCK	0.26			MPL	0.26	SD 000.00.10.650
				MSO = 3410	TCB 5.9		HSP	0.00	TOTAL	141.92	ENDED	388	
				SRB = 2493	SRB 0.2		HSP MISS	0.00	CENTRAL	78.25	END/SEC	0.43	QUE 002.30.02.113
				TOT = 89829	TCB + SRB% 0.6		EXP SNGL	50.73	EXPAND	63.67	#SWAPS	397	
				PER SEC = 99			EXP BLK	0.00					TOT 002.30.04.031

Figure A4.7(e). RMF Monitor I workload activity report—the application performance groups.

WORKLOAD ACTIVITY

```
MVS/ESA                SYSTEM ID MAC1              DATE 28/06/93           INTERVAL 15.00.000
SP4.2.0                RPT VERSION 4.2.1           TIME 09.00.000          IPS = IEAIPS00

OPT = IEAOPT00         REPORT BY PERFORMANCE GROUP     SERVICE DEFINITION COEFFICIENTS    SU/SEC = 1162.3
ICS = IEAICS00                   PERIOD                IOC = 5.0   CPU = 10.0  SRB = 10.0  MSO = 0.1000
```

PGN	PGP	DMN	TIME SLICE GROUP	INTERVAL SERVICE	AVERAGE AVE TRX TCB + SRB	ABSORPTION SERV RATE SECONDS, %	PAGE-IN RATES	RATES	STORAGE		TRANSACTIONS		AVE TRANS TIME, STD DEVIATION HHH.MM.SS.TTT	
0000	1	000	**	IOC = 1435 CPU = 260715 MSO = 28413 SRB = 214659 TOT = 505222 PER SEC = 561	ABSRPTN TRX SERV TCB SRB TCB + SRB%	109 109 22.4 18.4 4.5	SINGLE BLOCK HSP HSP MISS EXP SNGL EXP BLK	0.00 0.00 0.00 0.00 0.33 0.00	AVERAGE TOTAL CENTRAL EXPAND	309.92 1595.7 1214.7 381.08	AVE MPL ENDED ENDED/SEC #SWAPS	5.14 5.14 0 0.00 43	TRX SD QUE TOT	000.00.00.000 000.00.00.000 000.00.00.000 000.00.00.000
SUBSYS = STC USERID =				TRXCLASS = TRXNAME =										
0100	1	100	**	IOC = 22426 CPU = 152676 MSO = 4709 SRB = 42501 TOT = 222312 PER SEC = 247	ABSRPTN TRX SERV TCB SRB TCB + SRB%	24 24 13.1 3.6 1.8	SINGLE BLOCK HSP HSP MISS EXP SNGL EXP BLK	0.00 0.00 0.00 0.00 0.12 0.00	AVERAGE TOTAL CENTRAL EXPAND	3011.2 30526 4733.6 25793	AVE MPL ENDED END/SEC #SWAPS	10.13 10.13 1 0.00 0	TRX SD QUE TOT	000.03.55.622 000.00.00.000 547.50.56.559 547.54.52.181
SUBSYS = STC USERID =				TRXCLASS = TRXNAME = LLA										
0102	1	100	**	IOC = 965 CPU = 2435 MSO = 118 SRB = 111 TOT = 3629 PER SEC = 4	ABSRPTN TRX SERV TCB SRB TCB + SRB%	4 4 0.2 0.0 0.0	SINGLE BLOCK HSP HSP MISS EXP SNGL EXP BLK	0.00 0.09 0.00 0.00 0.56 0.00	AVERAGE TOTAL CENTRAL EXPAND	320.21 320.21 179.29 140.92	AVE MPL ENDED END/SEC #SWAPS	1.00 1.00 0 0.00 0	TRX SD QUE TOT	000.00.00.000 000.00.00.000 000.00.00.000 000.00.00.000
SUBSYS = STC USERID =				TRXCLASS = TRXNAME = NET										
0104	1	100	**	IOC = 0 CPU = 8424 MSO = 475 SRB = 17389 TOT = 26288 PER SEC = 29	ABSRPTN TRX SERV TCB SRB TCB + SRB%	29 29 0.7 1.4 0.2	SINGLE BLOCK HSP HSP MISS EXP SNGL EXP BLK	0.01 0.01 0.00 0.00 1.68 0.00	AVERAGE TOTAL CENTRAL EXPAND	457.40 457.40 326.90 130.50	AVE MPL ENDED END/SEC #SWAPS	1.00 1.00 0 0.00 0	TRX SD QUE TOT	000.00.00.000 000.00.00.000 000.00.00.000 000.00.00.000

Figure A4.8(a). RMF Monitor I workload activity report—the system performance groups.

WORKLOAD ACTIVITY

MVS/ESA
SP4.2.0
OPT = IEAOPT00
ICS = IEAICS00

SYSTEM ID MAC1
RPT VERSION 4.2.1
REPORT BY PERFORMANCE GROUP PERIOD

DATE 28/06/93
TIME 09.00.000

INTERVAL 15.00.000
IPS = IEAIPS00

SERVICE DEFINITION COEFFICIENTS
IOC = 5.0   CPU = 10.0   SRB = 10.0
SU/SEC = 1162.3   MSO = 0.1000

SUBSYS = STC
USERID =

PGN	PGP	DMN	TIME SLICE GROUP	INTERVAL SERVICE	AVERAGE AVE TRX TCB + SRB	ABSORPTION SERV RATE SECONDS, %	PAGE-IN RATES	RATES		STORAGE		TRANSACTIONS		AVE TRANS TIME, STD DEVIATION HHH.MM.SS.TTT	
0105	1	100	**	TRXCLASS = TRXNAME = JES2											
				IOC = 89059	ABSRPTN	270	SINGLE	0.00		AVERAGE	423.01	AVE	1.00	TRX	000.00.00.000
				CPU = 133 513	TRX SERV	270	BLOCK	0.02				MPL	1.00	SD	000.00.00.000
				MSO = 9572	TCB	11.4	HSP	0.00		TOTAL	423.01	ENDED	0		
				SRB = 11340	SRB	0.9	HSP MISS	0.00		CENTRAL	312.14	END/SEC	0.00	QUE	000.00.00.000
				TOT = 243 484	TCB + SRB%	1.3	EXP SNGL	0.46		EXPAND	110.87	#SWAPS	0		
				PER SEC = 270			EXP BLK	0.00						TOT	000.00.00.000
0106	1	100	**	IOC = 415	ABSRPTN	27	SINGLE	0.00		AVERAGE	132.21	AVE	1.00	TRX	000.00.00.000
				CPU = 11546	TRX SERV	27	BLOCK	0.00				MPL	1.00	SD	000.00.00.000
				MSO = 63	TCB	0.9	HSP	0.00		TOTAL	132.21	ENDED	0		
				SRB = 12523	SRB	1.0	HSP MISS	0.00		CENTRAL	52.01	END/SEC	0.00	QUE	000.00.00.000
				TOT = 24547	TCB + SRB%	0.2	EXP SNGL	0.08		EXPAND	80.20	#SWAPS	0		
				PER SEC = 27			EXP BLK	0.00						TOT	000.00.00.000

Figure A4.8(b). RMF Monitor I workload activity report—the application performance groups.

WORKLOAD ACTIVITY

MVS/ESA
SP4.2.0

SYSTEM ID MAC1
RPT VERSION 4.2.1
SYSTEM SUMMARY

DATE 28/06/93
TIME 09.00.000

INTERVAL 15.00.000
IPS = IEAIPS00

OPT = IEAOPT00
ICS = IEAICS00

SERVICE DEFINITION COEFFICIENTS
IOC = 5.0   CPU = 10.0   SRB = 10.0

SU/SEC = 1162.3
MSO = 0.1000

PGN	PGP	DMN	TIME SLICE GROUP	INTERVAL SERVICE		AVERAGE AVE TRX TCB+SRB	ABSORPTION SERV RATE SECONDS, %	PAGE-IN RATES	RATES	STORAGE		TRANSACTIONS		AVE TRANS TIME, STD DEV HHH.MM.SS.TTT	
ALL	ALL	ALL	ALL	IOC	2 760 090	ABSRPTN	247	SINGLE	0.05	AVERAGE	982.41	AVE	50.59	TRX	000.00.01.688
				CPU	6 638 865	TRX SERV	226	BLOCK	0.04			MPL	46.20	SD	000.00.12.340
				MSO	305 398	TCB	571.1	HSP	0.00	TOTAL	45 396	ENDED	15 815		
				SRB	600 186	SRB	51.6	HSP MISS	0.00	CENTRAL	13 844	END/SEC	17.57	QUE	000.21.16.965
				TOT	10 304 539	TCB+SRB%	69.1	EXP SNGL	14.78	EXPAND	31 552	#SWAPS	16 288		
				PER SEC	11 449			EXP BLK	0.38					TOT	000.21.18.654

Figure A4.9. RMF Monitor I workload activity report—system summary.

Appendix 5
The M Value as an alternative to relative processor power

Relative processor power (RPP) is the main accepted method of calculating the power of processors, not just IBM processors, but any manufacturer's mainframes. IBM Canada has used an alternative to this called *M Values*, but this method is losing favour against the RPP method. It is essential as capacity planners that you are aware of this method, as you may meet some of its advocates during your travels, and it behoves a professional to understand all options.

The rationale of M Values is the same as for ITRRs (and hence RPP), and that is to use an established workload. As for ITRRs, the IBM 3090 Model 180S is the basis for calibration at the time of writing. This may change, but the principle does not. The IBM 3090 Model 180S is stated to have 24.5 RPP, and at the same time an M Value of 1000. Each of the 1000 units is referred to as a *quantum*, therefore the processor is said to have an M Value of 1000 quanta.

Both methods base their principle on the amount of processor power required to sustain a given I/O rate on a machine. The RPP method uses the relative I/O content (RIOC) method (see Chapter 7), whereas the M Value uses the I/Os per quantum (I/O per Q) method, as shown in Sec. A5.1. The formula for the RIOC is:

$$\text{RIOC} = \frac{\text{Sustained I/O rate}}{\text{Processor RPP} \times \text{CPU busy percentage}}$$

where (Processor RPP × CPU busy percentage) = Utilized RPP (URPP).
The formula for I/O per Q is:

$$\text{I/O per Q} = \frac{\text{Sustained I/O rate}}{\text{Processor M Value} \times \text{CPU busy percentage}}$$

where (Processor M Value × CPU busy percentage) = Utilized M Value (UMV).

So you see, the UMV is the same as the URPP, and is arrived at in exactly the same manner; the total processor power of the machine multiplied by CPU busy.

A5.1 The RIOC versus the I/O per Q

Let us suppose we have a 75 per cent loaded IBM 3090 Model 180S, supporting 200 I/Os per second.

Using the RIOC method:

$$\text{RIOC} = 200/(24.5 \times 75) = 10.88 \text{ I/Os per URPP}$$

Using the M Value method:

$$\text{I/O per Q} = 200/(1000 \times 0.75) = 0.27 \text{ I/Os per quantum}$$

It is essential to understand that, as for the RIOC method, the M Value method requires that the workload is constant. As workloads change, then so will the RIOC and the M Value.

A5.2 How is the M Value of another processor derived?

First we have to find the I/O per quantum on the original machine. We will use as our example a migration from a 3090 Model 180S (24.5 RPP) to a 3090 Model 200J (52 RPP). The 180S is 90 per cent busy and sustains an I/O rate of 250 I/Os per second.

A5.2.1 M Value method

$$\text{I/O per Q} = \frac{\text{Sustained I/O rate}}{\text{Processor M Value} \times \text{CPU busy percentage}}$$

$$= \frac{\text{Sustained I/O rate}}{\text{UMV}}$$

Therefore:

$$\text{I/O per Q of 3090 Model 180S} = 250/(1000 \times 0.9) = 0.278 \text{ I/Os per Q}$$

To find the total processor power, we need to rearrange the above formula:

$$\text{Processor M Value} = \frac{\text{Sustained I/O rate}}{\text{I/O per Q} \times \text{CPU busy percentage}}$$

Therefore, as the CPU busy percentage will now be $(24.5/52) \times 0.9$, then:

$$\text{Processor M Value} = 250/(0.278 \times ((24.5/52) \times 0.9))$$
$$= 2121 \text{ I/O per Q} \quad \text{or} \quad \text{M Value of 2121}$$

A5.2.2 The RPP (RIOC) method

$$\text{RIOC} = \frac{\text{Sustained I/O rate}}{\text{Processor RPP} \times \text{CPU busy percentage}}$$
$$= \text{Sustained I/O rate} \times \text{URPP}$$

Therefore:
$$\text{RIOC} = 250/(24.5 \times 0.9) = 11.338 \text{ I/Os per URPP}$$

But:
$$\text{Processor RPP} = \frac{\text{Sustained I/O rate}}{\text{RIOC} \times \text{CPU busy percentage}}$$

Therefore:
$$\text{Processor RPP} = 250/(11.338 \times ((24.5/52) \times 0.9))$$
$$= 52 \text{ RPP}$$

A5.3 Summary

Using RIOC instead of I/Os per quantum is easier to use and to understand. It is quite acceptable to grasp that there will be a certain number of discrete I/Os supported by each utilized RPP of a processor for a given type of workload. It is a simple matter to plot these RIOCs as a moving average, and you will gain more information on how your system is working for you, and more data to help you arrive at the optimum mainframe system.

Quanta are too small to be used easily in capacity planning (1000 *vis-à-vis* 24.5), and so using them generates unnecessarily large numbers. We have enough of them in capacity planning/performance studies, and this probably explains the acceptance of the RPP values using RIOC in most countries, even the USA.

Appendix 6
Calculating capture ratios by regression analysis

The total CPU seconds used by all the applications, after incorporating the capture ratios, can be shown by the following formula, where S is the total CPU seconds used (including the capture ratios). A_n are three applications, and CR_n are the individual capture ratios, which range between 0 and 1; $0 < CR_n \leq 1$.

$$S = \frac{A_1}{CR_1} + \frac{A_2}{CR_2} + \frac{A_3}{CR_3}$$

In order to carry out regression analysis, you must collect a number of RMF Monitor I reports for the peak period, and work out the CPU seconds for each application, for each RMF Monitor I report. One very important point is that the relative I/O content (RIOC) must be stable across all the reports.

Y Total CPU seconds	X1 A_1 CPU seconds	X2 A_2 CPU seconds	X3 A_3 CPU seconds
400.0	51.5	61.9	172.0
336.0	36.2	57.4	115.2
316.8	37.3	52.3	85.2
398.4	48.2	45.4	203.3
395.6	58.1	51.5	169.0
354.8	39.9	28.4	185.6
400.0	41.9	52.3	209.3
354.4	42.5	47.1	144.9
323.6	41.0	64.8	69.4
338.0	33.7	52.9	129.6
353.6	44.3	45.6	129.8
398.8	36.6	59.6	200.7
333.6	35.5	57.0	103.0
399.6	40.4	56.0	219.5
370.0	57.0	60.8	124.7

Figure A6.1. The 15 RMF Monitor I reports data.

Appendix 6

This example shows 15 samples (15 RMF Monitor I reports), and uses Statistical Analysis System (SAS) to perform the least squares regression. See Fig. A6.1 for the data that was extracted from the RMF Monitor I reports. This example is included in the *Washington Systems Centre Technical Bulletin*, GG22-9299-03.

A6.1   The SAS JOB SUBMITted for execution

```
//XXXX1    JOB   (????,????),XXXX,MSGLEVEL=1,MSGCLASS=0,NOTIFY=XXXX
//SAS      EXEC SAS
//SYSIN DD *
DATA CAPTURE;
  INPUT Y X1-X3;
  CARDS;
    400.0              51.5              61.9              172.0
    336.0              36.2              57.4              115.2
    316.8              37.3              52.3               85.2
    398.4              48.2              45.4              203.3
    395.6              58.1              51.5              169.0
    354.8              39.9              28.4              185.6
    400.0              41.9              52.3              209.3
    354.4              42.5              47.1              144.9
    323.6              41.0              64.8               69.4
    338.0              33.7              52.9              129.6
    353.6              44.3              45.6              129.8
    398.8              36.6              59.6              200.7
    333.6              35.5              57.0              103.0
    399.6              40.4              56.0              219.5
    370.0              57.0              60.8              124.7
PROC REG;
  MODEL Y = X1-X3/NOINT;
/*

... and to eliminate X3 ...

//XXXX2    JOB   (????,????),XXXX,MSGLEVEL=1,MSGCLASS=0,NOTIFY=XXXX
//SAS      EXEC SAS
//SYSIN DD *
DATA CAPTURE;
  INPUT Y X1-X3;
  Y1=Y-X3
  CARDS;
    400.0              51.5              61.9              172.0
    336.0              36.2              57.4              115.2
    316.8              37.3              52.3               85.2
    398.4              48.2              45.4              203.3
    395.6              58.1              51.5              169.0
    354.8              39.9              28.4              185.6
    400.0              41.9              52.3              209.3
    354.4              42.5              47.1              144.9
    323.6              41.0              64.8               69.4
    338.0              33.7              52.9              129.6
    353.6              44.3              45.6              129.8
    398.8              36.6              59.6              200.7
    333.6              35.5              57.0              103.0
    399.6              40.4              56.0              219.5
    370.0              57.0              60.8              124.7
PROC REG;
  MODEL Y1 = X1-X2/NOINT;
/*
```

Results

- The first iteration yielded the capture ratio for A_3 (X3) of 0.805.
- The second iteration (removing X3) yielded the following values: 1.780 and 2.579.
- We have to take the reciprocals (remember that the terms in the formula are A_n/CR_n etc.), therefore the two remaining capture ratios are:

    $1/1.780 = 0.562$ for A_2 (X1)
    $1/2.579 = 0.388$ for A_3 (X2)

Appendix 7
Recording the number of CICS ended transactions

To MVS, *CICS is single transaction*, and the CICS transactions are internal to CICS; MVS knows nothing about them. The effect of this is that without some form of interference from the systems programmer, the number of ended CICS transactions within your CICS performance group(s) will usually be one. The exceptions are when you have CICS transactions in more than one report performance group, or when CICS goes down! What to do? By using the *report* performance group feature of MVS, allied to some entries in the CICS DFHSITxx member, we can not only get around this problem, but also take into account multiple CICS systems. We can even get around the problem of external networks requiring common names for the CICSs.

A7.1 The link between RMF, VTAM and CICS

When RMF is started, it asks VTAM for the application id (APPLID) of the applications listed in the IEAICSxx member of SYS1.PARMLIB, identified by the SUBSYS parameter within the member. VTAM knows of these applications, by having their names in SYS1.VTAMLST, and if you have multiple CICSs, then you differentiate between them by having unique names. SMF/RMF will look at the first four characters of these names to identify each CICS.

A7.2 Setting up CICS and RMF to collect CICS transactions

Define a report performance group for each of your CICSs; in fact you can define a report performance group for a subset of transactions within any CICS if you wish. Figure A7.1 shows how this can be done. This figure also shows the linking between RMF, VTAM and CICS, via the relevant library members.

```
IEAICSxx member entries:

SUBSYS-CIC1,RPGN=500      Report PG for CIC1
TRXNAME=CIC1A,RPGN=501    Report PG for transaction CIC1A
TRXNAME=CIC1B,RPGN=502    Report PG for transaction CIC1B
  .
  .
  .
SUBSYS=CIC2,RPGN=600      Report PG for CIC2
TRXNAME=CIC2A,RPGN=601    Report PG for transaction CIC2A
TRXNAME=CIC2B,RPGN=602    Report PG for transaction CIC2B
  .
  .
  .
```

↓

```
The SYS1.VTAMLST entries:

CIC1 APPL AUTH=(...       To define CIC1 to VTAM
CIC2 APPL AUTH=(...       To define CIC2 to VTAM
```

↓

```
The DHFSITxx member of the CICS load library entries:

MCT=YES   for the CICS systems
MONITOR=EVE  CICS SYSEVENTS will count CICS transactions
```

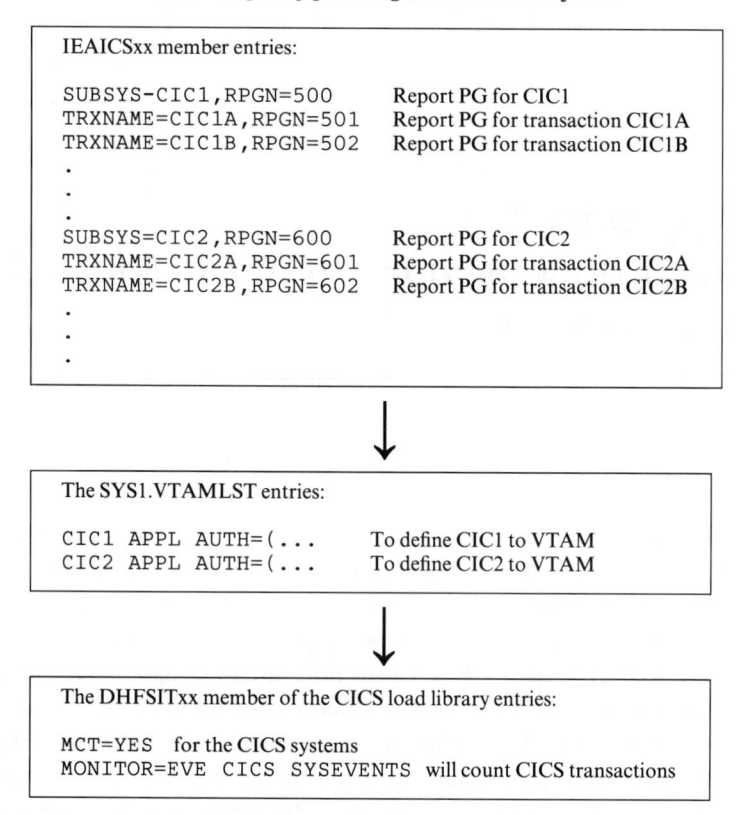

Figure A7.1. Linking RMF, VTAM and CICS for CICS transactions counts.

A7.2.1 DFHSITxx entries

In addition, you must add the following two parameters in the DFHSITxx member of your CICS load library:

- MONITOR=EVE (CICS SYSEVENTS will count transactions)
- MCT=YES (To switch CICS monitoring on)

An alternative to placing entries in the DFHSITxx member is to enter a CICS transaction at the CICS master terminal, which can be automated. For example:

```
CSTT MONITOR,ON=EVE
APPLID=CIC1
APPLID=CIC2
```

Finally, each CICS should be identified as a subsystem to MVS in the IEFSSNxx member of SYS1.PARMLIB, in order to ensure that the master subsystem is used to start it.

A7.3 What about external networks?

Some installations need to standardize the names of their CICSs, as they are referenced by external networks. This presents a possible problem, in that quite often the standards are laid down from outside your company. For example, if the VTAM network needs to have the first four characters of each CICS the same, and differentiate between them by having (say) the last four characters unique, then we apparently cannot use the method defined earlier, because SMF/RMF looks at the first four characters, and expects them to be unique. What to do?

Prior to the introduction of CICS/ESA 3.2, you had to SUPERZAP the DFHCMON member to look at the last four characters instead of the first four. This neatly got around the problem. Figure A7.2 shows the SMP ZAP. This was applied on an installation which the author was associated with, and worked.

In addition, the name associated with each SUBSYS parameter in the IEAICSxx member has to be changed to the last four characters of the names of the CICSs.

```
++USERMOD(UMODMON) .
++VER(C150) FMID(HC2113) .
++MACUPD(DFHCMON) DISTLIB(SOURCE) ASSEM(DFHCMON) .
./ CHANGE NAME=DFHCMON
*        MVC   MCTVNSSN(4),SITGAPLD    lift 1st. 4 chars. of name   @xxx 521000
         MVC   MCTVNSSN(4),SITGAPLD+4  lift last 4 chars. of name   @xxx 521000
./ ENDUP '
```

Figure A7.2. SUPERZAP to DFHCMON to read last four characters of CICS name.

A7.4 CICS/ESA 3.2 and 3.3

If you still have the requirement that the first four characters of your CICS be identical, because of external network dictates possibly, then it is easier to achieve this with CICS/ESA 3.2 and subsequent releases.

With CICS/ESA 3.2, it is now possible to set up the first four characters of the name of each CICS, as the name associated with the SUBSYS parameter identifying the CICS in the IEAICSxx member of SYS1.PARMLIB, and then assign each full CICS VTAM APPLID name to separate TRXCLASS names within this SUBSYS name: the name that is to be associated to the TRXCLASS; the VTAM APPLID NAME; the name by which VTAM identifies each individual CICS could (for simplicity) be the name of the program being invoked by the EXEC statement in the selected JCL.

In addition, you must indicate the VTAM ACB name, the name specified with the START command for the particular CICS that you wish to start (the name that could be associated with the JOB statement in the JCL invoking this CICS), by a TRXNAME parameter within the SUBSYS identifying the started tasks (STC). This tells MVS which CICS to start via the master subsystem.

The TRXCLASS parameter is normally used to assign JES2 or JES3 JOB scheduling classes to jobs coming into the system. Therefore, it may seem strange

```
SUBSYS=STC,PGN=10
 TRXNAME=CIC1,RPGN=300,PGN=30
 TRXNAME=CIC2,RPGN=400,PGN=40
 TRXNAME=CIC3,RPGN=500,PGN=50
```

Figure A7.3. Assigning CICSs to a report PG (CICS/ESA 3.2).

```
SUBSYS=CAPL
 TRXCLASS=CAPLAN1,RPGN=300
 TRXCLASS=CAPLAN2,RPGN=400
 TRXCLASS=CAPLAN3,RPGN=500
```

Figure A7.4. Assigning individual transactions to a report PG (CICS/ESA 3.2).

assigning the VTAM APPLID name to a TRXCLASS parameter, rather than the TRXNAME parameter, but this has in fact been tried in an installation, and works.

Figures A7.3 and A7.4 show the IEAICSxx entries, and Fig. A7.5 shows the linking of the IEAICSxx entries for the CICS/ESA 3.2 system named CAPLAN1, which is started by the command START CIC1.

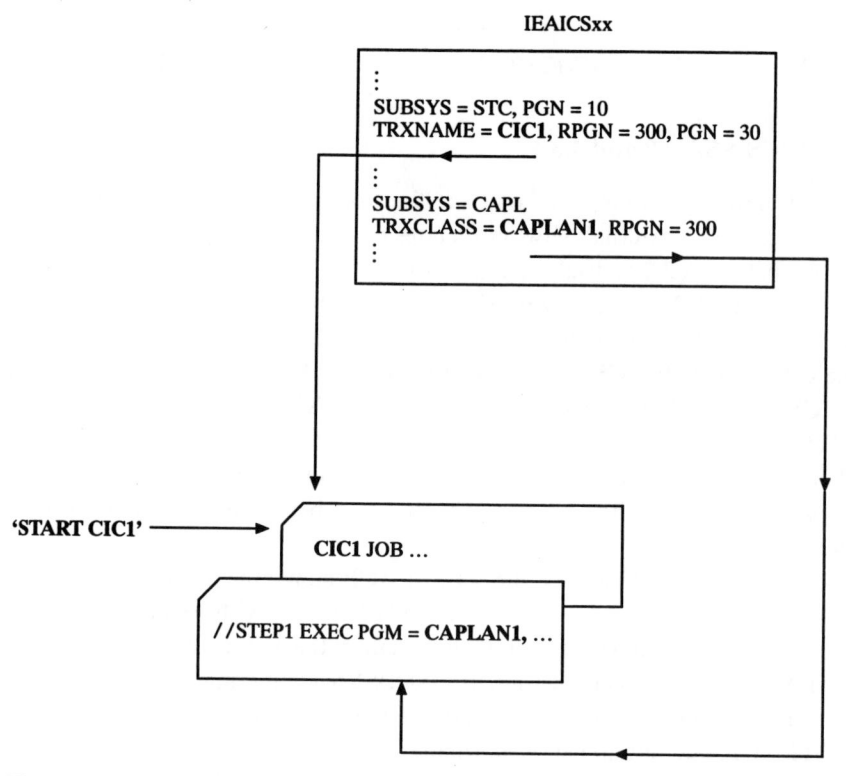

Figure A7.5. The IEAICSxx entries for the CICS/ESA 3.2 system named CAPLAN1.

Figures A7.3 and A7.4 show the three separate CICS/ESA 3.2 systems being identified in the IEAICSxx member of SYS1.PARMLIB. The identifications shown in Fig. A7.3 are the VTAM ACB names, which could be the names on the JCL JOB card (invoked by the MVS START command). In addition, it is recommended that the separate CICSs go into different control performance groups, as in Fig. A7.3.

Figure A7.4 shows the VTAM APPLID names, which in this case indicate the programs that are invoked by the JCL EXEC statement. Notice also, that the report performance group numbers in Fig. A7.3 are the same as those in Fig. A7.4; they have to be.

A7.4.1 Other CICS releases

CICS/ESA 3.3 has not been tested, but according to discussions with other CICS specialists, what works for CICS/ESA 3.2 should also work for CICS/ESA 3.3.

Index

80, arriving at divisor of, 115
3880 controller, 87
3990 controller, 83
9570 DASD, 122

ACNT command, 163
Address space swapped:
   where do they go?, 116
Allocations:
   average number of, 97
APAR OY36668, 147
Appendix 1: SYS1.PARMLIB members, *vii–viii*, 166–172:
   C0FDLF00, 171
   C0FVLF00, 170
   IEAICS00, 167
   IEAIPS00, 166–167
   IEAOPT00, 168
   IEASYS00, 169
   VATLST00, 172
Appendix 2:
   CPU analysis worksheet, 173–174
Appendix 3:
   IBM ITRs, 175–176
Appendix 4: Quarter hour RMF report, 177–194:
   Channel path activity report, 180
   CPU report, 178
   Direct access device report, 181–182
   I/O queuing activity report, 179
   Page/swap data set activity report, 186
   Paging activity report, 183, 184
   PGs 0/100/102/104, 192
   PG 1, 187
   PG 2, 188
   PG 11, 189
   PG 42, 190
   PGs 105/106, 193
   PGs 111/999, 191
   Swap placement activity report, 185
   system summary, 194
Appendix 5:
   M value as alternative to RPP, 195–197
Appendix 6:
   Capture ratios by regression analysis, 198–200

Appendix 7:
   Recording CICS transactions, 201–205
Arrival rate, 15
Asymptote, 19

Balanced system, 76–77
BASIC mode:
   distinction with LPAR mode, 160
Block paging:
   explicit, 124
   implicit, 124
Budget, get it in, 1

Cache:
   rules for, 120
   which data sets to?, 120
Capacity planning:
   for a partition (LPAR), 154
   in LPAR mode, 150
   in VM guest partition, 159–165
   roadmap, 4
   versus performance study, 3
Capture ratio, 31
   and TSO users, 31
   applying, 35, 37
   by regression analysis, 198–200
   calculating average, 35
   calculating TSO, 52
   forcing out TSO, 52
   formula, 32
   individual, 52
   NATIVE mode, 164
   under VM, 164–165
Central electronic complex (CEC), 1–4
   justifying analysis of, 1
   non partitionable, 14
   partitionable, 15
   what to analyse, 2
Central processing unit (CPU):
   activity report, 34
   activity report (LPAR), 151
   analysis of for capacity planning, 30–49
   analysis worksheet, 33, 39, 41, 45, 49
   calculating busy seconds, 32

factor, 5–12
  per engine, 10
  queue time, 60
  seconds, 32, 35–37
    easy way to find, 37
  service time for a transaction, 59
  service units, 5–12
  timer units and DIAGNOSE 'OC', 164
  utilization, and LPAR mode, 147
Central storage:
  acceptable rate to/from expanded storage, 136
  and expanded storage installed, 135
  managing, 125, 143
  monitoring, 133
  rate of movement to/from expanded storage, 135
  summary—more required?, 137
  summary of movement to expanded storage, 143
  to buy or not to buy, 144
  use of, 131–132
  with expanded storage installed, 135
Channel:
  all busy versus individual busy, 87
  calculating probability of all busy, 88
  ESCON, 121
  extracting data from RMF, 89
  path activity report, 85
  probability of not reconnecting, 88
  subsystem service time, 80
  upper bound of I/O rate, 84
CICS transactions:
  recording number of, 210–205
Clocks MVS, 161–162
Clock comparator, 162
Common page data set, 119
Connect time, 80
  breakdown, 95
  or EXCP for absorbing SUs, 96
Controllers:
  DASD, 80–82
CP mode and involuntary wait time (IW), 161
CP times:
  extracting from CPU busy time (VM), 163
  how it extends CPU busy time, 164
CPU analysis worksheet, 33, 39, 41, 45, 49, 173–174
CPU timer clock, 162
Criteria age (CA), 126
  default settings for page outs, 128

DASD:
  acceptable activity rate, 90
  acceptable response time, 90
  acceptable utilization, 90
  0D5—how busy?, 91
  activity report, 69–71, 92–93, 100–102
  controllers, 82–83
  in LCU 0D5, how busy, 91
  logical aspects of, 79
  response time, 78
Data collection, *xv*

Data facility systems managed storage (DFSMS), 120
  data sets not used for, 121
  used for, 121
Data-in-virtual (DIV):
  in page data set calculations, 119
Demand page rate, 123
Device service time, 80
Diagnose instruction, 163
  CPU timer units, 164
Disconnect time, 80, 94
Duplex page dataset, 119
DURATION parameter, 53

Erlang's table, 61
ESCON channels:
  greater than 9 kilometres in length, 122
  support in MVS version 4, 121
EXCP:
  or connect time, for absorbing SUs, 96
Expanded storage:
  acceptable movement rate to central storage, 136
  and central storage installed, 135
  managing, 125, 143
  monitoring, 137
  page migration to auxiliary storage, 143
  rate of movement to/from central storage, 135
  summary of movement to central storage, 143
  to buy or not to buy, 144
  use of, 131–132
Explicit block paging, 124
External throughput rate (ETR), 13–22
  and a single server, 13
  calculating, 17, 21, 46
  for PG 1, 46
  for period 3 of PG 42, 74
  function of, 17
  how to use, 21
  relationship to ITR, 20
  what can we do with it?, 48

High storage area (HSA):
  and LPAR mode, 152

IBM:
  3880 DASD controllers, 87
  3990 DASD controller, detail, 83
  9570 DASD, 122
  ES/9000, power of, 11–12
IEAIPS00, 63
IEASYSxx:
  and PAGE parameter, 120
IEAVNP10 module, 7
Implicit block paging, 124
IND USER command, 163
Initialization and tuning guide, 6–7
Internal throughput rate (ITR), 13–22
  calculating, 18, 21, 46
  effect of multi-engined processors, 19
  for PG 1, 46
  how to use, 21

Index

Internal throughput rate (ITR) *continued*
  IBM, 176–176
  relationship to ETR, 20
  to calculate service time, 19
  what can we do with it?, 48
Internal throughput rate ratio (ITRR), 23–29
  aggregated, 24–25
  and LSPR, 24
  calculating, 24–25
  how it can be used, 48
  or RPP, which to use?, 27
  relationship to ETR and ITR, 28–29
  relationship to RPP, 26
  weighted, 24–28
Involuntary wait time (IW):
  and CP mode, 161
I/O, 76–122
  anatomy of, 77
  and the balanced system, 76
  calculated versus actual paths, 106
  calculated versus actual volumes, 106
  definitions, 78–80
  operation, 80–81
  optimum number of paths, 105
  optimum number of volumes for, 104
  rate through the channels, 84
  recommended upper bound, 84
  service units, 6
  subsystem designers' questions, 77
  system designers' questions, 77
I/O queuing:
  activity report, 68, 86
I/O rate:
  acceptable, 90
  average per transaction, 65
  calculating system upper bound, 103
  calculating weighted averages, 104
  finding total system, 67
  maximum system will sustain, 98
    summary of (and paths), 106
  share of for period 3 of PG 42, 65, 67
  system adequate for?, 103
  through the channels, 84
  total system, 67
I/O response:
  time for period 3 of PG 42, 74
I/O system:
  adequate for I/O rate?, 103
IOSQ time, 78
IRARMCPU control block, 7, 10

Large system performance reference (LSPR), 23–24
Latency time, 79
Local page data sets:
  initial size of, 119
  performance recommendations, 119
Local system queue area, 107
Logical control unit (LCU):
  097, 89
  0D5, 89–90
    DASD incorporated within, 92–93

  detail, 90
  how busy?, 91
Logical partitioning (LPAR), 146–158
  BAM3 partition:
    analysis of, 152
    capture ratio for, 154
    captured seconds for, 154
    RPP used by, 156–157
    WAR for, 153
  capacity planning:
    for all partitions, 156
    under, 150, 154
  capture ratio, 147
    calculating, 152–154
  CPU activity report, 146, 151:
    efficiency of, 157–158
  CPU utilization, 147
  high storage area, 152
  logical processor data, 154
  low utilization effect, 150
  management, percentage use of, 155
  mode, distinction with BASIC mode, 160
  other manufacturers, 147
  partition data report, 148, 149
  partition efficiency, 157, 158
  performance aspects of, 148
  physical processor:
    data, 155
    load, 157
    percentage use of, 155
    RPP used, 156
  RMF, 147
  RPP calculations, 156
  running VM V = R or V = F in a partition, 150
  system summary, 153
Low utilization effect, 150
LPAR (*see* logical partitioning)
LPAR mode:
  or BASIC mode?, 160
LSPR (*see* Large system performance reference)
LSQA (*see* Local system queue area)

M value, as alternative to RPP, 195–197
M1/M2/N, 61
Managing:
  central storage, 125
  expanded storage, 125
MCCAECTH, 138
MCCAFCTH, 138
Migration age (MA), 136
  association with UIC, 126
  what are our values?, 137
Migration rate, 140
  upper bound of, 140
Multi-engined processors, 8, 14
  queue time, 60
Multi-programming level:
  and paging rate, 116
Multiple domain facility (MDF), 147
Multiple logical processor facility (MLPF), 146

Index

Multiple high performance guests (MHPG), 159
  feature of VM/XA, 146
  systems it will support, 159
MVS:
  clocks, 161–162
  locks, 8

NATIVE mode, 164
  capture ratio in, 164
  distinction with LPAR mode, 160

Page data sets:
  calculating the size, 111
    arriving at divisor of 80, 115
    MVS version 2, 113
    MVS version 3 or 4, 111, 113
    how many and what size?, 110
    initial sizing of, 119
  local, 119
  performance recommendations, 119
  paging activity report, 108, 114
  primary, common and duplex, 119
  usage report, 99, 112
Page fault, 123
Page management:
  and page migration, 140
  distinction with page migration, 140–141
  processor time used for, 141
Page migration, 143
  distinction with page management, 140–141
  to auxiliary storage, 143
Page movement, 143
  acceptable rate, 136
  rates of, 135
Page rate:
  and multi-programming level, 116
  and system multi-programming level, 116
  demand, 123
    calculating, 65
  VIO, 124
Page reclaim, 124
Page outs:
  page steals, 127
  VIO pages, 127
  virtual fetch, 127
Page steal, 123
  page outs, 127
Page/swap data sets:
  activity report, 66
  do we need them?, 107
Page/swap I/O rate:
  calculating, 65
Page rate:
  and system multi-programming level, 116
  demand, 123
  VIO, 124
Paging activity report:
  page 1, 117
  page 2, 131, 134, 139
    central and expanded storage use, 131
  page 3, 108, 114

Partition data report, 149
  system summary, 153
Partitioning, ways of, 146
Pending time, 78
Performance aspects of LPAR, 148
Performance group (PG):
  calculating queue time for, 62
  PG 0 WAR, 142
  PG 1 WAR, 47
  PG 42 WAR, 38, 51
  PG 100 WAR, 44
  recording resources used by, 30
  system performance groups, 42
  system summary WAR, 36
Performance study:
  information required for, 53
Processor time:
  percentage used by PG 42, 37
Production system, 129
Primary page data set, 119
  performance recommendations, 120
  used for PLPA, 120
Processor resource systems management (PR/SM), 146

Quantum, 195–196
  calculated, 196
QUERY TIME command, 163
Queue, 14
Queue time, 16, 60
  calculated for period 3 of PG 42, 62
  for multi-engined processors, 60
  for uni-processors, 60
Queuing theory, 14

RCCPTRT, 116
Real storage manager (RSM), 107
Reconnect time, 79
Redundant array of independent disks (RAID), 122
Relative I/O content (RIOC), 98
  calculating, 98
Relative Processor Power (RPP), xv, 23–29
  setting, 26
RESERVE, 97
Residency time:
  breakdown, 64
  calculating for period 3 of PG 42, 56
  extracting from RMF, 55
  quick method of finding, 59
Resource Measurement Facility (RMF):
  channel path activity report, 85
  CPU activity report, 34
  CPU activity report (LPAR), 151
  direct access device report, 69–71, 92–93, 100–102
  I/O queuing activity report, 68, 86
  Monitor II, 132
  page data set usage report, 99
  page/swap data set activity report, 66
  paging activity report—page 1, 117
  paging activity report—page 2, 131, 134, 139

Resource Measurement Facility (RMF) *continued*
  paging activity report—page 3, 108, 114
  partition data report (LPAR), 149
  report described, *xiv*
  swap placement activity report, 108, 114
  system summary (LPAR), 153
  WAR for performance group 0, 142
  WAR for performance group 42, 51, 73
  WAR for performance group 100, 44
  WAR system summary, 36, 72
Response time:
  acceptable, 90
  breaking down, 91
  I/O for period 3 of PG 42, 74
RESUMIO, 110–111
Review of swap process, 125
RMF weakness under VM, 162
Rotational position sensing (RPS), 94
  calculating for device, 6, 37, 94

Seek time, 78
  forcing it out, 95
Servee, 14
Server, 14
Service rate, 15
Service request block (SRB):
  service units, 6
Service time, 15
  calculating, 21
  for single server, 15
  for multi server, 15
Service unit (SU), 5–12
  absorbed by a transaction, 58
  and multi-engined processors, 8
  calculation of, 6
  execution time per, 11
  relationship to SRM second, 5, 7
SIGP instruction, 161
Start interpretive execution (SIE):
  mode defined, 160
STARTIO, 110–111
Storage analysis, 123–145
  how is it being used?, 130
  managing central storage, 125
  managing expanded storage, 125
  UIC values—what are they?, 133
Storage isolation (SI), 144–145
Storage requirements:
  analysis for, 129
  calculating minimum, 130
  to buy or not to buy, 144
Summit (520-based processors), 11, 12
Swap data sets:
  do we need them?, 107
  placement activity report, 108, 114
    analysis of, 118
    size of, 109
Swap decision process, 126
Swap placement activity report, 118
Swap process, 125
Swap rate:
  calculating, 65

Swapped address spaces:
  where do they go?, 116
Swapping:
  address spaces, 116
  and criteria age, 126
  and migration age, 126
  and user think time, 126
  the decision process, 126
  to expanded or auxiliary storage?, 126
Swaps per transaction, 48
SYS1.PARMLIB:
  IEAIPS00, 63
  members, 166–172
System multi-programming level:
  and page rate, 116
System performance groups (PG), 42
  apportioning, 42
Systems resources manager (SRM), 6
  second, 5–12
  parameters, *xv*
  relationship to real seconds, 7
  relationship to SU, 7

Terminal:
  input wait, 118
  output wait, 118
Think time, 126
Time in the system (TS), 16
Time-of-day clock, 161
Transaction:
  CPU service time, 59
  residency time:
    breakdown, 64
    quick method of finding, 59
  swaps per, 58
Transaction time, 50
  component parts of, 54
  extracting from RMF, 55
TSOKEYxx, 118
TTIME, 163

U (*see* Utilization)
Unreferenced interval count (UIC), 125
  how to use it, 133
  values—what do they tell us?, 133
User think time, 126
Utilization, 15
  acceptable, 90
  calculating, 61
  CPU, and LPAR mode, 147
  expansion of, 96
  formula, 15
  low effect (LPAR), 150
Utilized RPP (URPP):
  for a PG, 37
  for PG 42, 37–40
  total for application PG, 43
  easy way to find, 37

VIO:
  page outs, 127
  page rate, 124

Index

Virtual fetch page outs, 127
VM guest partitions, 159–165
  and the RMF weakness, 162
  capture ratio in guest partitions, 164–165
  CP mode and involuntary wait time (IW), 161
  extracting CP time from CPU busy time, 163
  finding VTIME, 163
  multiple high performance guests (MHPG), 159
  start interpretive execution, 160
VTIME, 163
  finding it, 163

Wait to start time (WTST):
  calculating for period of PG 42, 56
  extracting from RMF, 55
  quick method of finding, 59
Working sets:
  primary, 107
  secondary, 107
Workload activity report (WAR), 177–194
  CPU activity, 34, 39, 41
  performance group 1, 47
  performance group 42, 38, 51, 73
  system PG 100, 44
  system summary, 36, 72
Worksheet, CPU analysis, 33, 39, 41, 45, 49, 173–174

Further Titles in the IBM McGraw-Hill Series

OS/2 Presentation Manager Programming Bryan Goodyer
Hints and Tips

PC User's Guide Peter Turner
Simple Steps to Powerful Personal Computing

The IBM RISC System/6000 Clive Harris

The IBM RISC System/6000 User Guide Mike Leaver
Hardev Sanghera

MVS Systems Programming Dave Elder-Vass

CICS Concepts and Uses Jim Geraghty
A Management Guide

Dynamic Factory Automation Alastair Ross